morning glories

volume nine

assembly

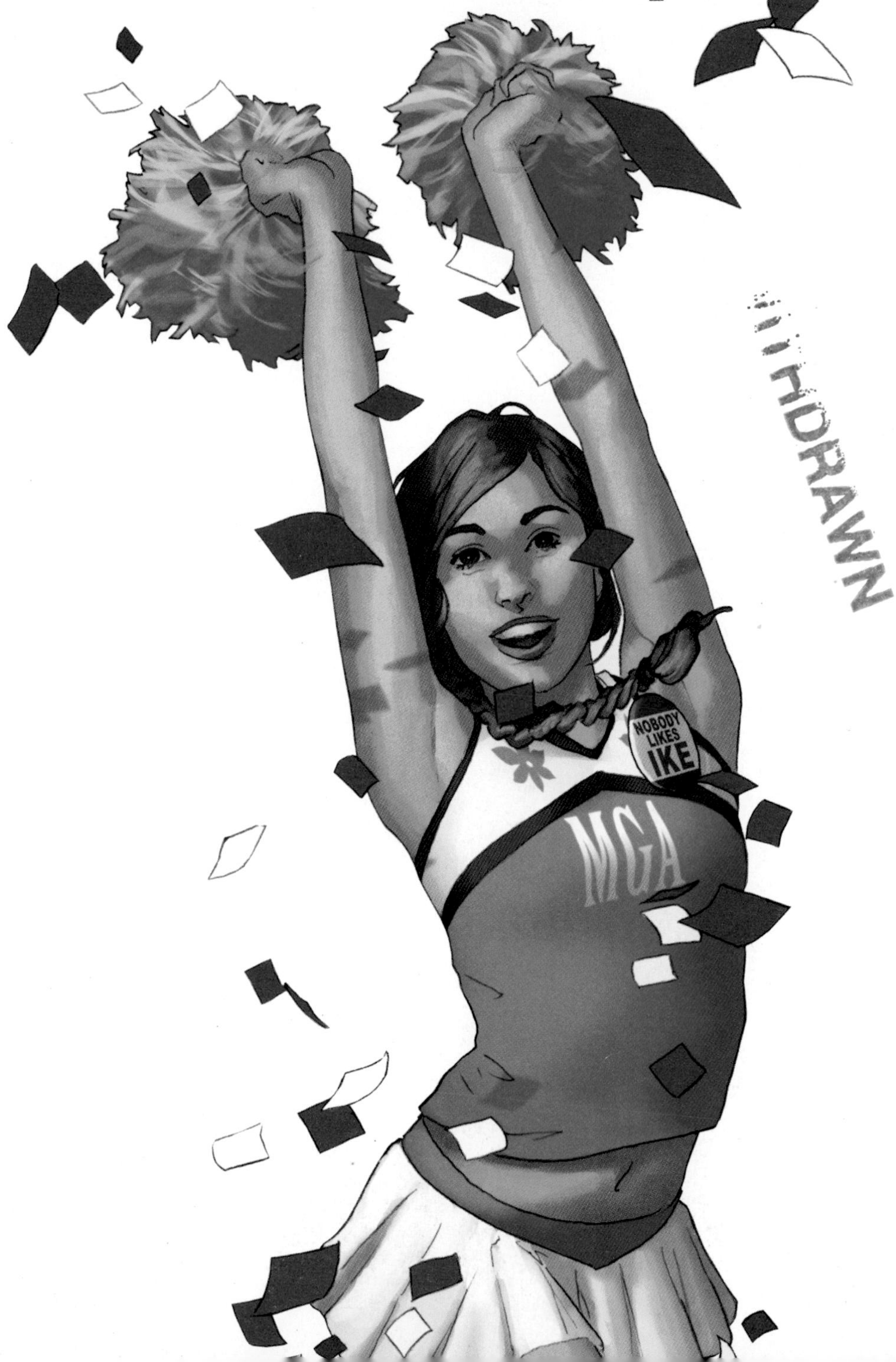
NOBODY LIKES IKE
MGA

WORDS
NICK SPENCER

ART
JOE EISMA

COVERS
RODIN ESQUEJO

PAUL LITTLE
COLORS

JOHNNY LOWE
LETTERS

TIM DANIEL
DESIGN

IMAGE COMICS, INC.
Robert Kirkman – Chief Operating Officer
Erik Larsen – Chief Financial Officer
Todd McFarlane – President
Marc Silvestri – Chief Executive Officer
Jim Valentine – Vice-President

Eric Stephenson – Publisher
Corey Murphy – Director of Sales
Jeff Boison – Director of Publishing Planning & Book Trade Sales
Jeremy Sullivan – Director of Digital Sales
Kat Salazar – Director of PR & Marketing
Emily Miller – Director of Operations
Branwyn Bigglestone – Senior Accounts Manager
Sarah Mello – Accounts Manager
Drew Gill – Art Director
Jonathan Chan – Production Manager
Meredith Wallace – Print Manager
Briah Skelly – Publicity Assistant
Randy Okamura – Marketing Production Designer
David Brothers – Branding Manager
Ally Power – Content Manager
Addison Duke – Production Artist
Vincent Kukua – Production Artist
Sasha Head – Production Artist
Tricia Ramos – Production Artist
Jeff Stang – Direct Market Sales Representative
Emilio Bautista – Digital Sales Associate
Chloe Ramos-Petersen – Administrative Assistant
IMAGECOMICS.COM

fortythree

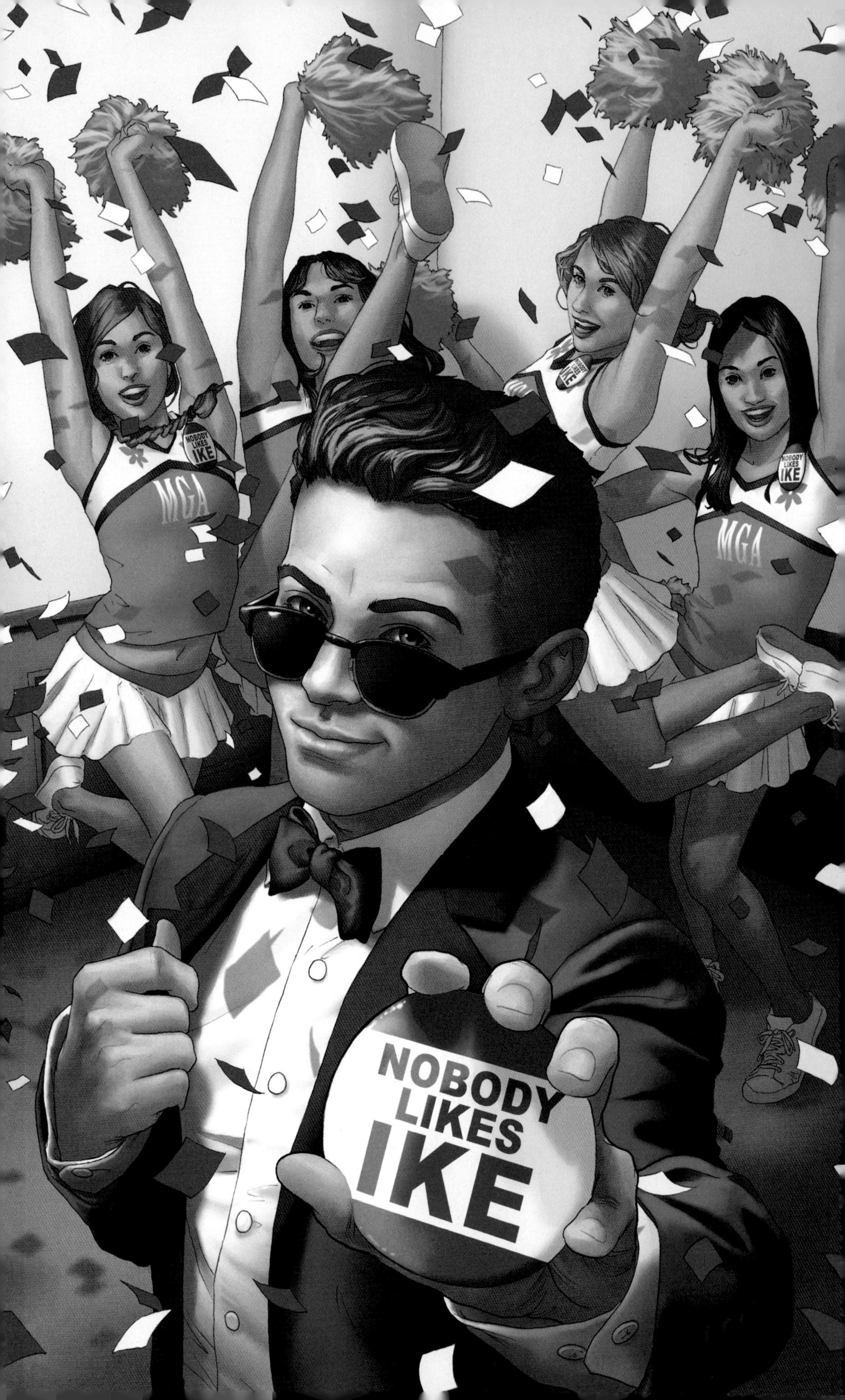
NOBODY LIKES IKE
MGA
NOBODY LIKES IKE
MGA
NOBODY LIKES IKE

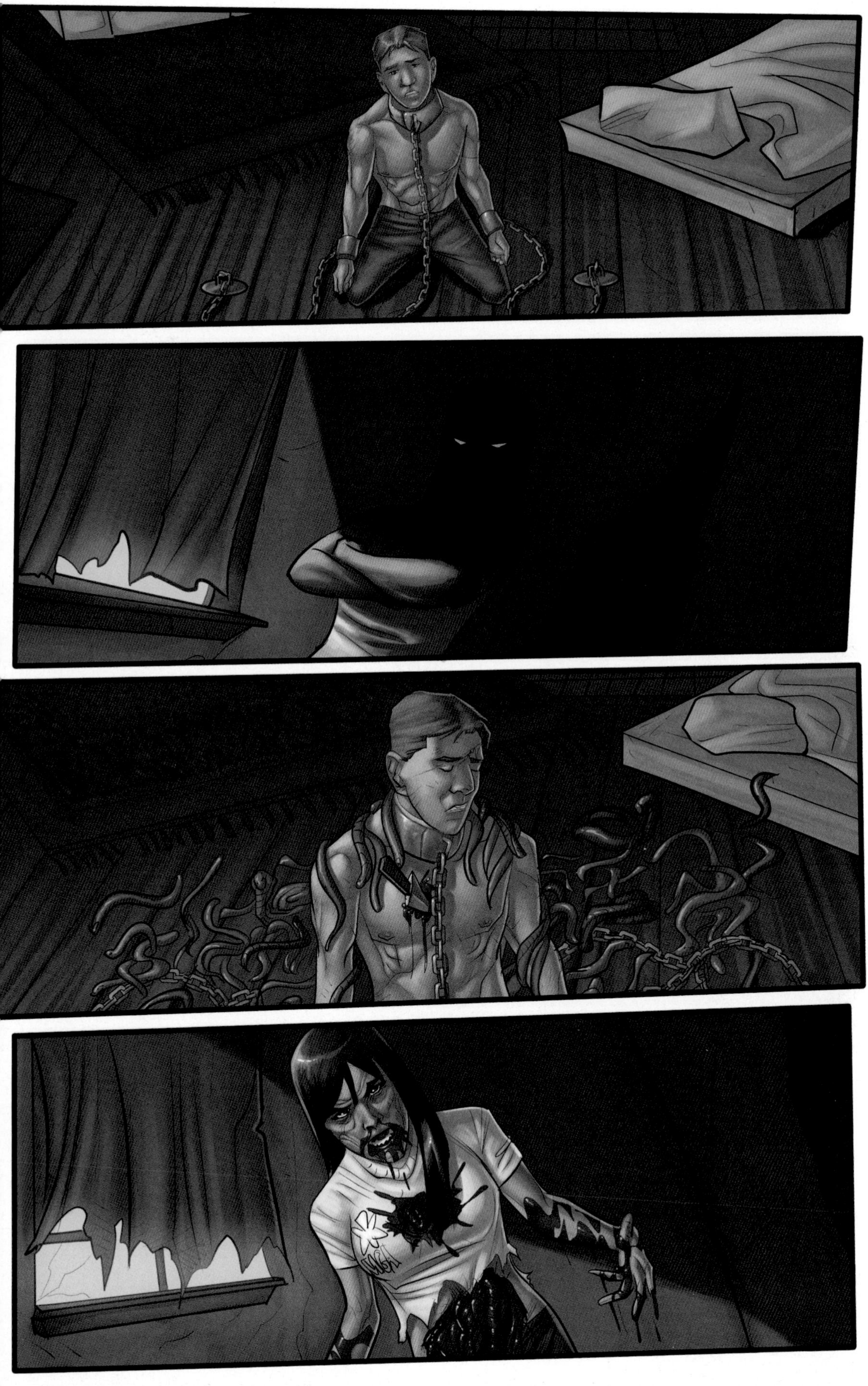

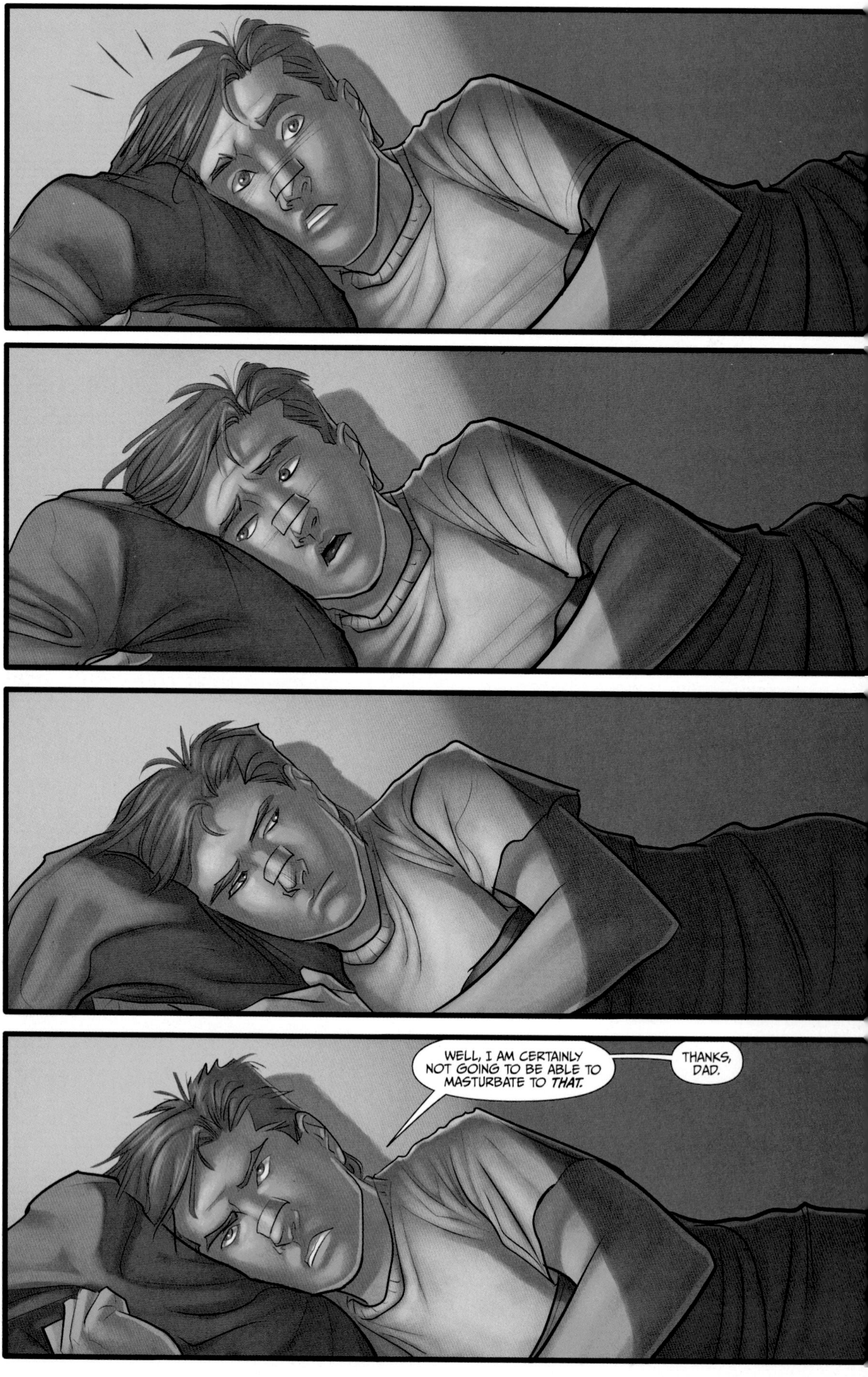
WELL, I AM CERTAINLY NOT GOING TO BE ABLE TO MASTURBATE TO *THAT.*
THANKS, DAD.

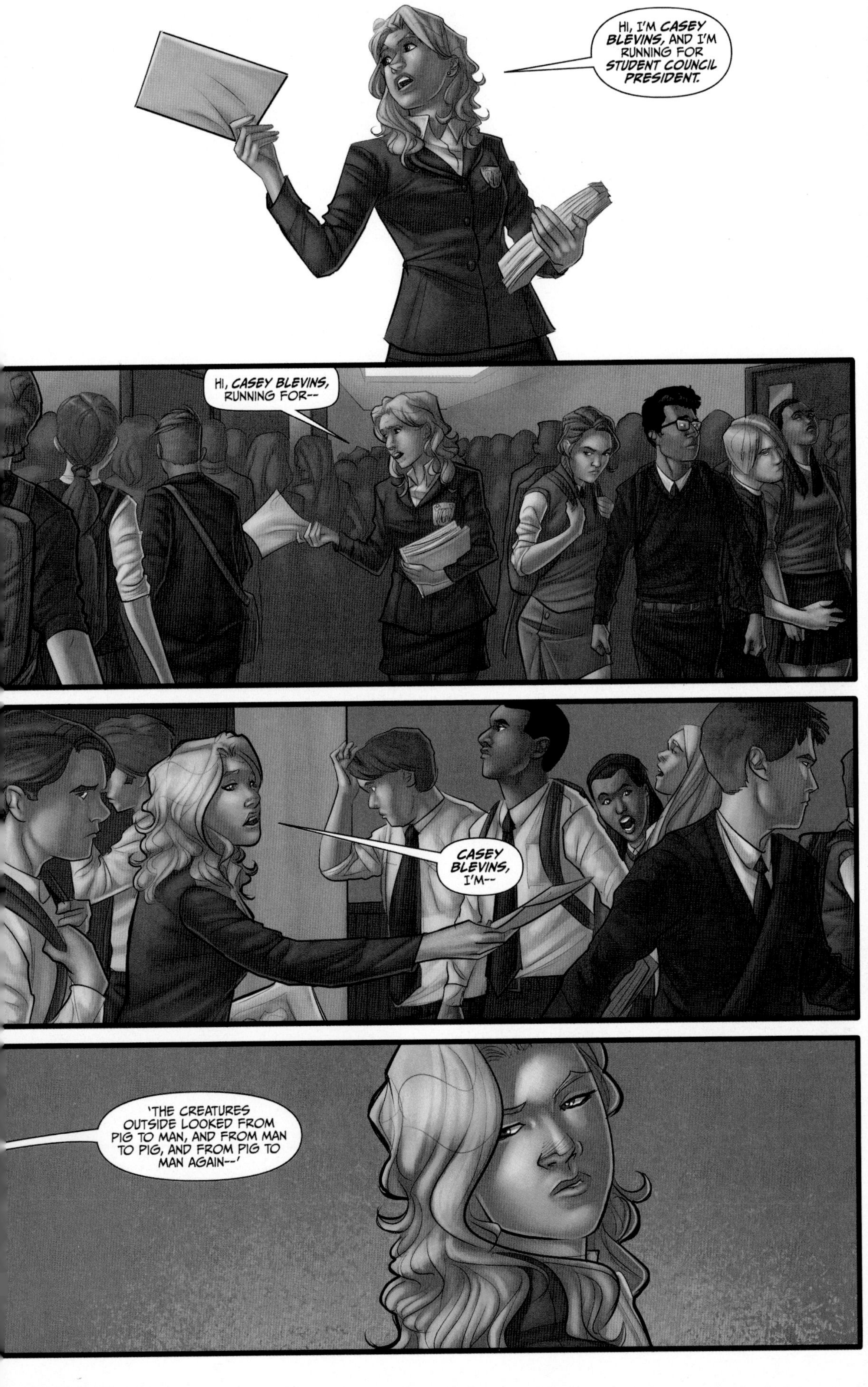
HI, I'M CASEY BLEVINS, AND I'M RUNNING FOR STUDENT COUNCIL PRESIDENT.
HI, CASEY BLEVINS, RUNNING FOR--
CASEY BLEVINS, I'M--
'THE CREATURES OUTSIDE LOOKED FROM PIG TO MAN, AND FROM MAN TO PIG, AND FROM PIG TO MAN AGAIN--'

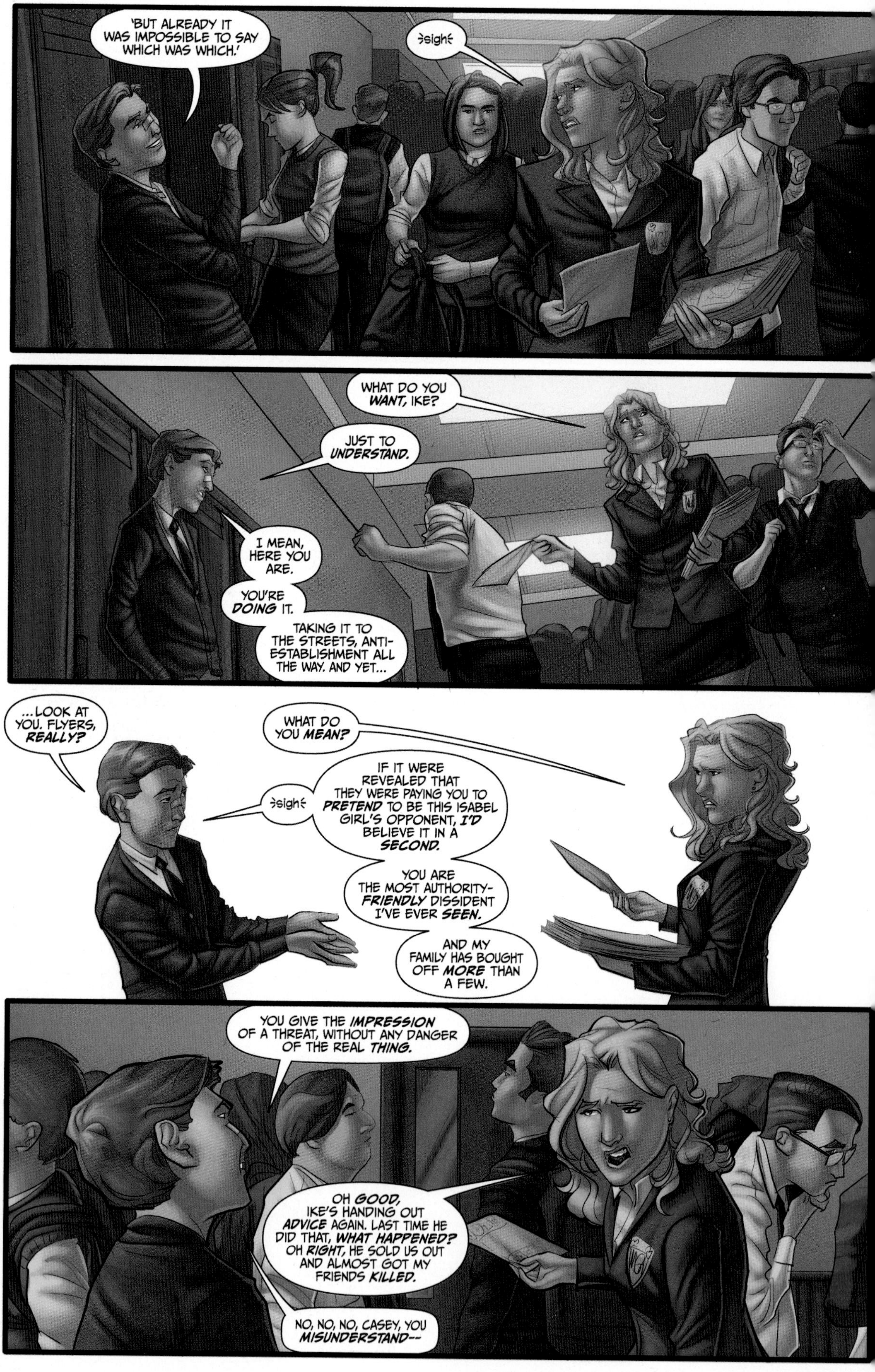
'BUT ALREADY IT WAS IMPOSSIBLE TO SAY WHICH WAS WHICH.'
›sigh‹
WHAT DO YOU WANT, IKE?
JUST TO UNDERSTAND.
I MEAN, HERE YOU ARE.
YOU'RE DOING IT.
TAKING IT TO THE STREETS, ANTI-ESTABLISHMENT ALL THE WAY. AND YET...
...LOOK AT YOU. FLYERS, REALLY?
WHAT DO YOU MEAN?
›sigh‹
IF IT WERE REVEALED THAT THEY WERE PAYING YOU TO PRETEND TO BE THIS ISABEL GIRL'S OPPONENT, I'D BELIEVE IT IN A SECOND.
YOU ARE THE MOST AUTHORITY-FRIENDLY DISSIDENT I'VE EVER SEEN.
AND MY FAMILY HAS BOUGHT OFF MORE THAN A FEW.
YOU GIVE THE IMPRESSION OF A THREAT, WITHOUT ANY DANGER OF THE REAL THING.
OH GOOD, IKE'S HANDING OUT ADVICE AGAIN. LAST TIME HE DID THAT, WHAT HAPPENED? OH RIGHT, HE SOLD US OUT AND ALMOST GOT MY FRIENDS KILLED.
NO, NO, NO, CASEY, YOU MISUNDERSTAND--

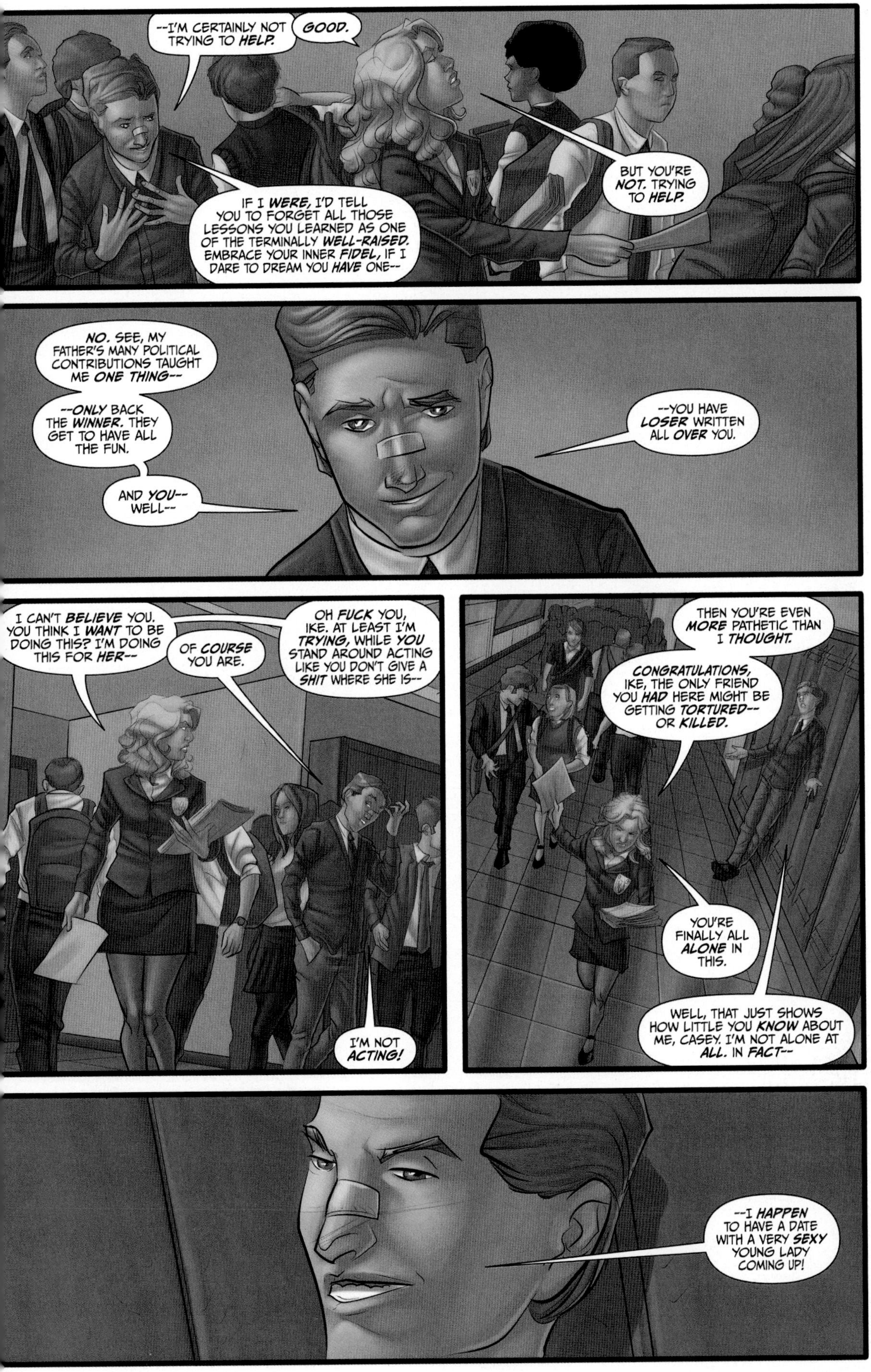
--I'M CERTAINLY NOT TRYING TO HELP.
GOOD.
IF I WERE, I'D TELL YOU TO FORGET ALL THOSE LESSONS YOU LEARNED AS ONE OF THE TERMINALLY WELL-RAISED. EMBRACE YOUR INNER FIDEL, IF I DARE TO DREAM YOU HAVE ONE--
BUT YOU'RE NOT. TRYING TO HELP.
NO. SEE, MY FATHER'S MANY POLITICAL CONTRIBUTIONS TAUGHT ME ONE THING--
--ONLY BACK THE WINNER. THEY GET TO HAVE ALL THE FUN.
AND YOU-- WELL--
--YOU HAVE LOSER WRITTEN ALL OVER YOU.
I CAN'T BELIEVE YOU. YOU THINK I WANT TO BE DOING THIS? I'M DOING THIS FOR HER--
OF COURSE YOU ARE.
OH FUCK YOU, IKE. AT LEAST I'M TRYING, WHILE YOU STAND AROUND ACTING LIKE YOU DON'T GIVE A SHIT WHERE SHE IS--
I'M NOT ACTING!
THEN YOU'RE EVEN MORE PATHETIC THAN I THOUGHT.
CONGRATULATIONS, IKE, THE ONLY FRIEND YOU HAD HERE MIGHT BE GETTING TORTURED-- OR KILLED.
YOU'RE FINALLY ALL ALONE IN THIS.
WELL, THAT JUST SHOWS HOW LITTLE YOU KNOW ABOUT ME, CASEY. I'M NOT ALONE AT ALL. IN FACT--
--I HAPPEN TO HAVE A DATE WITH A VERY SEXY YOUNG LADY COMING UP!

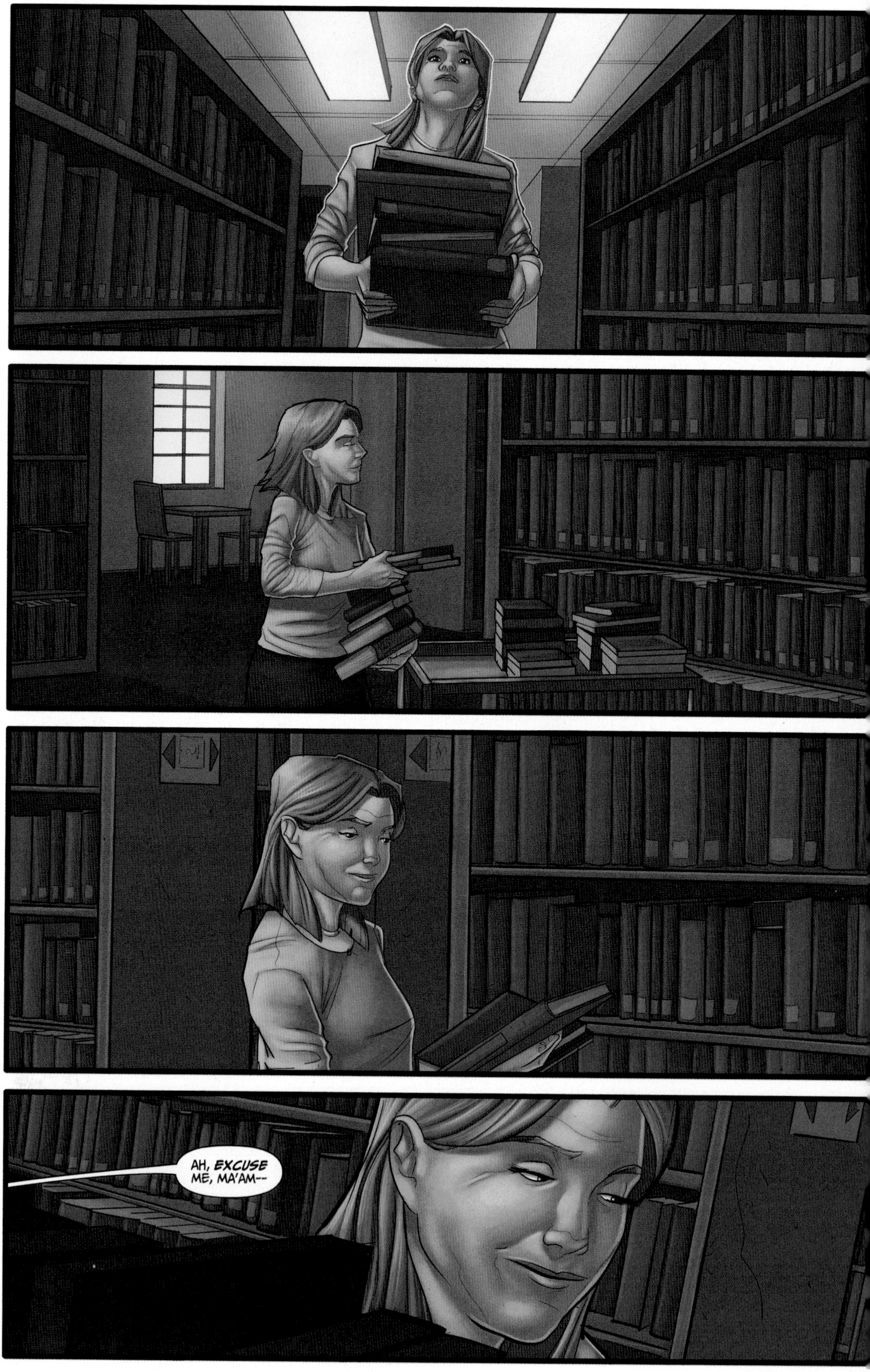
AH, EXCUSE ME, MA'AM--

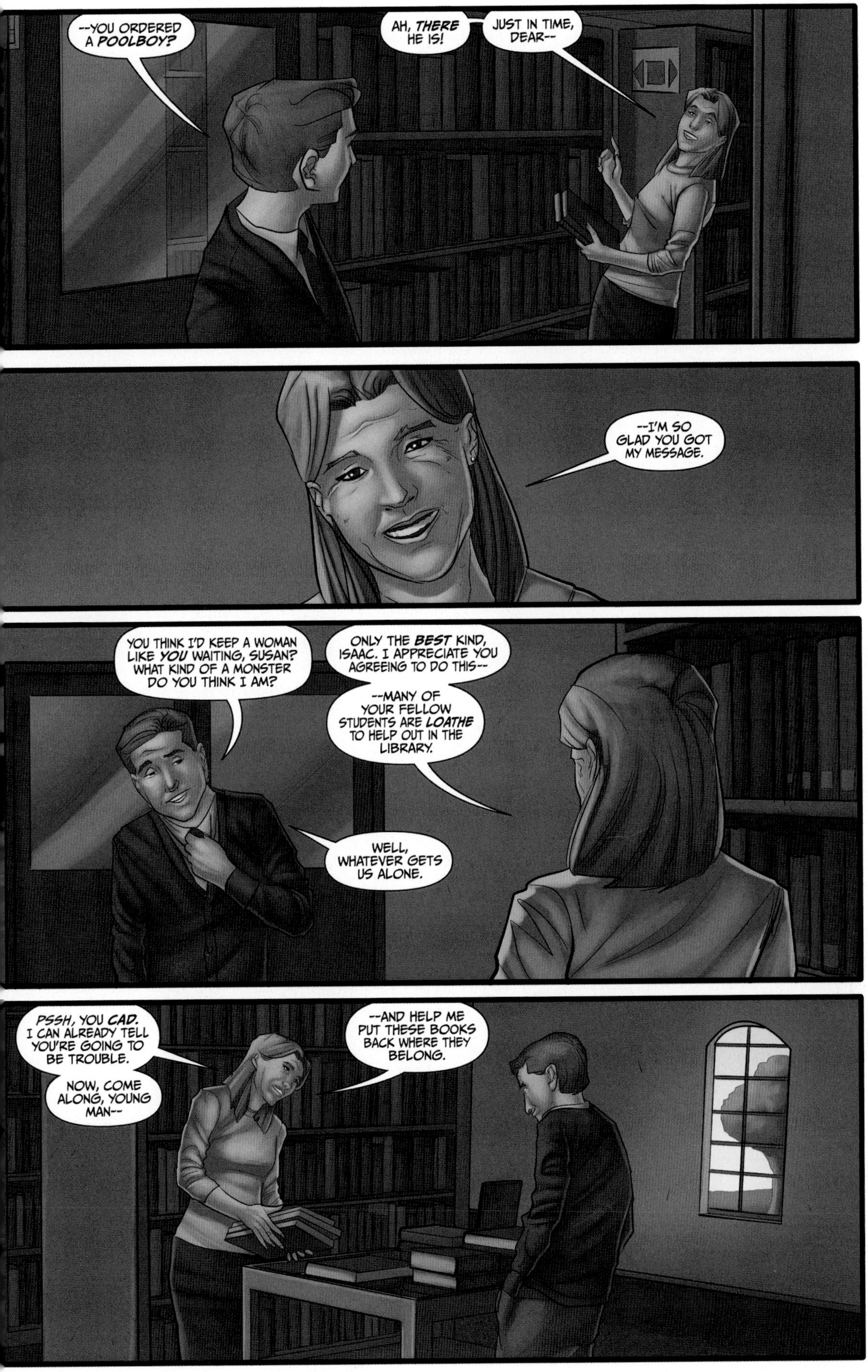
--YOU ORDERED A POOLBOY?
AH, THERE HE IS!
JUST IN TIME, DEAR--
--I'M SO GLAD YOU GOT MY MESSAGE.
YOU THINK I'D KEEP A WOMAN LIKE YOU WAITING, SUSAN? WHAT KIND OF A MONSTER DO YOU THINK I AM?
ONLY THE BEST KIND, ISAAC. I APPRECIATE YOU AGREEING TO DO THIS--
--MANY OF YOUR FELLOW STUDENTS ARE LOATHE TO HELP OUT IN THE LIBRARY.
WELL, WHATEVER GETS US ALONE.
PSSH, YOU CAD. I CAN ALREADY TELL YOU'RE GOING TO BE TROUBLE.
NOW, COME ALONG, YOUNG MAN--
--AND HELP ME PUT THESE BOOKS BACK WHERE THEY BELONG.

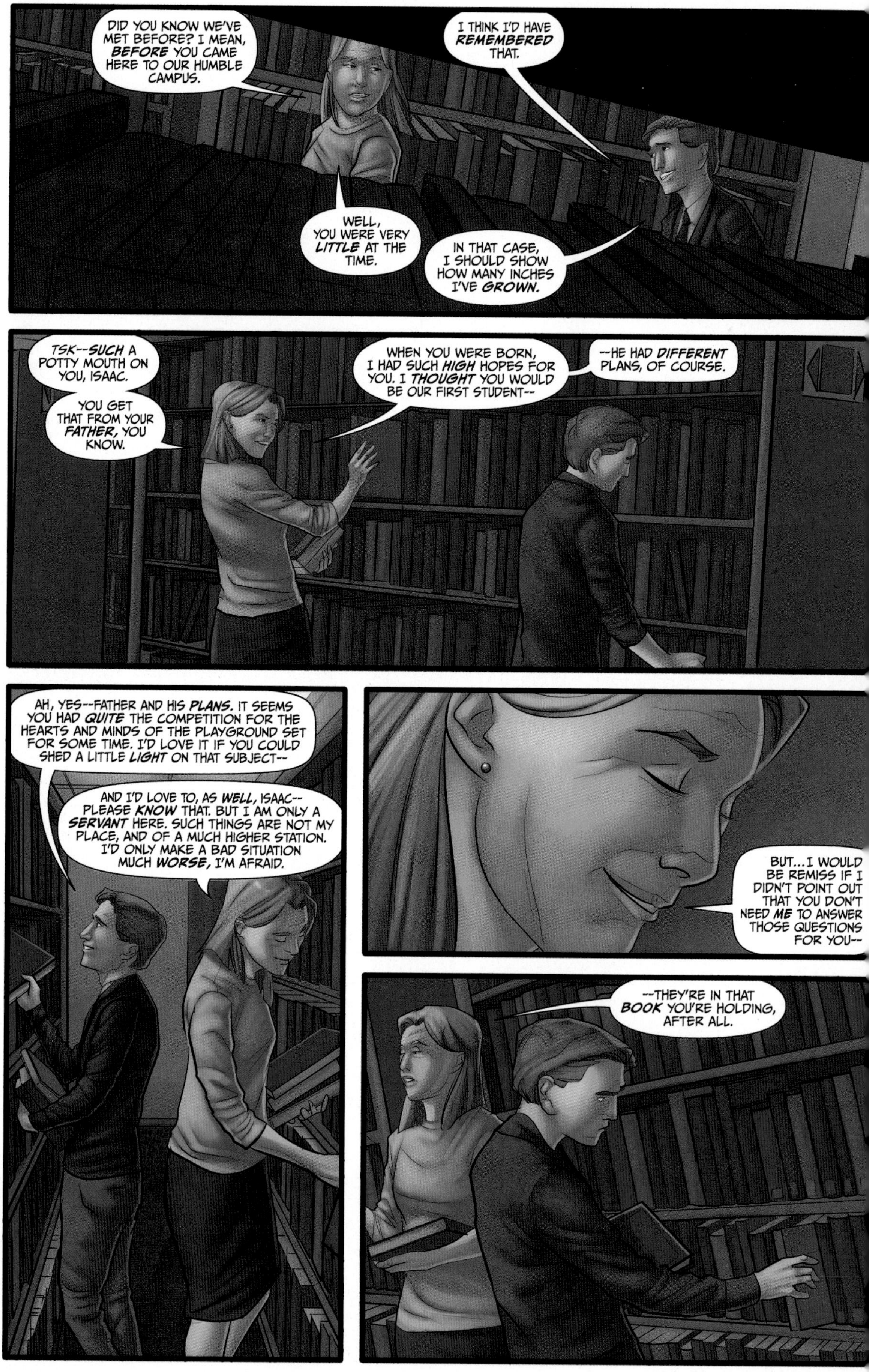
DID YOU KNOW WE'VE MET BEFORE? I MEAN, BEFORE YOU CAME HERE TO OUR HUMBLE CAMPUS.
I THINK I'D HAVE REMEMBERED THAT.
WELL, YOU WERE VERY LITTLE AT THE TIME.
IN THAT CASE, I SHOULD SHOW HOW MANY INCHES I'VE GROWN.
TSK--SUCH A POTTY MOUTH ON YOU, ISAAC.
YOU GET THAT FROM YOUR FATHER, YOU KNOW.
WHEN YOU WERE BORN, I HAD SUCH HIGH HOPES FOR YOU. I THOUGHT YOU WOULD BE OUR FIRST STUDENT--
--HE HAD DIFFERENT PLANS, OF COURSE.
AH, YES--FATHER AND HIS PLANS. IT SEEMS YOU HAD QUITE THE COMPETITION FOR THE HEARTS AND MINDS OF THE PLAYGROUND SET FOR SOME TIME. I'D LOVE IT IF YOU COULD SHED A LITTLE LIGHT ON THAT SUBJECT--
AND I'D LOVE TO, AS WELL, ISAAC--PLEASE KNOW THAT. BUT I AM ONLY A SERVANT HERE. SUCH THINGS ARE NOT MY PLACE, AND OF A MUCH HIGHER STATION. I'D ONLY MAKE A BAD SITUATION MUCH WORSE, I'M AFRAID.
BUT...I WOULD BE REMISS IF I DIDN'T POINT OUT THAT YOU DON'T NEED ME TO ANSWER THOSE QUESTIONS FOR YOU--
--THEY'RE IN THAT BOOK YOU'RE HOLDING, AFTER ALL.

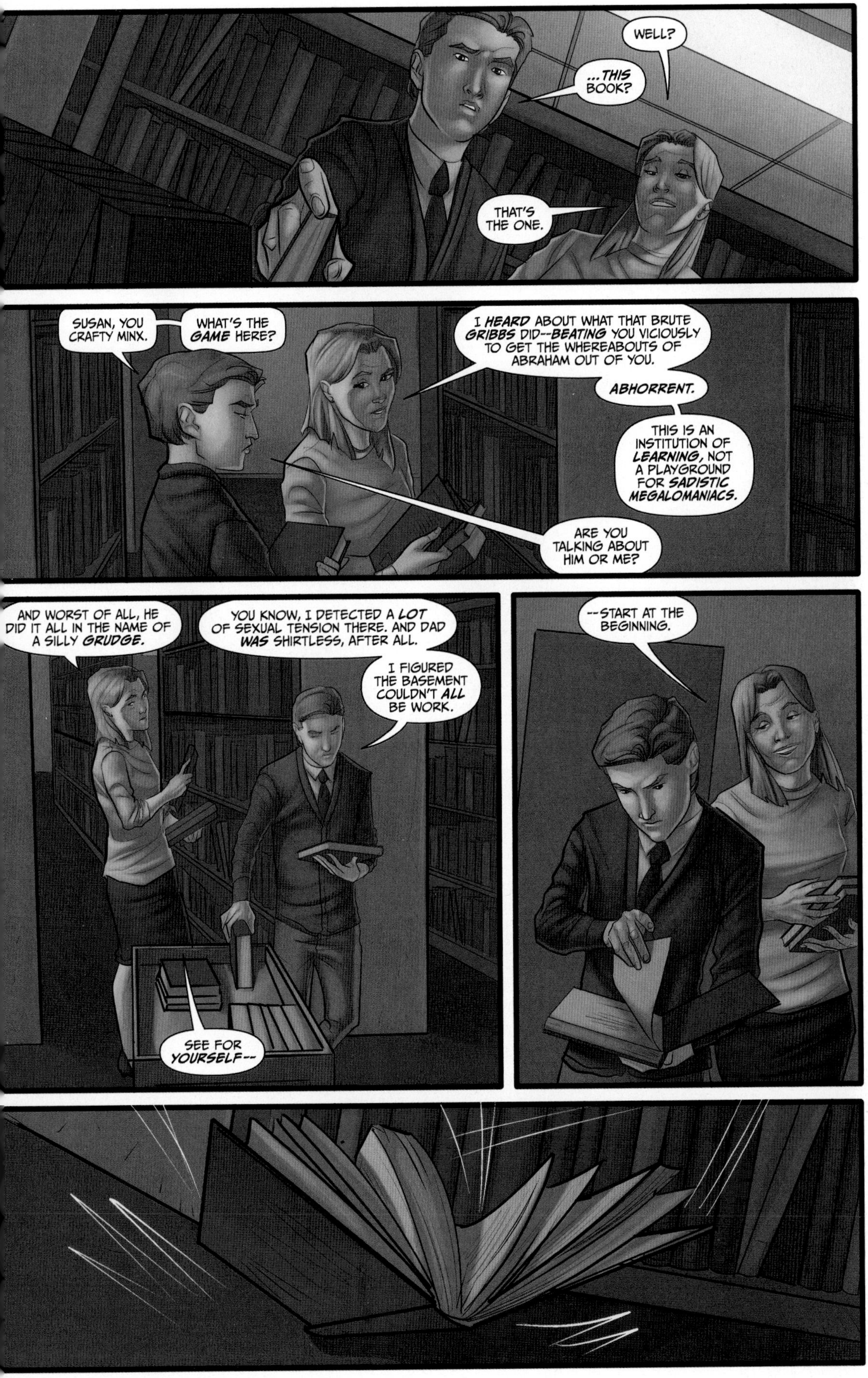
WELL?
...THIS BOOK?
THAT'S THE ONE.
SUSAN, YOU CRAFTY MINX.
WHAT'S THE GAME HERE?
I HEARD ABOUT WHAT THAT BRUTE GRIBBS DID--BEATING YOU VICIOUSLY TO GET THE WHEREABOUTS OF ABRAHAM OUT OF YOU.
ABHORRENT.
THIS IS AN INSTITUTION OF LEARNING, NOT A PLAYGROUND FOR SADISTIC MEGALOMANIACS.
ARE YOU TALKING ABOUT HIM OR ME?
AND WORST OF ALL, HE DID IT ALL IN THE NAME OF A SILLY GRUDGE.
YOU KNOW, I DETECTED A LOT OF SEXUAL TENSION THERE. AND DAD WAS SHIRTLESS, AFTER ALL.
I FIGURED THE BASEMENT COULDN'T ALL BE WORK.
SEE FOR YOURSELF--
--START AT THE BEGINNING.

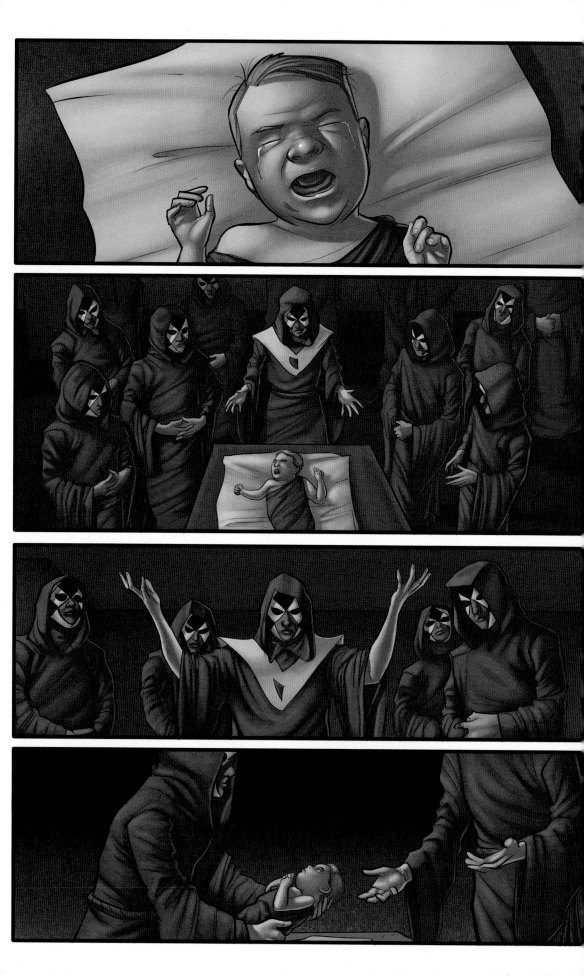

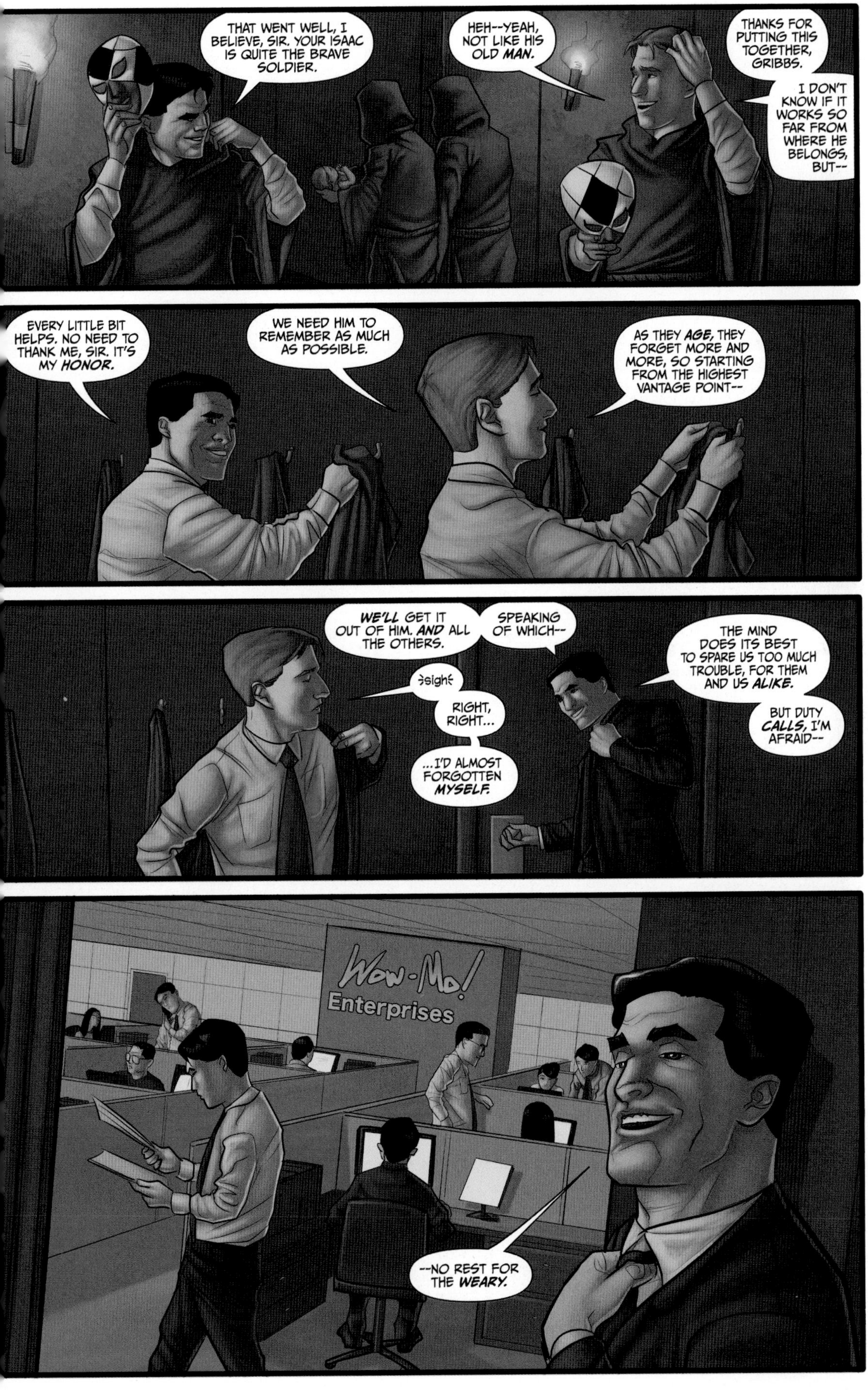
THAT WENT WELL, I BELIEVE, SIR. YOUR ISAAC IS QUITE THE BRAVE SOLDIER.
HEH--YEAH, NOT LIKE HIS OLD *MAN.*
THANKS FOR PUTTING THIS TOGETHER, GRIBBS.
I DON'T KNOW IF IT WORKS SO FAR FROM WHERE HE BELONGS, BUT--
EVERY LITTLE BIT HELPS. NO NEED TO THANK ME, SIR. IT'S MY *HONOR.*
WE NEED HIM TO REMEMBER AS MUCH AS POSSIBLE.
AS THEY *AGE,* THEY FORGET MORE AND MORE, SO STARTING FROM THE HIGHEST VANTAGE POINT--
WE'LL GET IT OUT OF HIM. *AND* ALL THE OTHERS.
SPEAKING OF WHICH--
THE MIND DOES ITS BEST TO SPARE US TOO MUCH TROUBLE, FOR THEM AND US *ALIKE.*
BUT DUTY *CALLS,* I'M AFRAID--
sigh
RIGHT, RIGHT...
...I'D ALMOST FORGOTTEN *MYSELF.*
Wow-Mo!
Enterprises
--NO REST FOR THE *WEARY.*

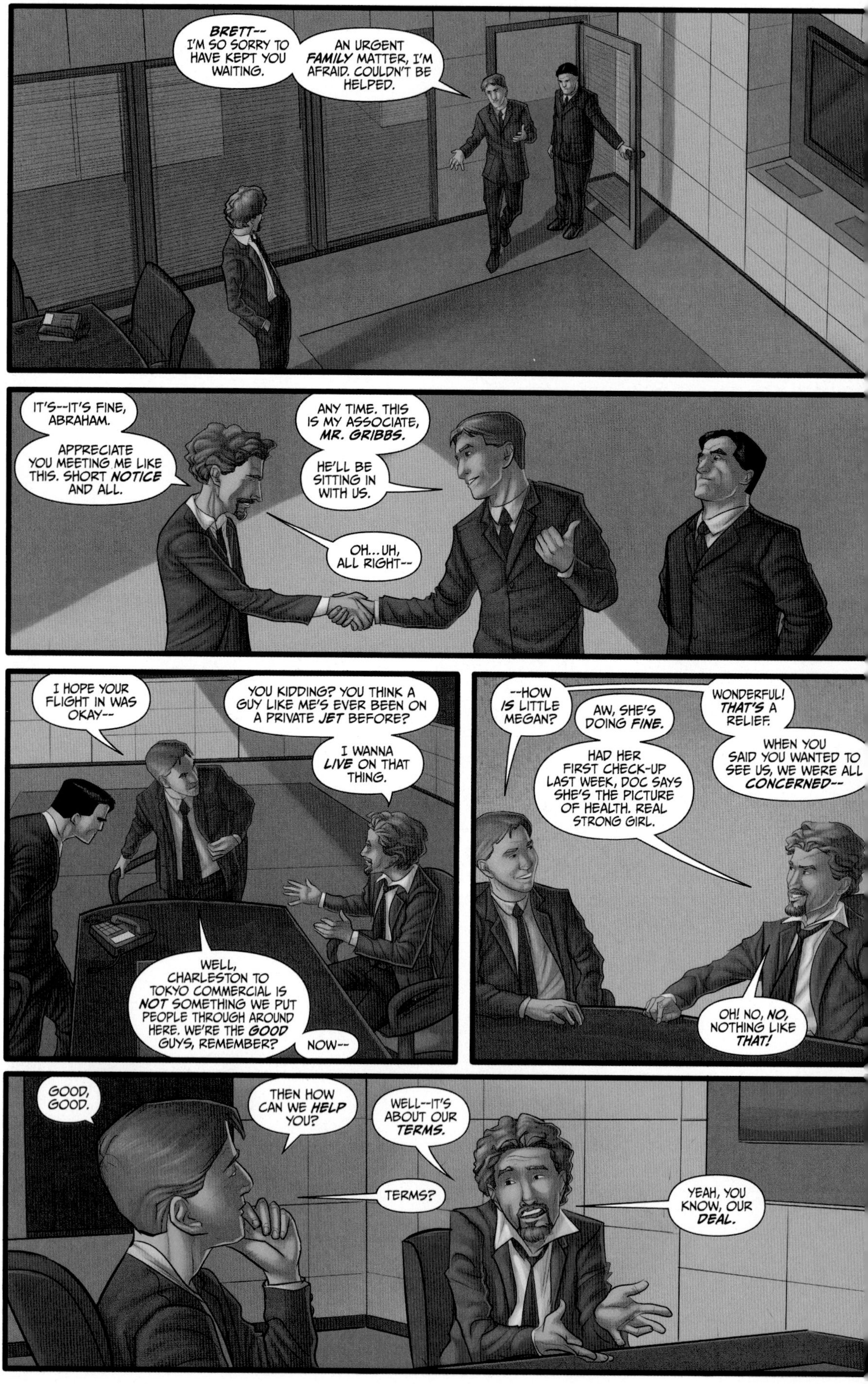

BRETT-- I'M SO SORRY TO HAVE KEPT YOU WAITING.
AN URGENT FAMILY MATTER, I'M AFRAID. COULDN'T BE HELPED.
IT'S--IT'S FINE, ABRAHAM.
APPRECIATE YOU MEETING ME LIKE THIS. SHORT NOTICE AND ALL.
ANY TIME. THIS IS MY ASSOCIATE, MR. GRIBBS.
HE'LL BE SITTING IN WITH US.
OH...UH, ALL RIGHT--
I HOPE YOUR FLIGHT IN WAS OKAY--
YOU KIDDING? YOU THINK A GUY LIKE ME'S EVER BEEN ON A PRIVATE JET BEFORE?
I WANNA LIVE ON THAT THING.
WELL, CHARLESTON TO TOKYO COMMERCIAL IS NOT SOMETHING WE PUT PEOPLE THROUGH AROUND HERE. WE'RE THE GOOD GUYS, REMEMBER?
NOW--
--HOW IS LITTLE MEGAN?
AW, SHE'S DOING FINE.
HAD HER FIRST CHECK-UP LAST WEEK, DOC SAYS SHE'S THE PICTURE OF HEALTH. REAL STRONG GIRL.
WONDERFUL! THAT'S A RELIEF.
WHEN YOU SAID YOU WANTED TO SEE US, WE WERE ALL CONCERNED--
OH! NO, NO, NOTHING LIKE THAT!
GOOD, GOOD.
THEN HOW CAN WE HELP YOU?
WELL--IT'S ABOUT OUR TERMS.
TERMS?
YEAH, YOU KNOW, OUR DEAL.

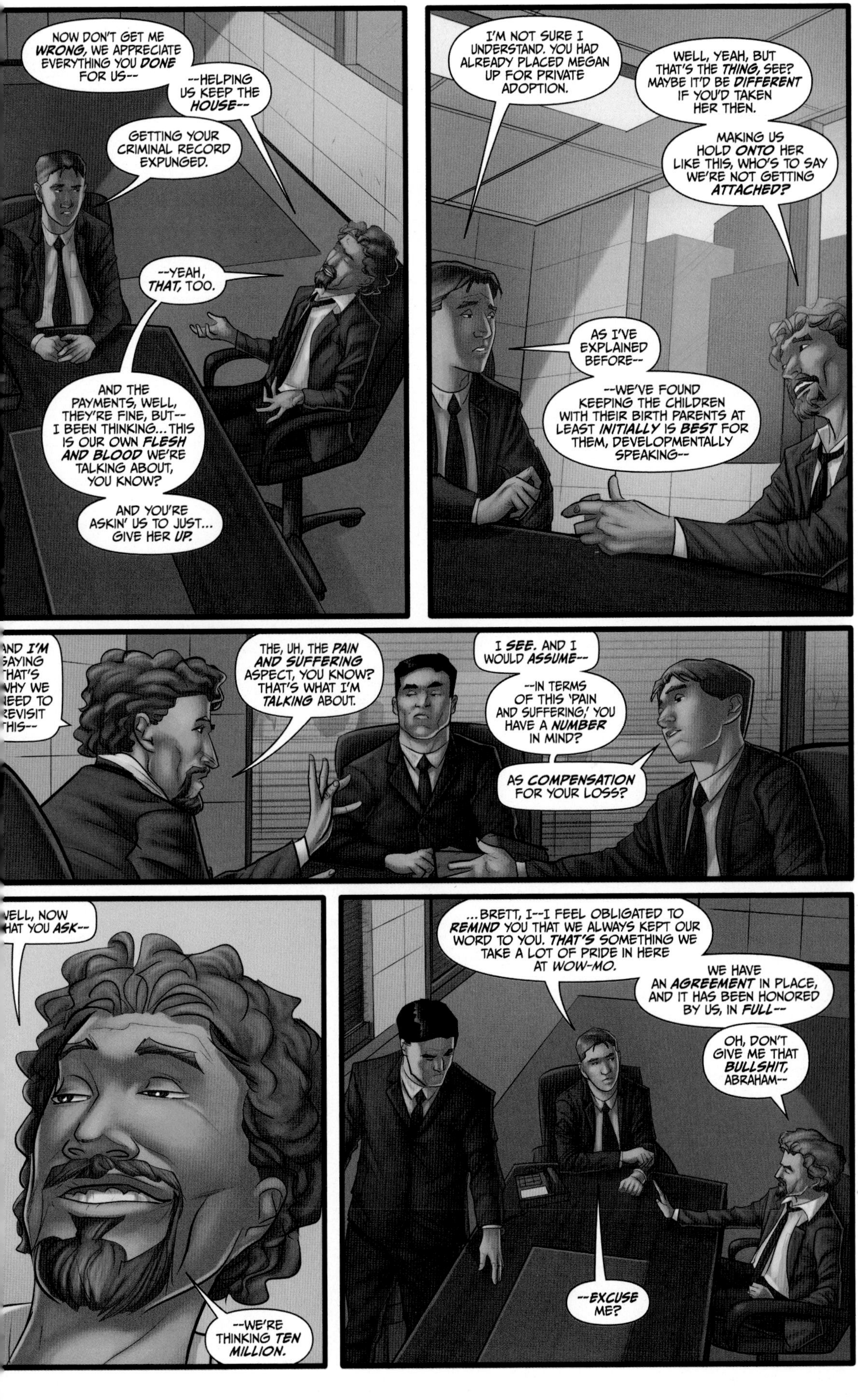

NOW DON'T GET ME WRONG, WE APPRECIATE EVERYTHING YOU DONE FOR US--
--HELPING US KEEP THE HOUSE--
GETTING YOUR CRIMINAL RECORD EXPUNGED.
--YEAH, THAT, TOO.
AND THE PAYMENTS, WELL, THEY'RE FINE, BUT-- I BEEN THINKING... THIS IS OUR OWN FLESH AND BLOOD WE'RE TALKING ABOUT, YOU KNOW?
AND YOU'RE ASKIN' US TO JUST... GIVE HER UP.
I'M NOT SURE I UNDERSTAND. YOU HAD ALREADY PLACED MEGAN UP FOR PRIVATE ADOPTION.
WELL, YEAH, BUT THAT'S THE THING, SEE? MAYBE IT'D BE DIFFERENT IF YOU'D TAKEN HER THEN.
MAKING US HOLD ONTO HER LIKE THIS, WHO'S TO SAY WE'RE NOT GETTING ATTACHED?
AS I'VE EXPLAINED BEFORE--
--WE'VE FOUND KEEPING THE CHILDREN WITH THEIR BIRTH PARENTS AT LEAST INITIALLY IS BEST FOR THEM, DEVELOPMENTALLY SPEAKING--
AND I'M SAYING THAT'S WHY WE NEED TO REVISIT THIS--
THE, UH, THE PAIN AND SUFFERING ASPECT, YOU KNOW? THAT'S WHAT I'M TALKING ABOUT.
I SEE. AND I WOULD ASSUME--
--IN TERMS OF THIS 'PAIN AND SUFFERING,' YOU HAVE A NUMBER IN MIND?
AS COMPENSATION FOR YOUR LOSS?
WELL, NOW THAT YOU ASK--
--WE'RE THINKING TEN MILLION.
...BRETT, I--I FEEL OBLIGATED TO REMIND YOU THAT WE ALWAYS KEPT OUR WORD TO YOU. THAT'S SOMETHING WE TAKE A LOT OF PRIDE IN HERE AT WOW-MO.
WE HAVE AN AGREEMENT IN PLACE, AND IT HAS BEEN HONORED BY US, IN FULL--
OH, DON'T GIVE ME THAT BULLSHIT, ABRAHAM--
--EXCUSE ME?

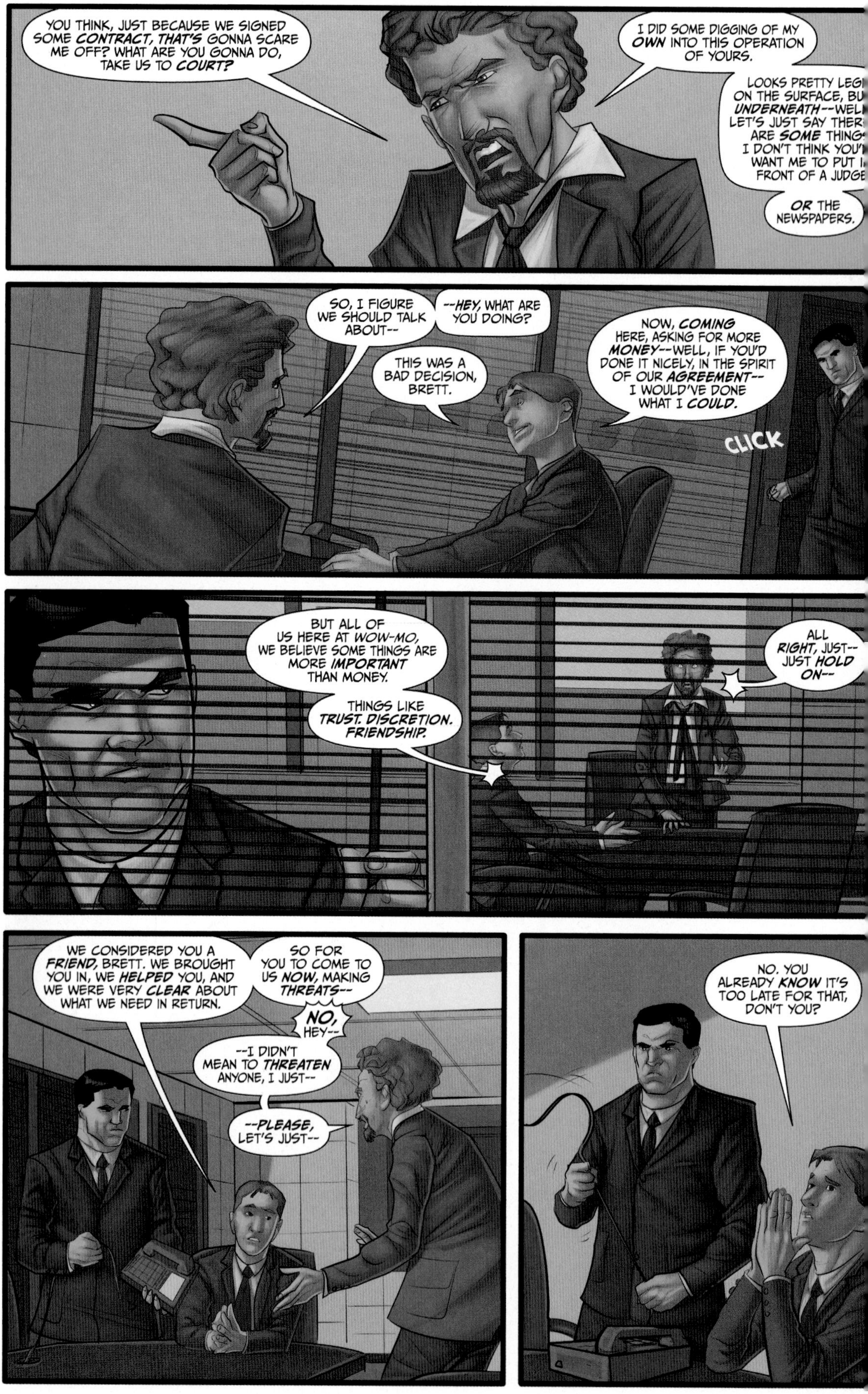
YOU THINK, JUST BECAUSE WE SIGNED SOME CONTRACT, THAT'S GONNA SCARE ME OFF? WHAT ARE YOU GONNA DO, TAKE US TO COURT?
I DID SOME DIGGING OF MY OWN INTO THIS OPERATION OF YOURS.
LOOKS PRETTY LEGI ON THE SURFACE, BU UNDERNEATH--WEL LET'S JUST SAY THER ARE SOME THING I DON'T THINK YOU' WANT ME TO PUT I FRONT OF A JUDGE
OR THE NEWSPAPERS.
SO, I FIGURE WE SHOULD TALK ABOUT--
--HEY, WHAT ARE YOU DOING?
THIS WAS A BAD DECISION, BRETT.
NOW, COMING HERE, ASKING FOR MORE MONEY--WELL, IF YOU'D DONE IT NICELY, IN THE SPIRIT OF OUR AGREEMENT-- I WOULD'VE DONE WHAT I COULD.
CLICK
BUT ALL OF US HERE AT WOW-MO, WE BELIEVE SOME THINGS ARE MORE IMPORTANT THAN MONEY.
THINGS LIKE TRUST. DISCRETION. FRIENDSHIP.
ALL RIGHT, JUST-- JUST HOLD ON--
WE CONSIDERED YOU A FRIEND, BRETT. WE BROUGHT YOU IN, WE HELPED YOU, AND WE WERE VERY CLEAR ABOUT WHAT WE NEED IN RETURN.
SO FOR YOU TO COME TO US NOW, MAKING THREATS--
NO, HEY--
--I DIDN'T MEAN TO THREATEN ANYONE, I JUST--
--PLEASE, LET'S JUST--
NO. YOU ALREADY KNOW IT'S TOO LATE FOR THAT, DON'T YOU?

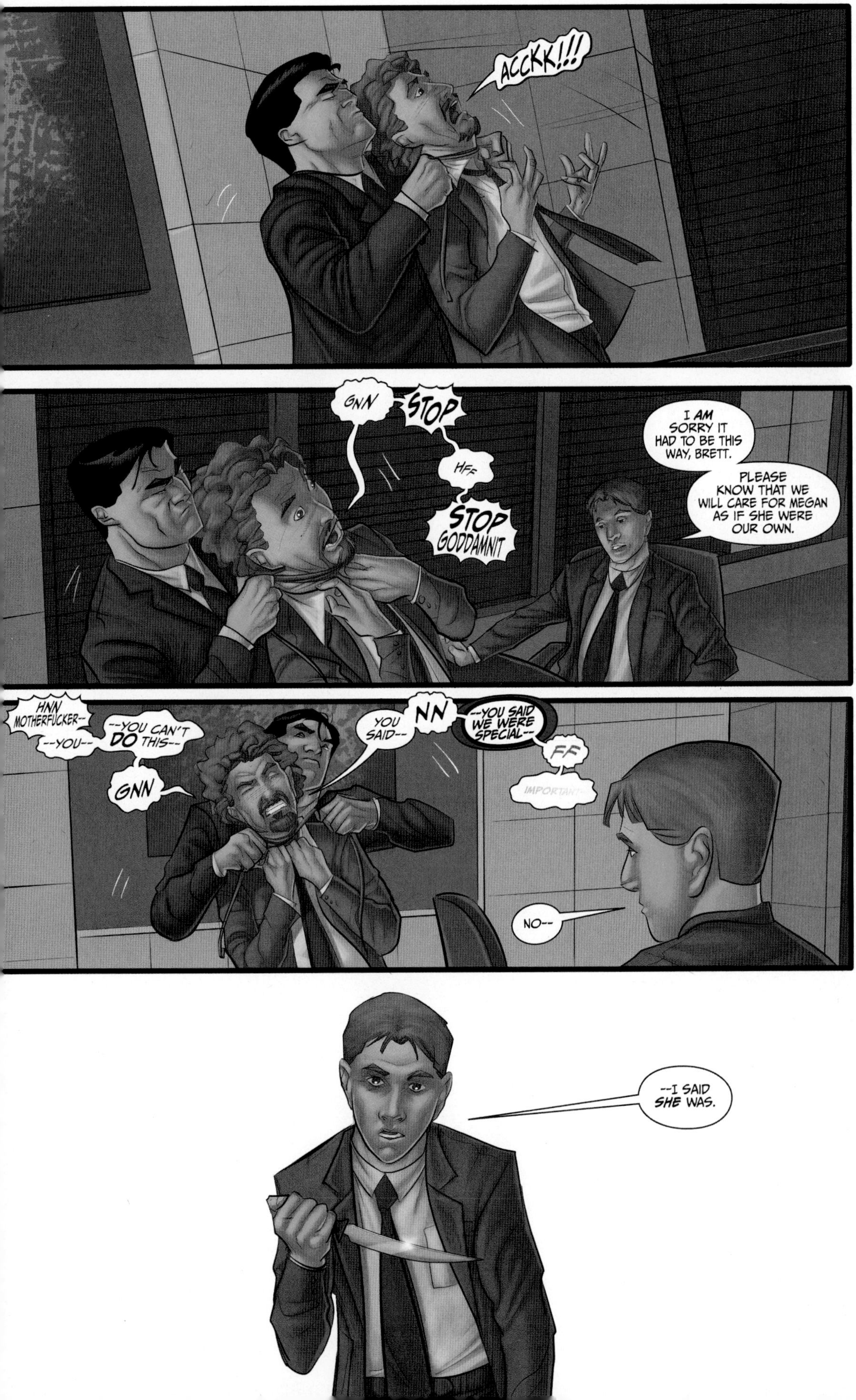
ACCKK!!!
GNN
STOP
HFF
STOP GODDAMNIT
I AM SORRY IT HAD TO BE THIS WAY, BRETT.
PLEASE KNOW THAT WE WILL CARE FOR MEGAN AS IF SHE WERE OUR OWN.
HNN MOTHERFUCKER--
--YOU--
--YOU CAN'T DO THIS--
GNN
YOU SAID--
NN
--YOU SAID WE WERE SPECIAL--
FF
IMPORTANT--
NO--
--I SAID SHE WAS.

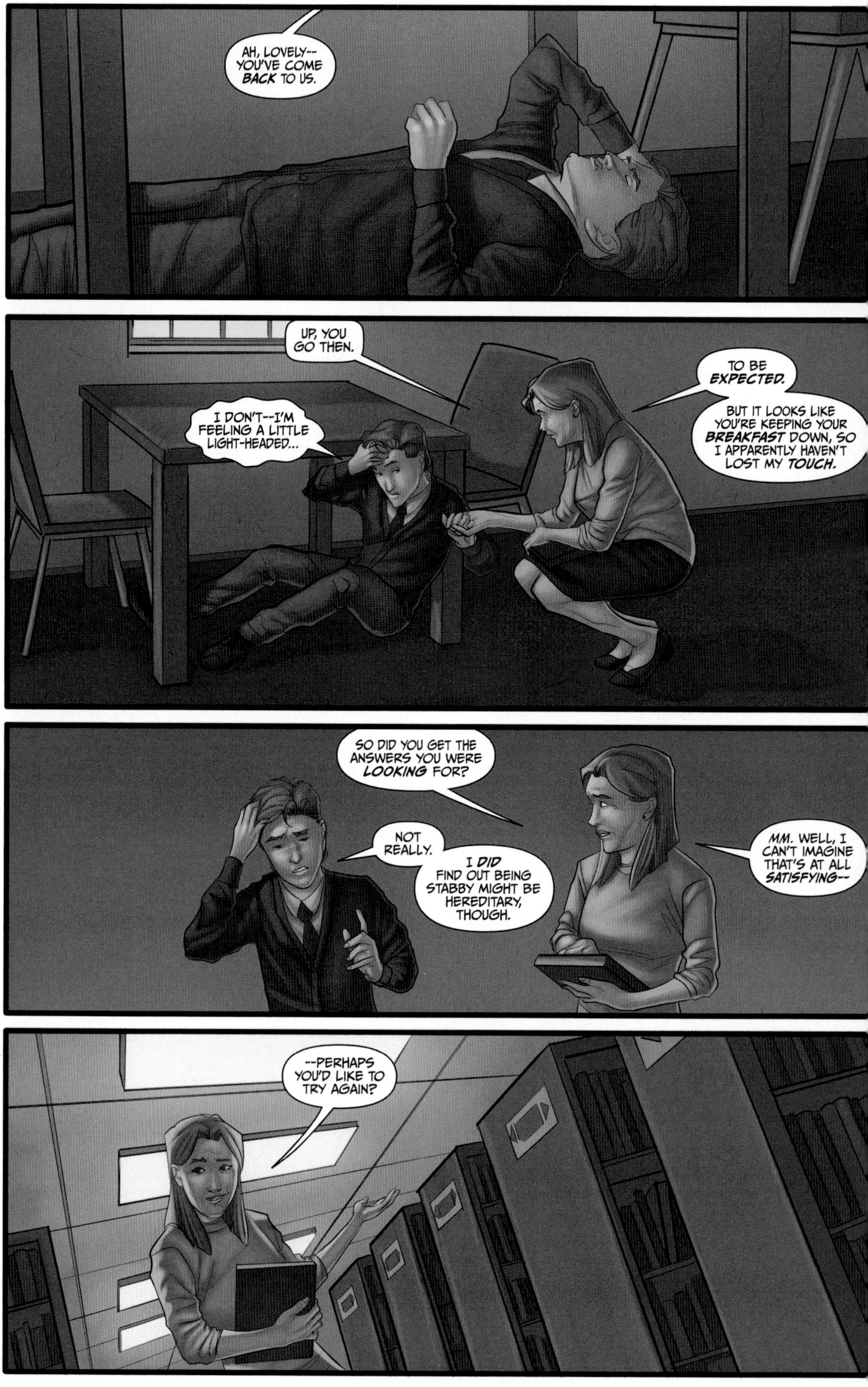
AH, LOVELY-- YOU'VE COME BACK TO US.
UP, YOU GO THEN.
I DON'T--I'M FEELING A LITTLE LIGHT-HEADED...
TO BE EXPECTED.
BUT IT LOOKS LIKE YOU'RE KEEPING YOUR BREAKFAST DOWN, SO I APPARENTLY HAVEN'T LOST MY TOUCH.
SO DID YOU GET THE ANSWERS YOU WERE LOOKING FOR?
NOT REALLY.
I DID FIND OUT BEING STABBY MIGHT BE HEREDITARY, THOUGH.
MM. WELL, I CAN'T IMAGINE THAT'S AT ALL SATISFYING--
--PERHAPS YOU'D LIKE TO TRY AGAIN?

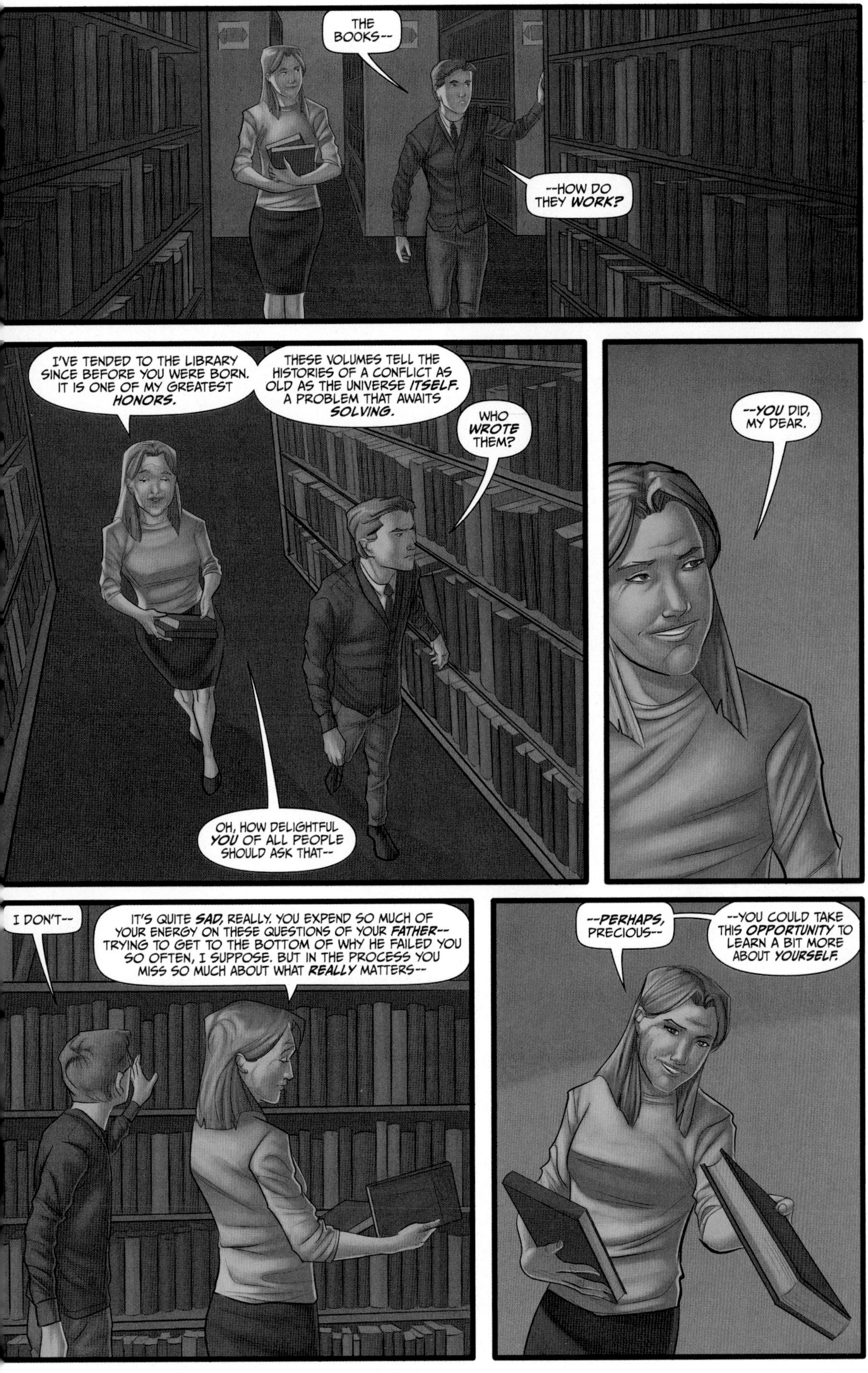
THE BOOKS--
--HOW DO THEY WORK?
I'VE TENDED TO THE LIBRARY SINCE BEFORE YOU WERE BORN. IT IS ONE OF MY GREATEST HONORS.
THESE VOLUMES TELL THE HISTORIES OF A CONFLICT AS OLD AS THE UNIVERSE ITSELF. A PROBLEM THAT AWAITS SOLVING.
WHO WROTE THEM?
OH, HOW DELIGHTFUL YOU OF ALL PEOPLE SHOULD ASK THAT--
--YOU DID, MY DEAR.
I DON'T--
IT'S QUITE SAD, REALLY. YOU EXPEND SO MUCH OF YOUR ENERGY ON THESE QUESTIONS OF YOUR FATHER-- TRYING TO GET TO THE BOTTOM OF WHY HE FAILED YOU SO OFTEN, I SUPPOSE. BUT IN THE PROCESS YOU MISS SO MUCH ABOUT WHAT REALLY MATTERS--
--PERHAPS, PRECIOUS--
--YOU COULD TAKE THIS OPPORTUNITY TO LEARN A BIT MORE ABOUT YOURSELF.

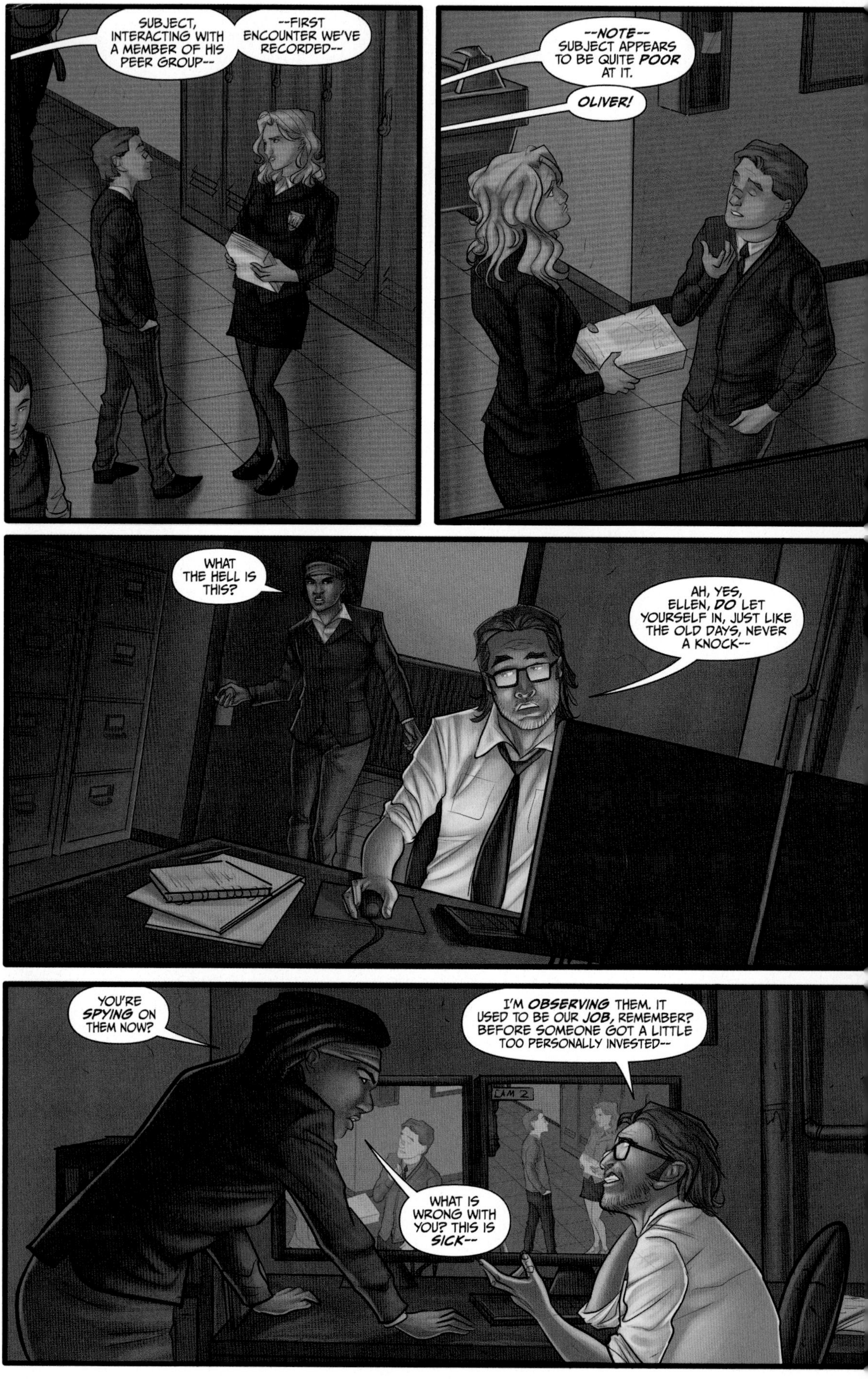
SUBJECT, INTERACTING WITH A MEMBER OF HIS PEER GROUP--
--FIRST ENCOUNTER WE'VE RECORDED--
--NOTE-- SUBJECT APPEARS TO BE QUITE POOR AT IT.
OLIVER!
WHAT THE HELL IS THIS?
AH, YES, ELLEN, DO LET YOURSELF IN, JUST LIKE THE OLD DAYS, NEVER A KNOCK--
YOU'RE SPYING ON THEM NOW?
I'M OBSERVING THEM. IT USED TO BE OUR JOB, REMEMBER? BEFORE SOMEONE GOT A LITTLE TOO PERSONALLY INVESTED--
WHAT IS WRONG WITH YOU? THIS IS SICK--

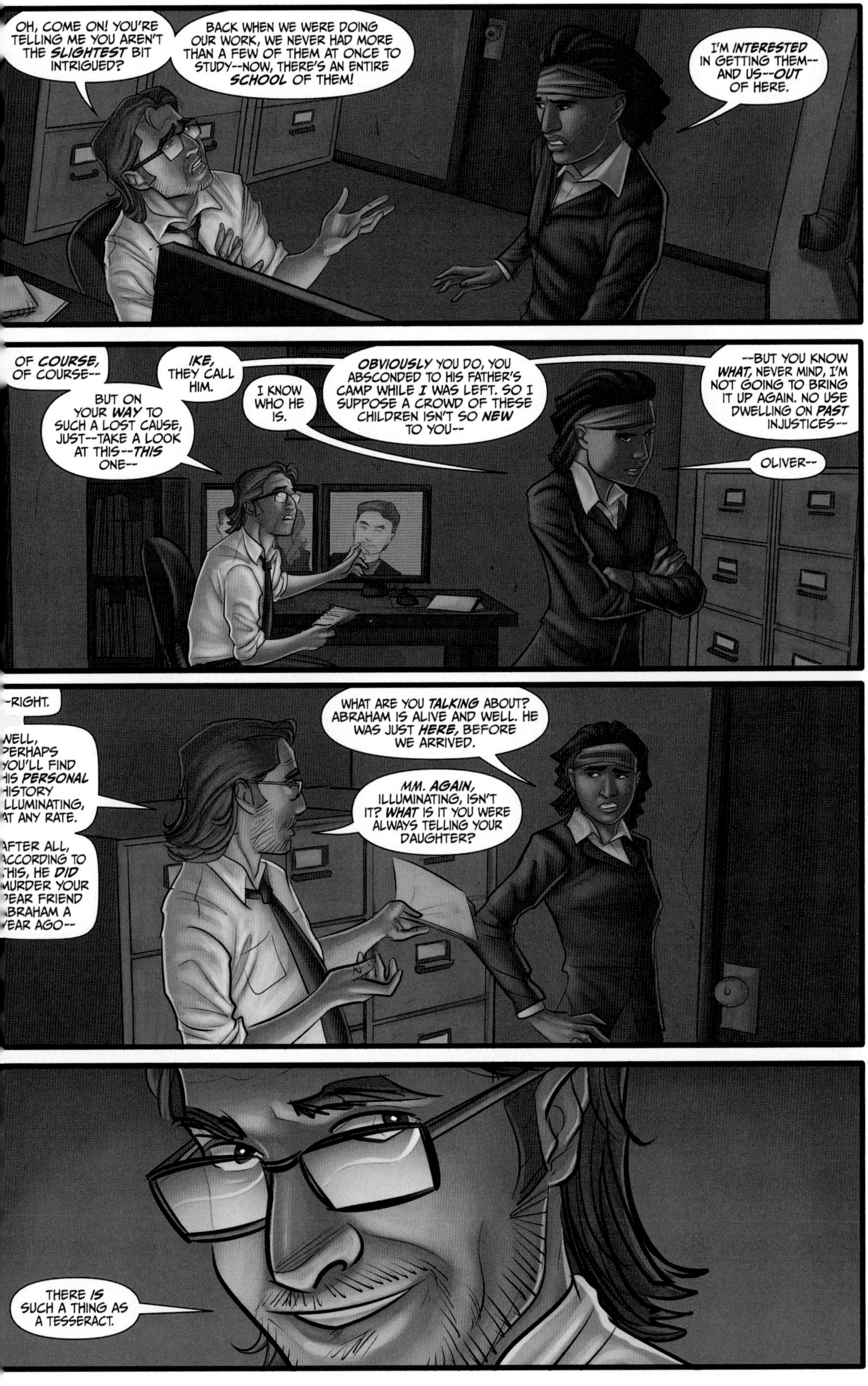
OH, COME ON! YOU'RE TELLING ME YOU AREN'T THE *SLIGHTEST* BIT INTRIGUED?
BACK WHEN WE WERE DOING OUR WORK, WE NEVER HAD MORE THAN A FEW OF THEM AT ONCE TO STUDY--NOW, THERE'S AN ENTIRE *SCHOOL* OF THEM!
I'M *INTERESTED* IN GETTING THEM--AND US--*OUT* OF HERE.
OF *COURSE*, OF COURSE--
BUT ON YOUR *WAY* TO SUCH A LOST CAUSE, JUST--TAKE A LOOK AT THIS--*THIS* ONE--
IKE, THEY CALL HIM.
I KNOW WHO HE IS.
OBVIOUSLY YOU DO, YOU ABSCONDED TO HIS FATHER'S CAMP WHILE *I* WAS LEFT. SO I SUPPOSE A CROWD OF THESE CHILDREN ISN'T SO *NEW* TO YOU--
--BUT YOU KNOW *WHAT*, NEVER MIND, I'M NOT GOING TO BRING IT UP AGAIN. NO USE DWELLING ON *PAST* INJUSTICES--
OLIVER--
--RIGHT.
WELL, PERHAPS YOU'LL FIND HIS *PERSONAL* HISTORY ILLUMINATING, AT ANY RATE.
AFTER ALL, ACCORDING TO THIS, HE *DID* MURDER YOUR DEAR FRIEND ABRAHAM A YEAR AGO--
WHAT ARE YOU *TALKING* ABOUT? ABRAHAM IS ALIVE AND WELL. HE WAS JUST *HERE*, BEFORE WE ARRIVED.
MM. AGAIN, ILLUMINATING, ISN'T IT? *WHAT* IS IT YOU WERE ALWAYS TELLING YOUR DAUGHTER?
THERE *IS* SUCH A THING AS A TESSERACT.

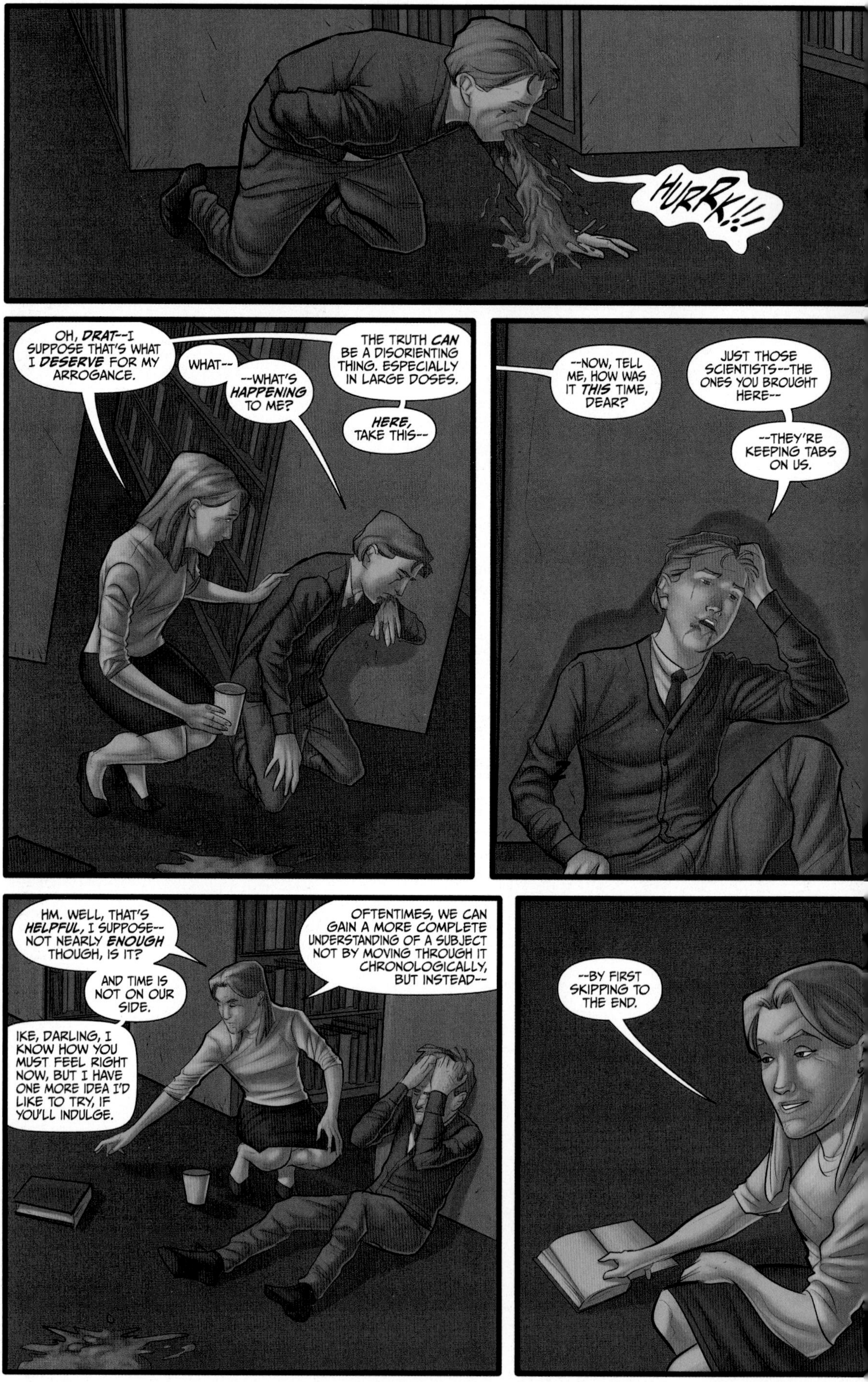
HURRK!!!
OH, DRAT--I SUPPOSE THAT'S WHAT I DESERVE FOR MY ARROGANCE.
WHAT--
--WHAT'S HAPPENING TO ME?
THE TRUTH CAN BE A DISORIENTING THING. ESPECIALLY IN LARGE DOSES.
HERE, TAKE THIS--
--NOW, TELL ME, HOW WAS IT THIS TIME, DEAR?
JUST THOSE SCIENTISTS--THE ONES YOU BROUGHT HERE--
--THEY'RE KEEPING TABS ON US.
HM. WELL, THAT'S HELPFUL, I SUPPOSE--NOT NEARLY ENOUGH THOUGH, IS IT?
AND TIME IS NOT ON OUR SIDE.
IKE, DARLING, I KNOW HOW YOU MUST FEEL RIGHT NOW, BUT I HAVE ONE MORE IDEA I'D LIKE TO TRY, IF YOU'LL INDULGE.
OFTENTIMES, WE CAN GAIN A MORE COMPLETE UNDERSTANDING OF A SUBJECT NOT BY MOVING THROUGH IT CHRONOLOGICALLY, BUT INSTEAD--
--BY FIRST SKIPPING TO THE END.

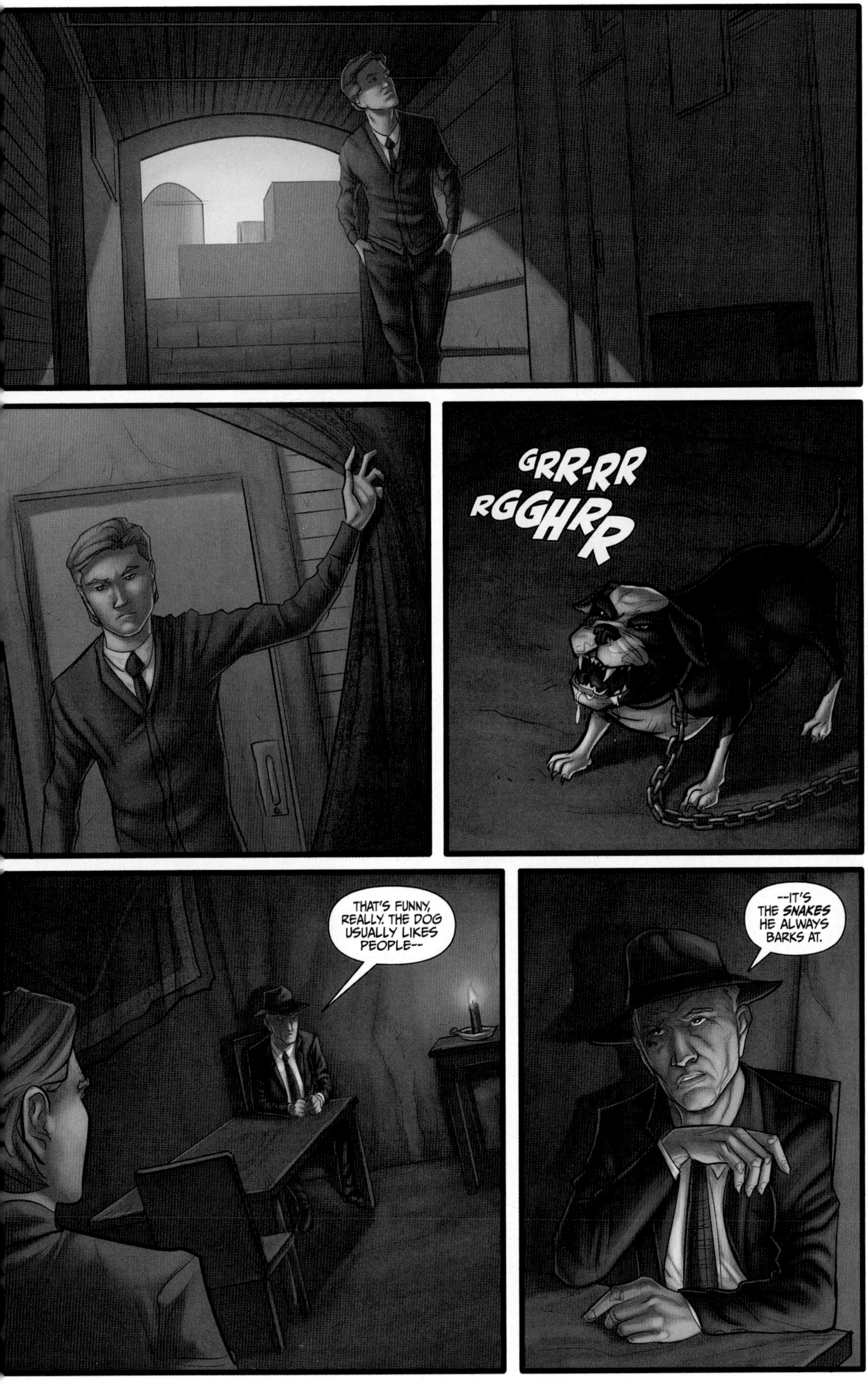
GRR-RR
RGGHRR
THAT'S FUNNY, REALLY. THE DOG USUALLY LIKES PEOPLE--
--IT'S THE SNAKES HE ALWAYS BARKS AT.

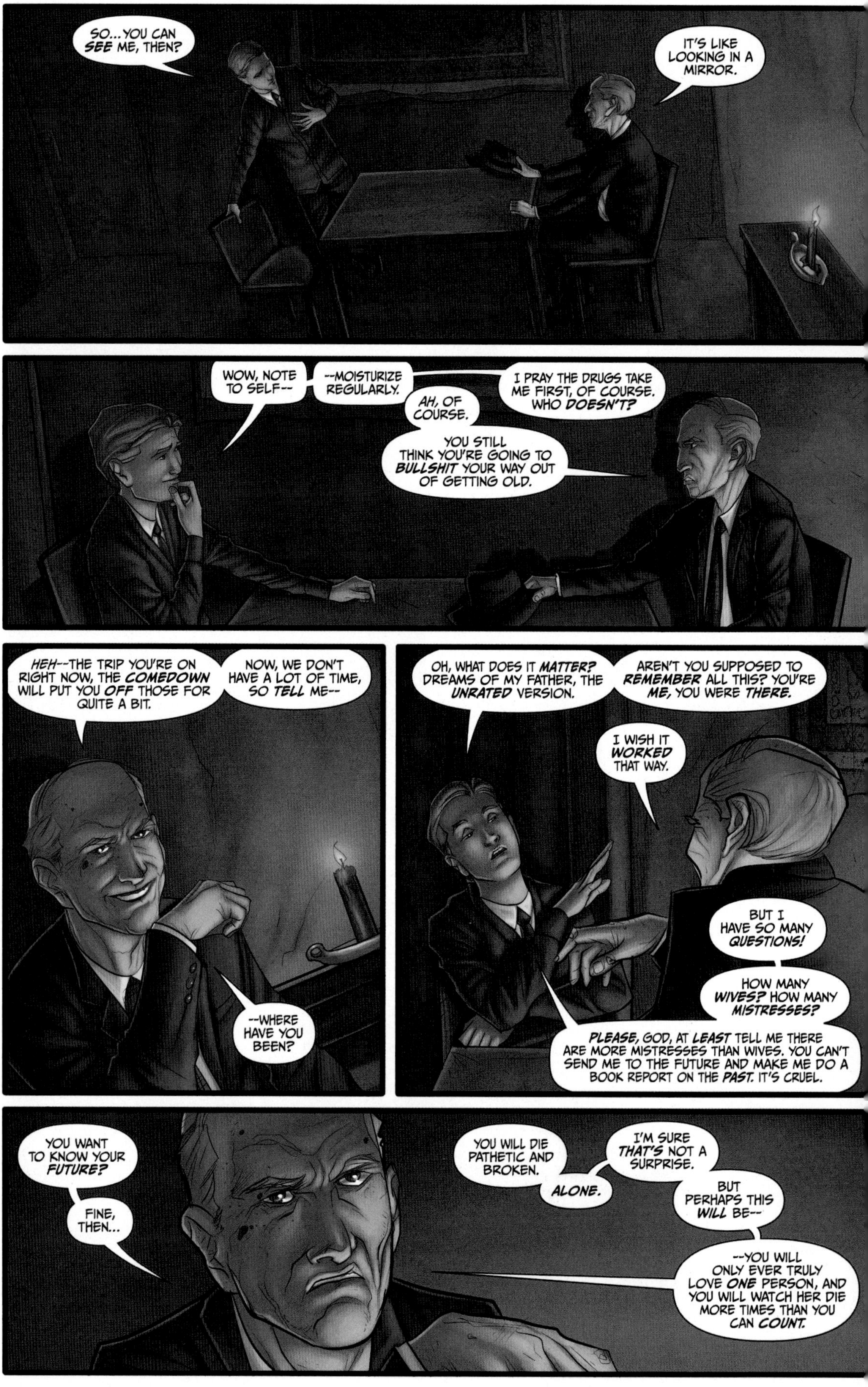
SO...YOU CAN SEE ME, THEN?
IT'S LIKE LOOKING IN A MIRROR.
WOW, NOTE TO SELF--
--MOISTURIZE REGULARLY.
I PRAY THE DRUGS TAKE ME FIRST, OF COURSE. WHO DOESN'T?
AH, OF COURSE.
YOU STILL THINK YOU'RE GOING TO BULLSHIT YOUR WAY OUT OF GETTING OLD.
HEH--THE TRIP YOU'RE ON RIGHT NOW, THE COMEDOWN WILL PUT YOU OFF THOSE FOR QUITE A BIT.
NOW, WE DON'T HAVE A LOT OF TIME, SO TELL ME--
--WHERE HAVE YOU BEEN?
OH, WHAT DOES IT MATTER? DREAMS OF MY FATHER, THE UNRATED VERSION.
AREN'T YOU SUPPOSED TO REMEMBER ALL THIS? YOU'RE ME, YOU WERE THERE.
I WISH IT WORKED THAT WAY.
BUT I HAVE SO MANY QUESTIONS!
HOW MANY WIVES? HOW MANY MISTRESSES?
PLEASE, GOD, AT LEAST TELL ME THERE ARE MORE MISTRESSES THAN WIVES. YOU CAN'T SEND ME TO THE FUTURE AND MAKE ME DO A BOOK REPORT ON THE PAST. IT'S CRUEL.
YOU WANT TO KNOW YOUR FUTURE?
FINE, THEN...
YOU WILL DIE PATHETIC AND BROKEN.
ALONE.
I'M SURE THAT'S NOT A SURPRISE.
BUT PERHAPS THIS WILL BE--
--YOU WILL ONLY EVER TRULY LOVE ONE PERSON, AND YOU WILL WATCH HER DIE MORE TIMES THAN YOU CAN COUNT.

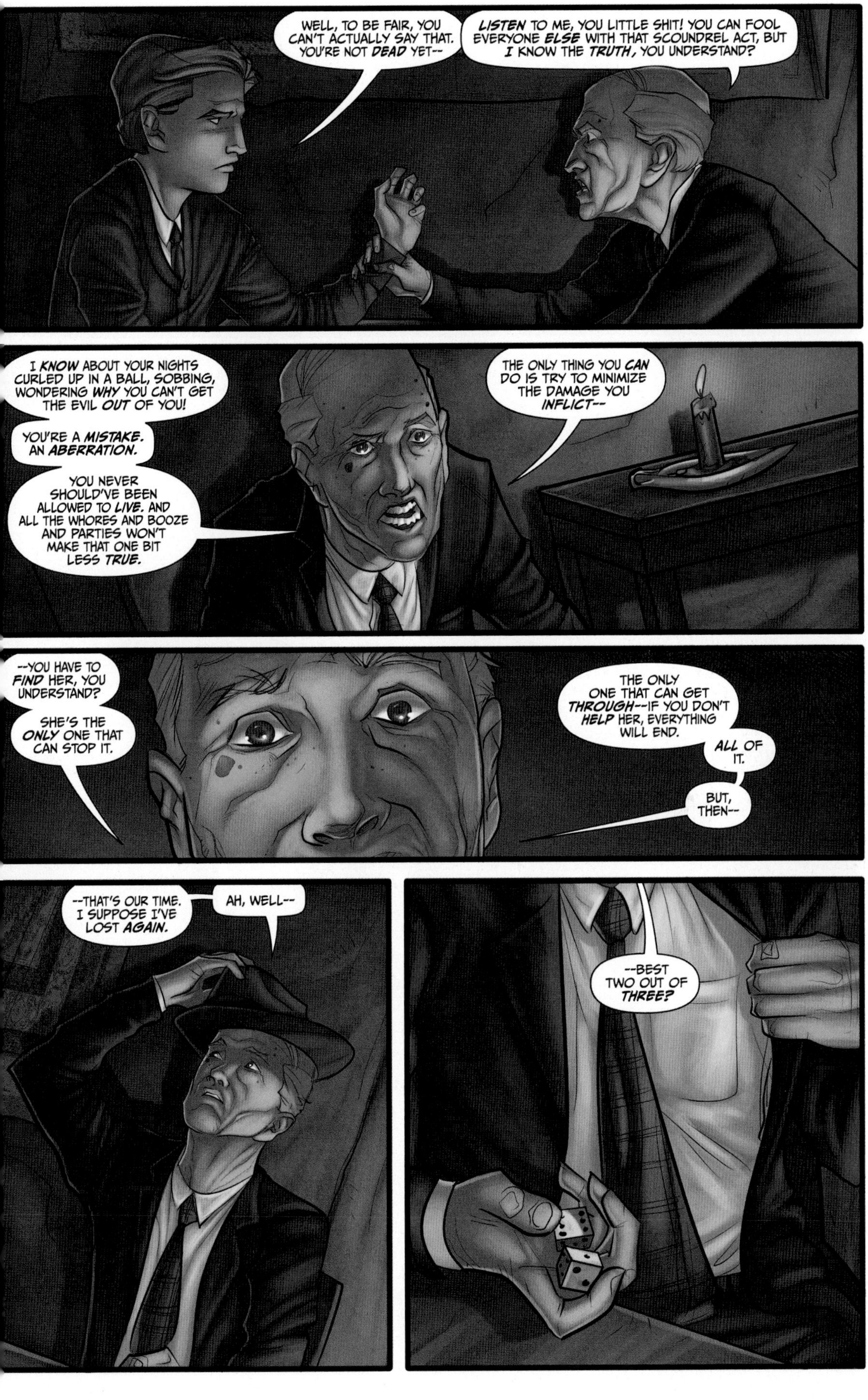

WELL, TO BE FAIR, YOU CAN'T ACTUALLY SAY THAT. YOU'RE NOT DEAD YET--
LISTEN TO ME, YOU LITTLE SHIT! YOU CAN FOOL EVERYONE ELSE WITH THAT SCOUNDREL ACT, BUT I KNOW THE TRUTH, YOU UNDERSTAND?
I KNOW ABOUT YOUR NIGHTS CURLED UP IN A BALL, SOBBING, WONDERING WHY YOU CAN'T GET THE EVIL OUT OF YOU!
YOU'RE A MISTAKE. AN ABERRATION.
YOU NEVER SHOULD'VE BEEN ALLOWED TO LIVE. AND ALL THE WHORES AND BOOZE AND PARTIES WON'T MAKE THAT ONE BIT LESS TRUE.
THE ONLY THING YOU CAN DO IS TRY TO MINIMIZE THE DAMAGE YOU INFLICT--
--YOU HAVE TO FIND HER, YOU UNDERSTAND?
SHE'S THE ONLY ONE THAT CAN STOP IT.
THE ONLY ONE THAT CAN GET THROUGH--IF YOU DON'T HELP HER, EVERYTHING WILL END.
ALL OF IT.
BUT, THEN--
--THAT'S OUR TIME. I SUPPOSE I'VE LOST AGAIN.
AH, WELL--
--BEST TWO OUT OF THREE?

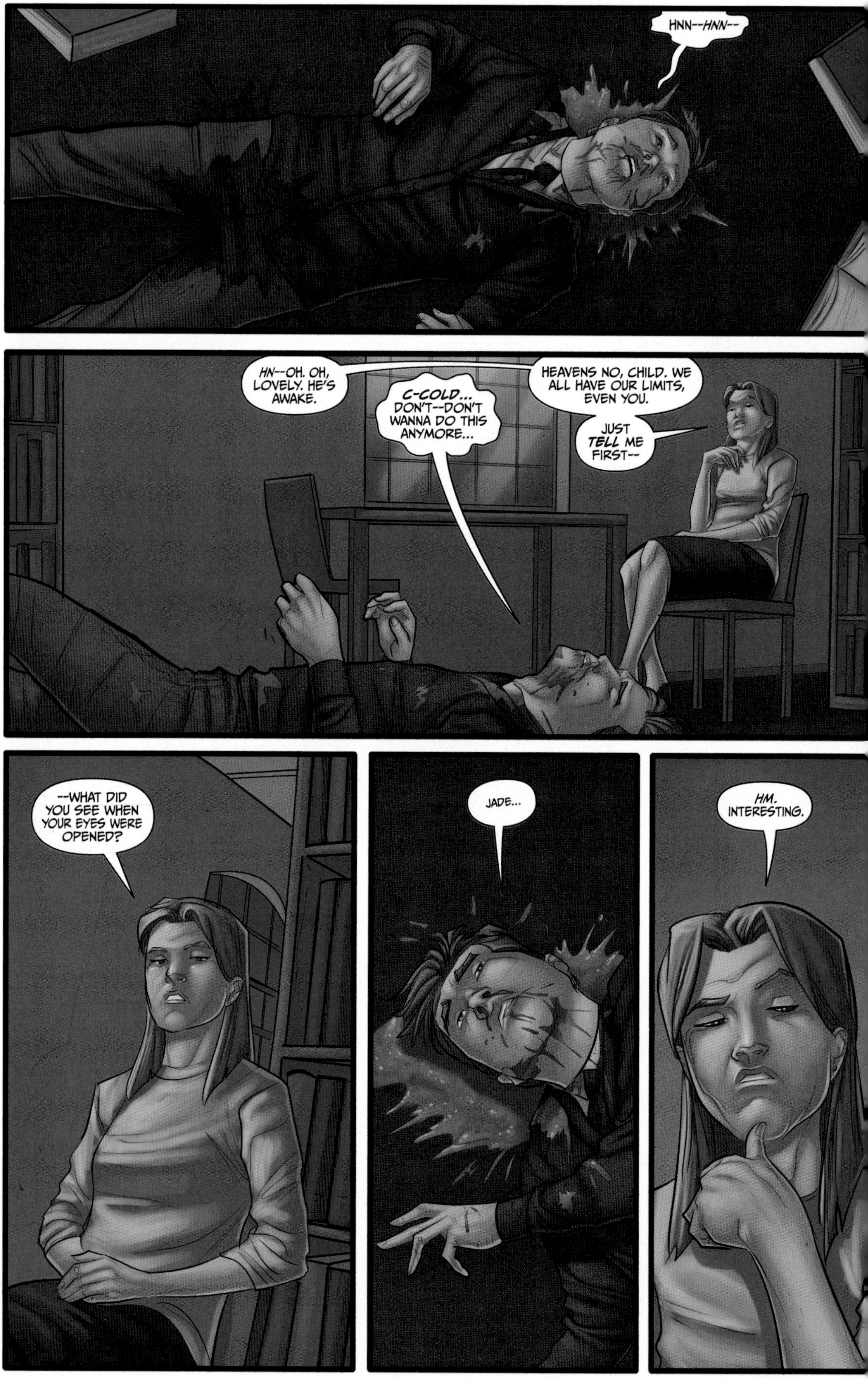
HNN--HNN--
HN--OH. OH, LOVELY. HE'S AWAKE.
C-COLD... DON'T--DON'T WANNA DO THIS ANYMORE...
HEAVENS NO, CHILD. WE ALL HAVE OUR LIMITS, EVEN YOU.
JUST TELL ME FIRST--
--WHAT DID YOU SEE WHEN YOUR EYES WERE OPENED?
JADE...
HM. INTERESTING.

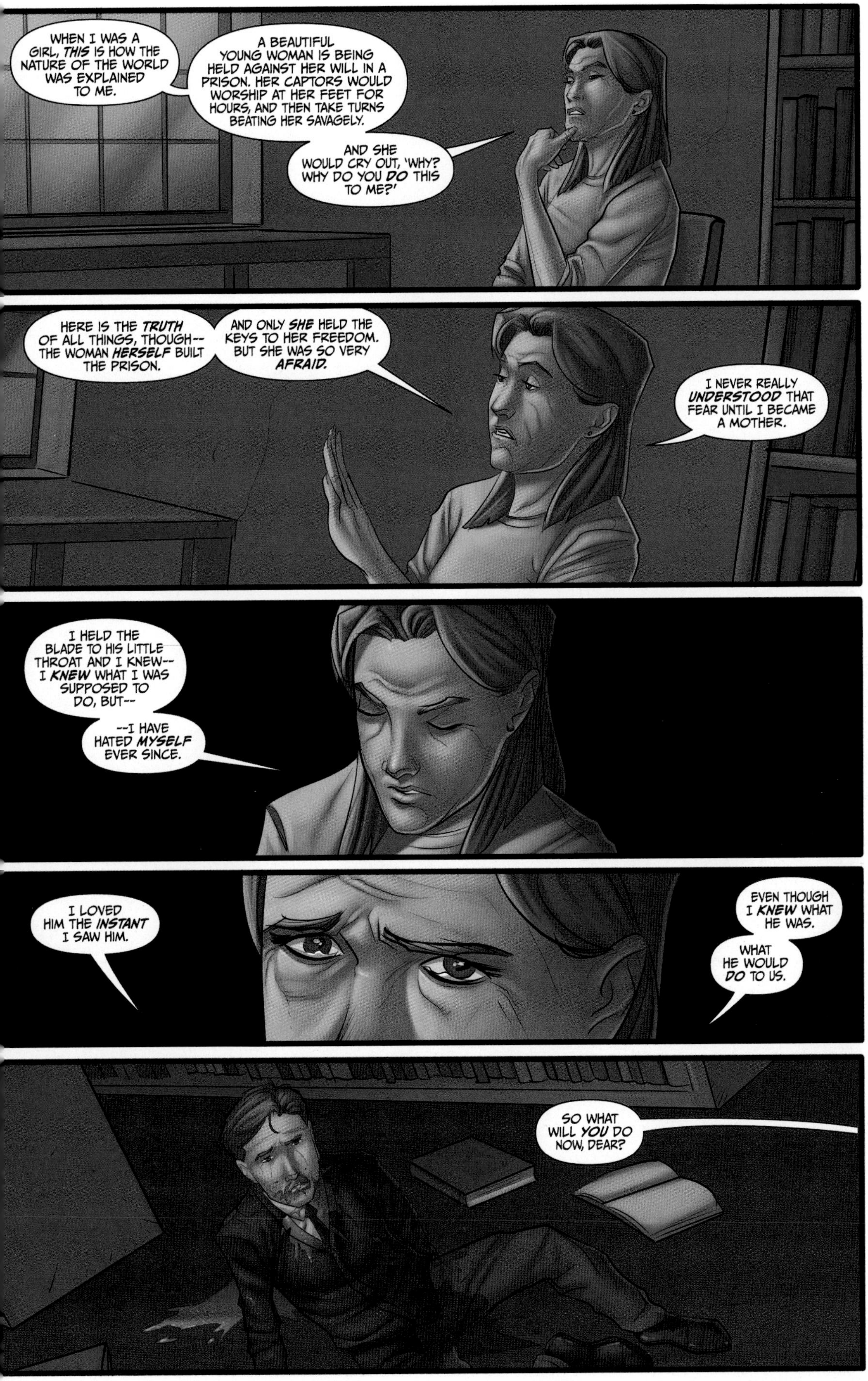
WHEN I WAS A GIRL, *THIS* IS HOW THE NATURE OF THE WORLD WAS EXPLAINED TO ME.
A BEAUTIFUL YOUNG WOMAN IS BEING HELD AGAINST HER WILL IN A PRISON. HER CAPTORS WOULD WORSHIP AT HER FEET FOR HOURS, AND THEN TAKE TURNS BEATING HER SAVAGELY.
AND SHE WOULD CRY OUT, 'WHY? WHY DO YOU *DO* THIS TO ME?'
HERE IS THE *TRUTH* OF ALL THINGS, THOUGH-- THE WOMAN *HERSELF* BUILT THE PRISON.
AND ONLY *SHE* HELD THE KEYS TO HER FREEDOM. BUT SHE WAS SO VERY *AFRAID.*
I NEVER REALLY *UNDERSTOOD* THAT FEAR UNTIL I BECAME A MOTHER.
I HELD THE BLADE TO HIS LITTLE THROAT AND I KNEW-- I *KNEW* WHAT I WAS SUPPOSED TO DO, BUT--
--I HAVE HATED *MYSELF* EVER SINCE.
I LOVED HIM THE *INSTANT* I SAW HIM.
EVEN THOUGH I *KNEW* WHAT HE WAS.
WHAT HE WOULD *DO* TO US.
SO WHAT WILL *YOU* DO NOW, DEAR?

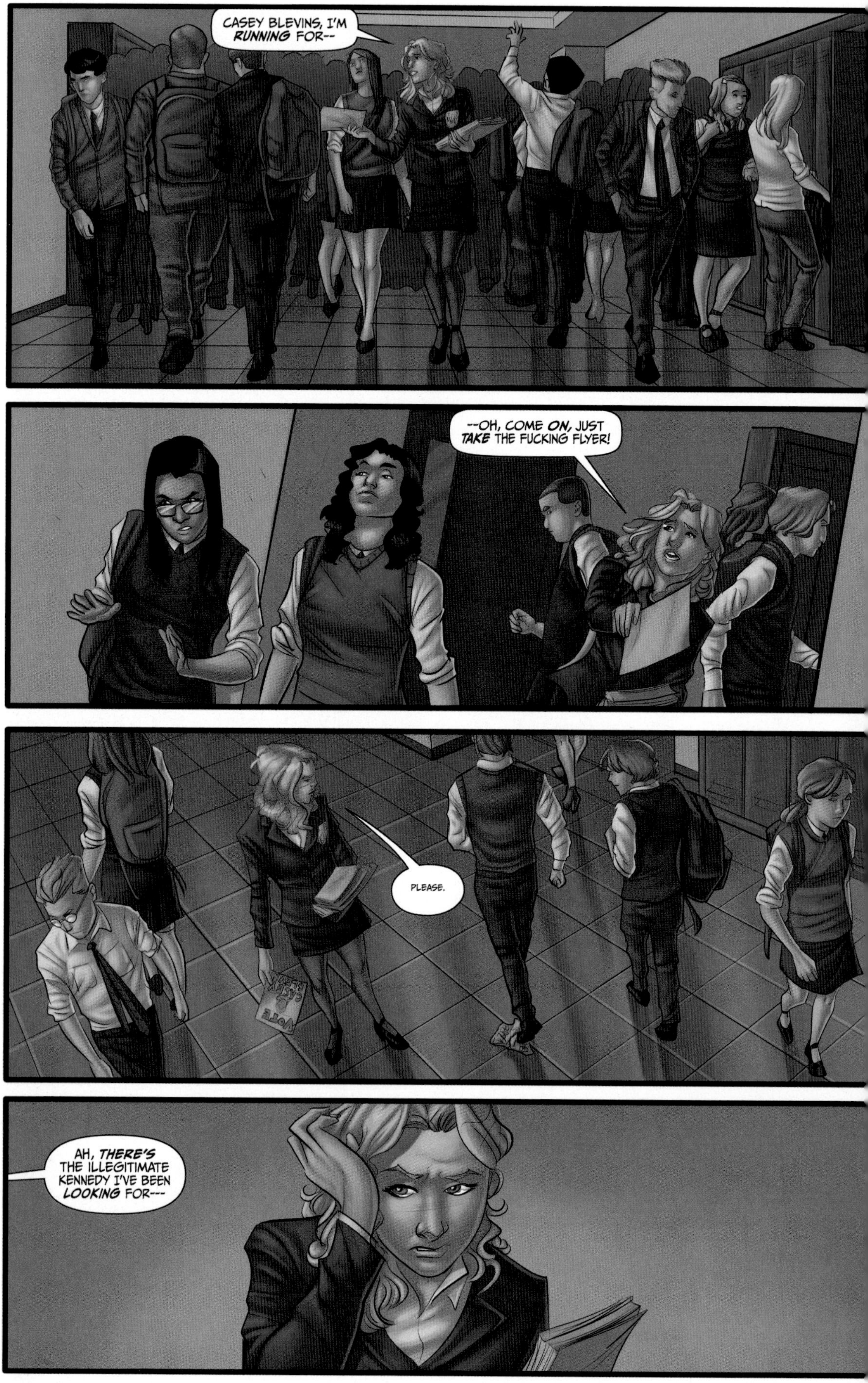
CASEY BLEVINS, I'M *RUNNING* FOR--
--OH, COME *ON*, JUST *TAKE* THE FUCKING FLYER!
PLEASE.
AH, *THERE'S* THE ILLEGITIMATE KENNEDY I'VE BEEN *LOOKING* FOR---

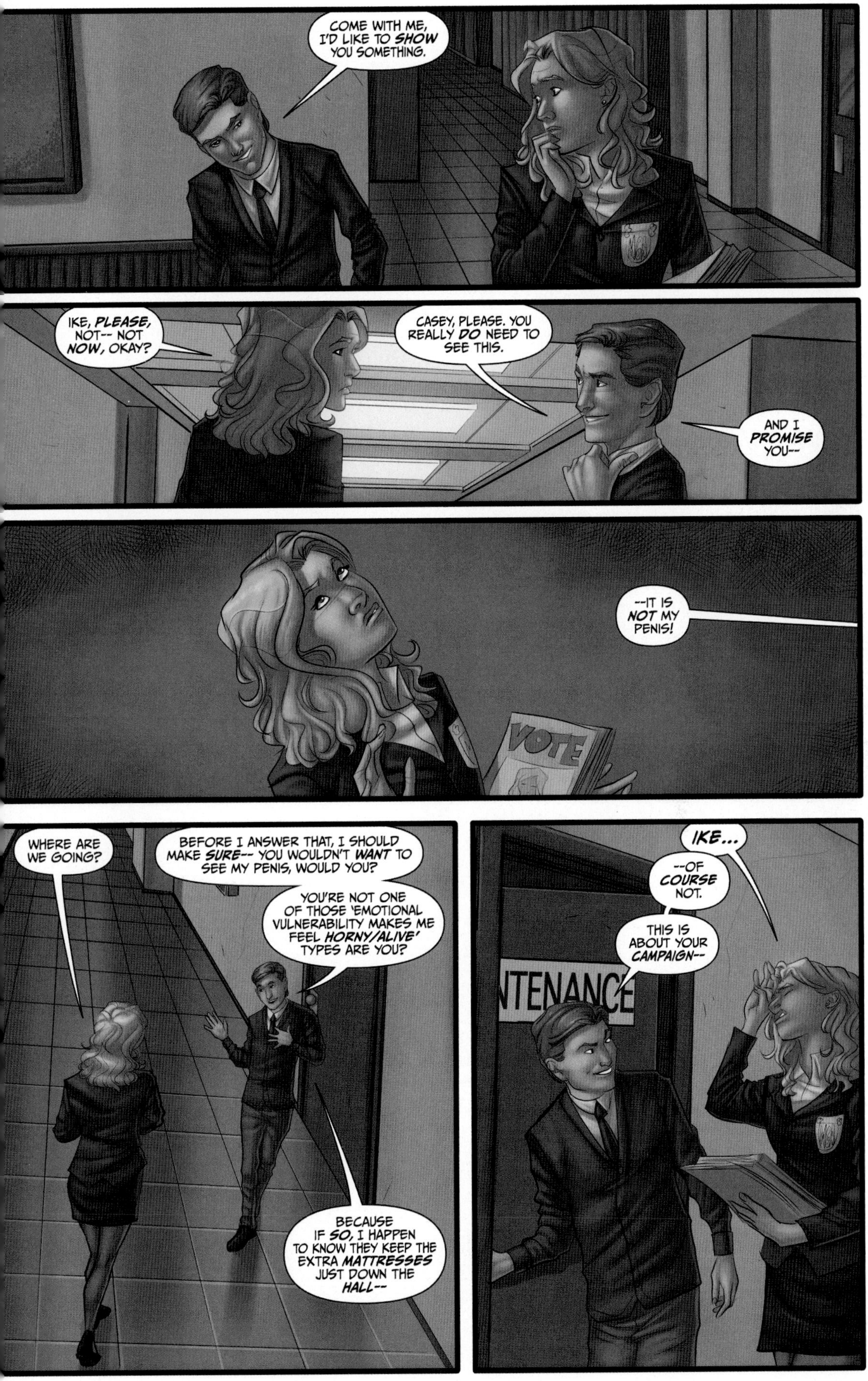
COME WITH ME, I'D LIKE TO SHOW YOU SOMETHING.
IKE, PLEASE, NOT-- NOT NOW, OKAY?
CASEY, PLEASE. YOU REALLY DO NEED TO SEE THIS.
AND I PROMISE YOU--
--IT IS NOT MY PENIS!
VOTE
WHERE ARE WE GOING?
BEFORE I ANSWER THAT, I SHOULD MAKE SURE-- YOU WOULDN'T WANT TO SEE MY PENIS, WOULD YOU?
YOU'RE NOT ONE OF THOSE 'EMOTIONAL VULNERABILITY MAKES ME FEEL HORNY/ALIVE' TYPES ARE YOU?
BECAUSE IF SO, I HAPPEN TO KNOW THEY KEEP THE EXTRA MATTRESSES JUST DOWN THE HALL--
IKE...
--OF COURSE NOT.
THIS IS ABOUT YOUR CAMPAIGN--
NTENANCE

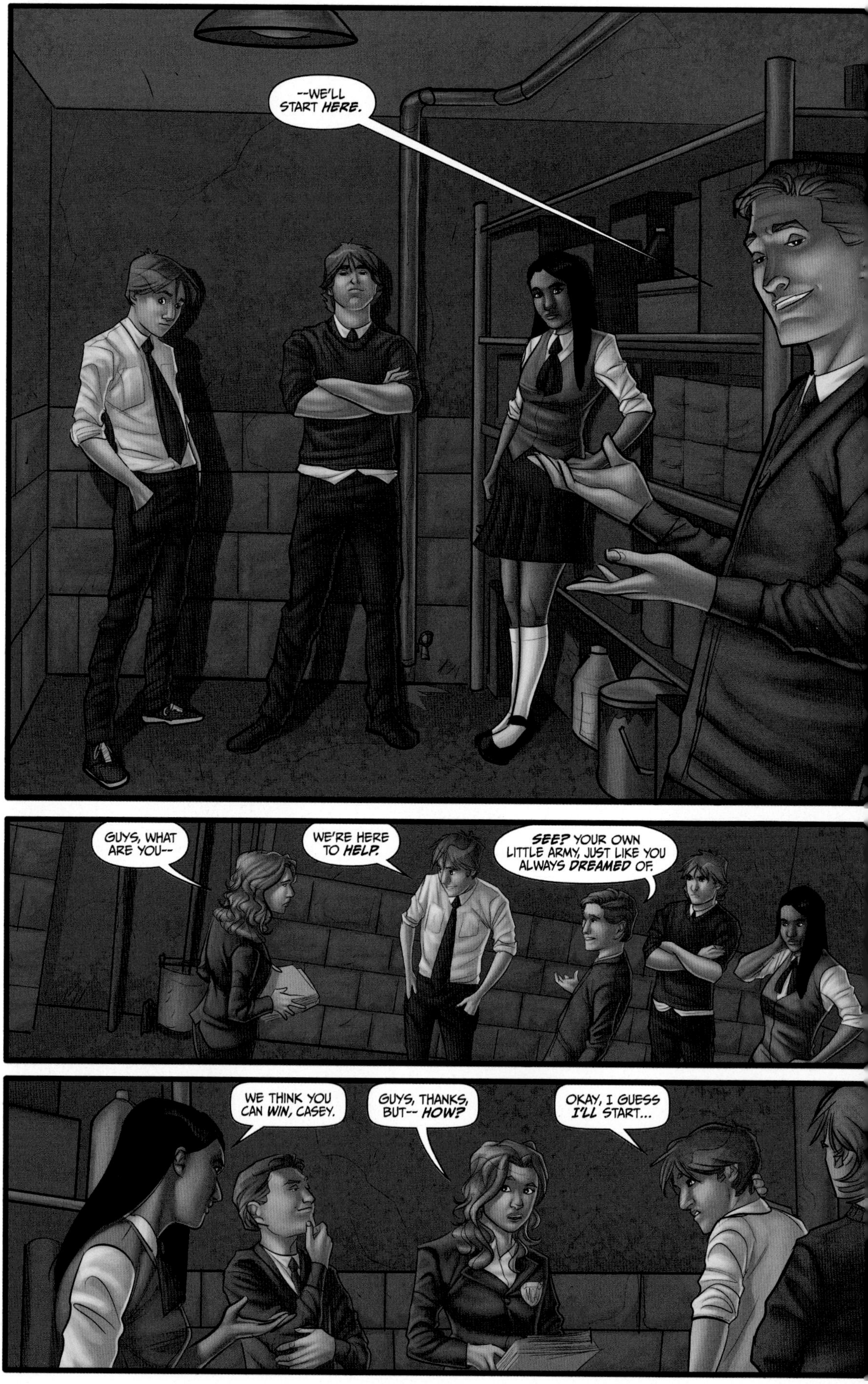
--WE'LL START *HERE.*
GUYS, WHAT ARE YOU--
WE'RE HERE TO *HELP.*
SEE? YOUR OWN LITTLE ARMY, JUST LIKE YOU ALWAYS *DREAMED* OF.
WE THINK YOU CAN *WIN,* CASEY.
GUYS, THANKS, BUT-- *HOW?*
OKAY, I GUESS *I'LL* START...

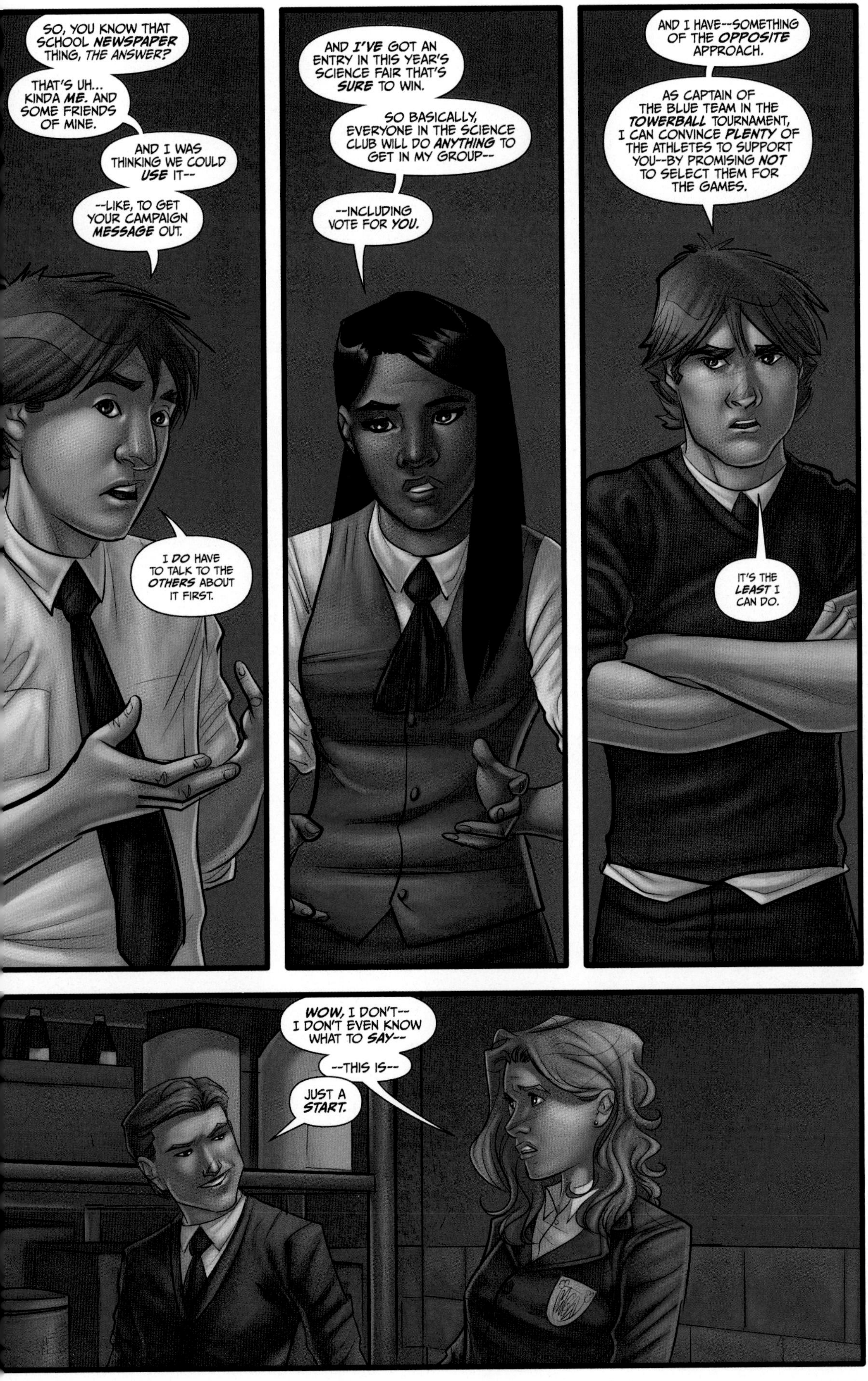
SO, YOU KNOW THAT SCHOOL NEWSPAPER THING, THE ANSWER?
THAT'S UH... KINDA ME. AND SOME FRIENDS OF MINE.
AND I WAS THINKING WE COULD USE IT--
--LIKE, TO GET YOUR CAMPAIGN MESSAGE OUT.
I DO HAVE TO TALK TO THE OTHERS ABOUT IT FIRST.
AND I'VE GOT AN ENTRY IN THIS YEAR'S SCIENCE FAIR THAT'S SURE TO WIN.
SO BASICALLY, EVERYONE IN THE SCIENCE CLUB WILL DO ANYTHING TO GET IN MY GROUP--
--INCLUDING VOTE FOR YOU.
AND I HAVE--SOMETHING OF THE OPPOSITE APPROACH.
AS CAPTAIN OF THE BLUE TEAM IN THE TOWERBALL TOURNAMENT, I CAN CONVINCE PLENTY OF THE ATHLETES TO SUPPORT YOU--BY PROMISING NOT TO SELECT THEM FOR THE GAMES.
IT'S THE LEAST I CAN DO.
WOW, I DON'T-- I DON'T EVEN KNOW WHAT TO SAY--
--THIS IS--
JUST A START.

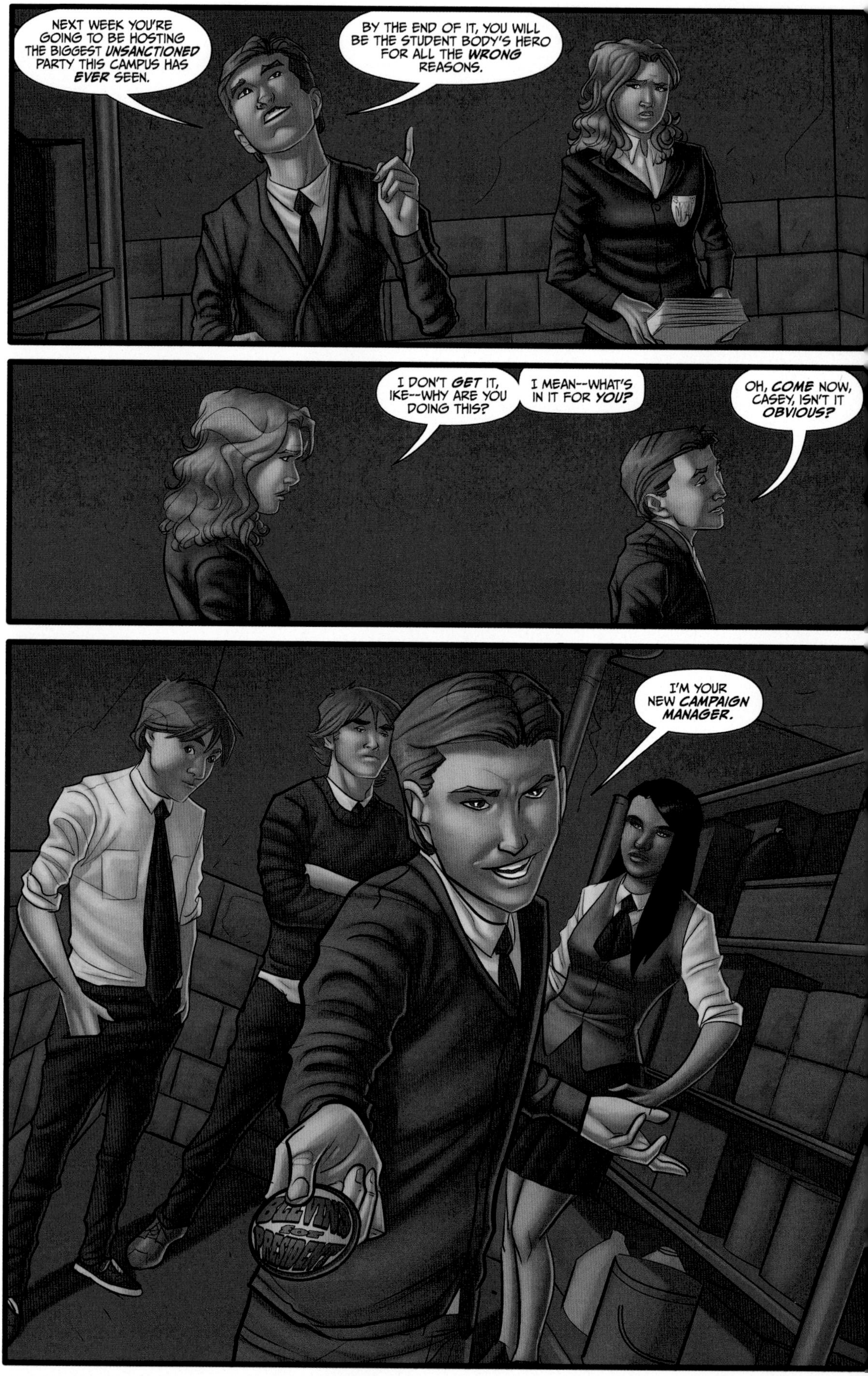
NEXT WEEK YOU'RE GOING TO BE HOSTING THE BIGGEST *UNSANCTIONED* PARTY THIS CAMPUS HAS *EVER* SEEN.
BY THE END OF IT, YOU WILL BE THE STUDENT BODY'S HERO FOR ALL THE *WRONG* REASONS.
I DON'T *GET* IT, IKE--WHY ARE YOU DOING THIS?
I MEAN--WHAT'S IN IT FOR *YOU?*
OH, *COME* NOW, CASEY, ISN'T IT *OBVIOUS?*
I'M YOUR NEW *CAMPAIGN MANAGER.*

forty**four**

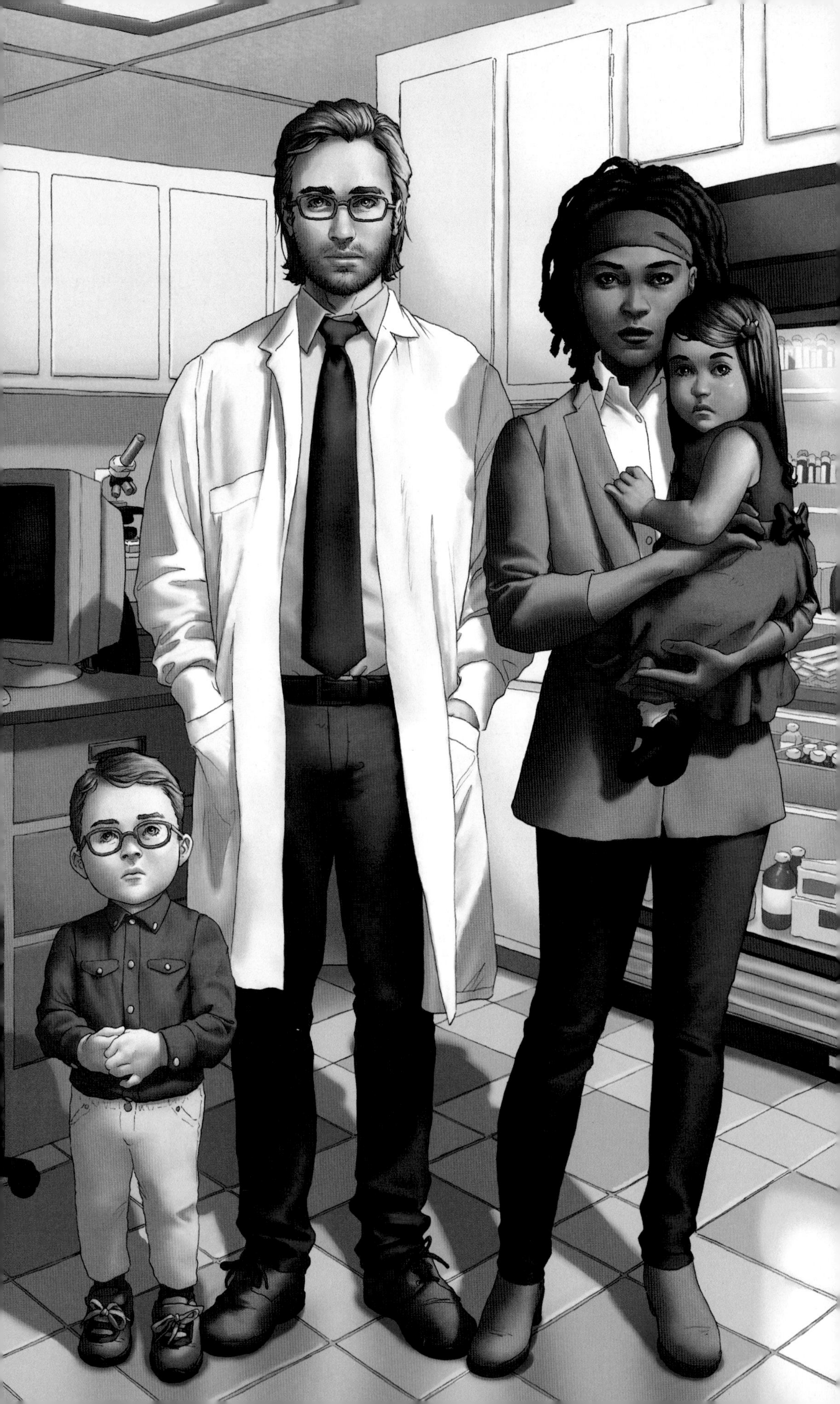

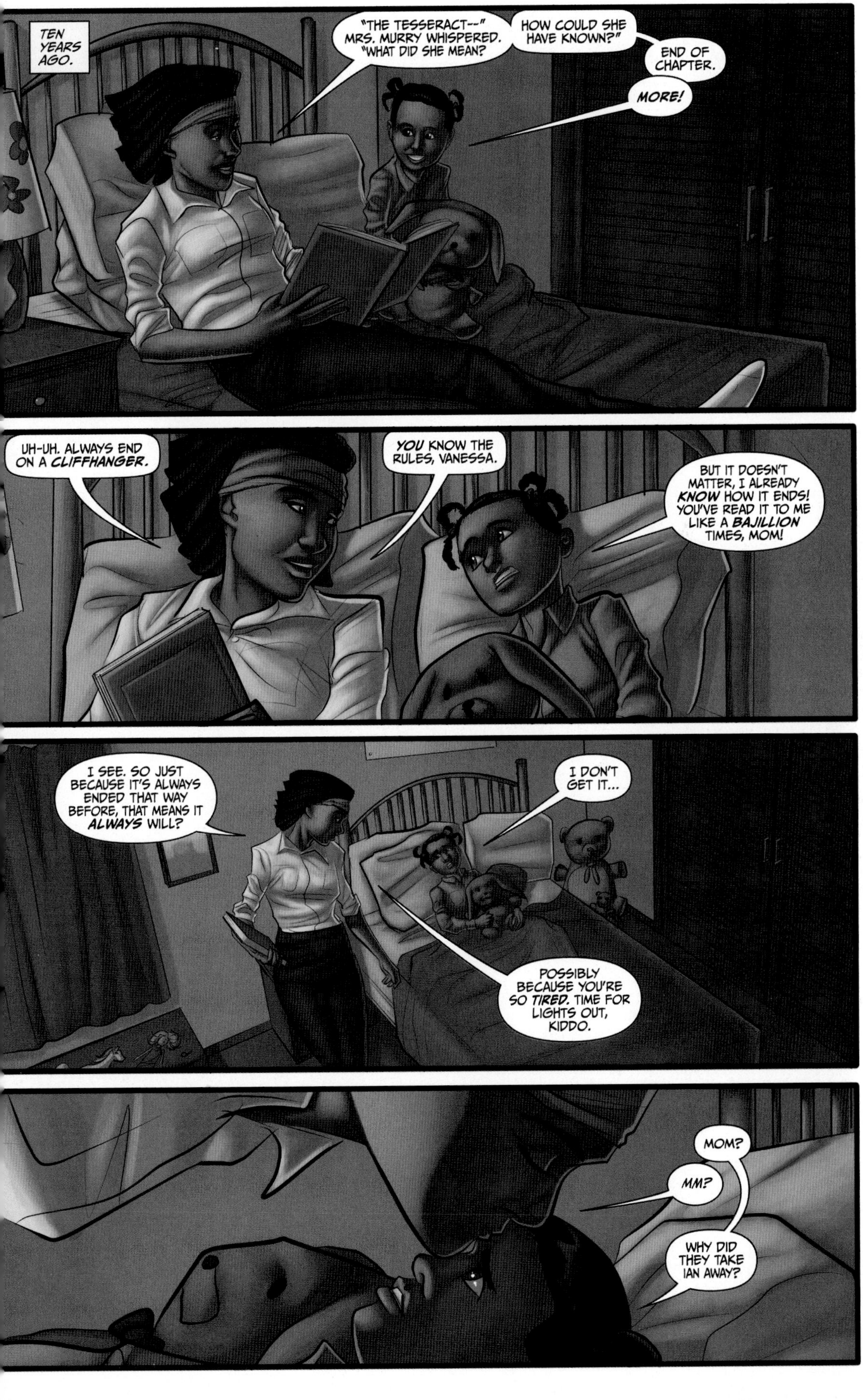
TEN YEARS AGO.
"THE TESSERACT--" MRS. MURRY WHISPERED. "WHAT DID SHE MEAN?
HOW COULD SHE HAVE KNOWN?"
END OF CHAPTER.
MORE!
UH-UH. ALWAYS END ON A CLIFFHANGER.
YOU KNOW THE RULES, VANESSA.
BUT IT DOESN'T MATTER, I ALREADY KNOW HOW IT ENDS! YOU'VE READ IT TO ME LIKE A BAJILLION TIMES, MOM!
I SEE. SO JUST BECAUSE IT'S ALWAYS ENDED THAT WAY BEFORE, THAT MEANS IT ALWAYS WILL?
I DON'T GET IT...
POSSIBLY BECAUSE YOU'RE SO TIRED. TIME FOR LIGHTS OUT, KIDDO.
MOM?
MM?
WHY DID THEY TAKE IAN AWAY?

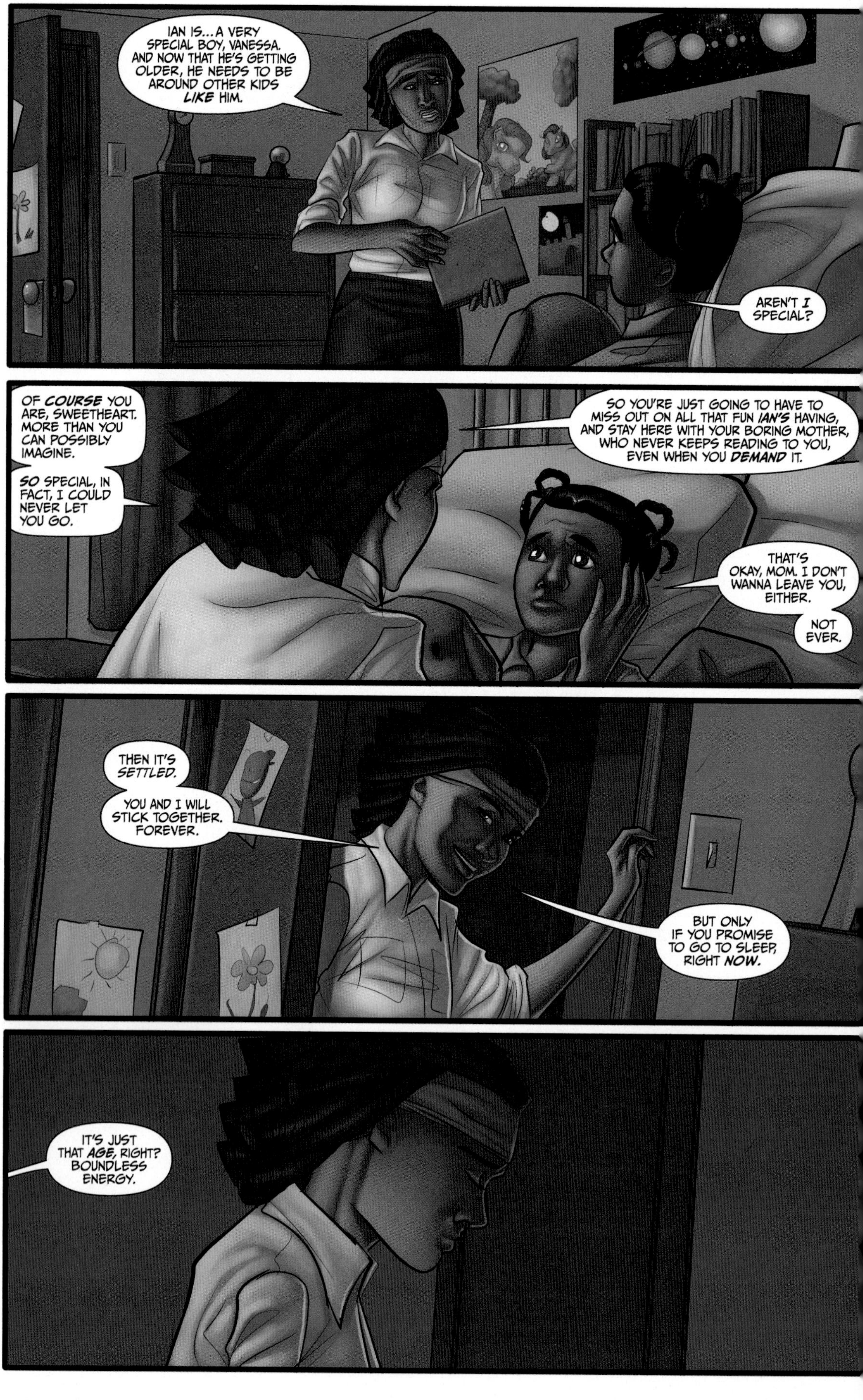
IAN IS... A VERY SPECIAL BOY, VANESSA. AND NOW THAT HE'S GETTING OLDER, HE NEEDS TO BE AROUND OTHER KIDS *LIKE* HIM.
AREN'T *I* SPECIAL?
OF *COURSE* YOU ARE, SWEETHEART. MORE THAN YOU CAN POSSIBLY IMAGINE.
SO SPECIAL, IN FACT, I COULD NEVER LET YOU GO.
SO YOU'RE JUST GOING TO HAVE TO MISS OUT ON ALL THAT FUN *IAN'S* HAVING, AND STAY HERE WITH YOUR BORING MOTHER, WHO NEVER KEEPS READING TO YOU, EVEN WHEN YOU *DEMAND* IT.
THAT'S OKAY, MOM. I DON'T WANNA LEAVE YOU, EITHER.
NOT EVER.
THEN IT'S *SETTLED.*
YOU AND I WILL STICK TOGETHER. FOREVER.
BUT ONLY IF YOU PROMISE TO GO TO SLEEP, RIGHT *NOW.*
IT'S JUST THAT *AGE*, RIGHT? BOUNDLESS ENERGY.

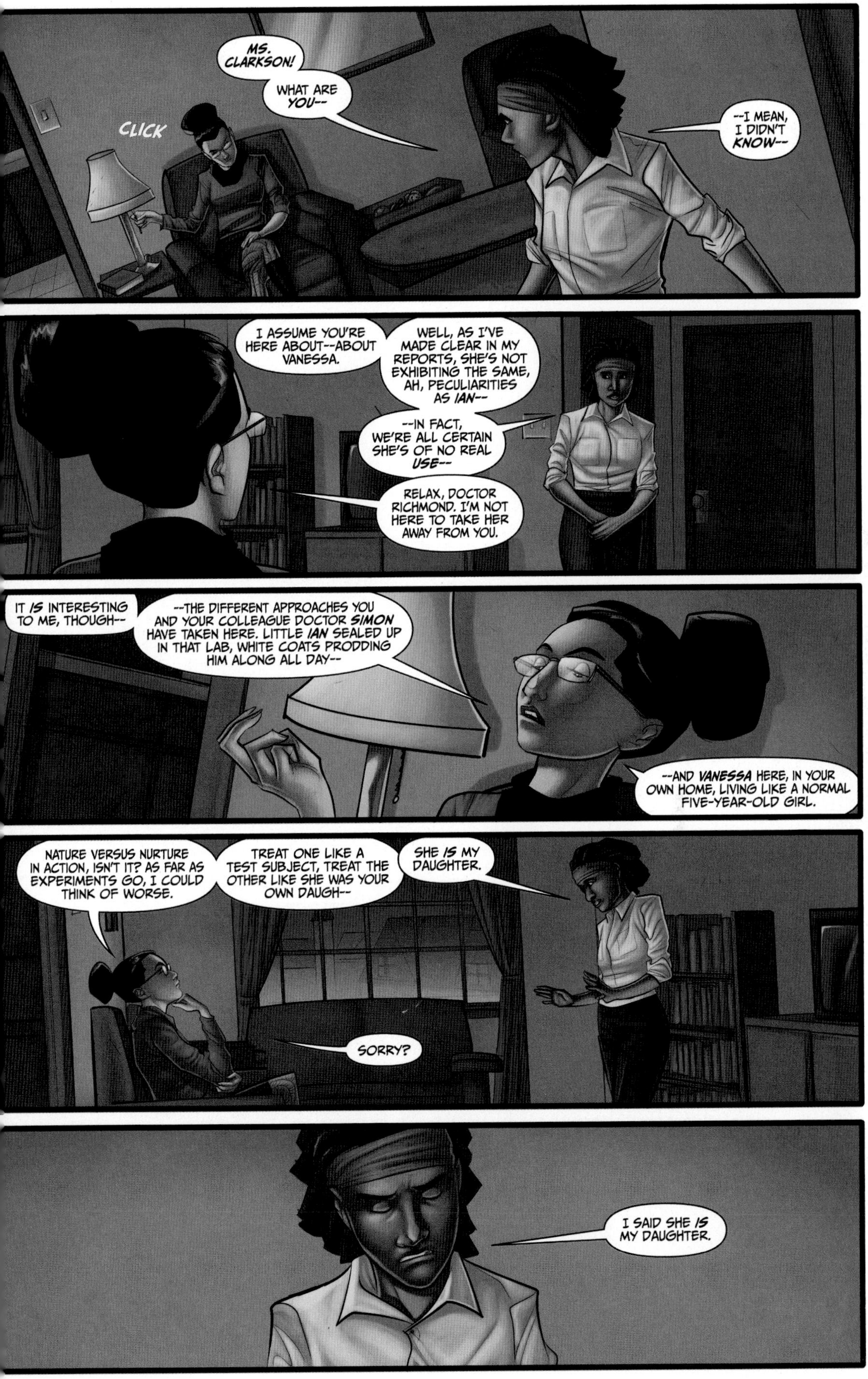
MS. CLARKSON!
WHAT ARE YOU--
CLICK
--I MEAN, I DIDN'T KNOW--
I ASSUME YOU'RE HERE ABOUT--ABOUT VANESSA.
WELL, AS I'VE MADE CLEAR IN MY REPORTS, SHE'S NOT EXHIBITING THE SAME, AH, PECULIARITIES AS IAN--
--IN FACT, WE'RE ALL CERTAIN SHE'S OF NO REAL USE--
RELAX, DOCTOR RICHMOND. I'M NOT HERE TO TAKE HER AWAY FROM YOU.
IT IS INTERESTING TO ME, THOUGH--
--THE DIFFERENT APPROACHES YOU AND YOUR COLLEAGUE DOCTOR SIMON HAVE TAKEN HERE. LITTLE IAN SEALED UP IN THAT LAB, WHITE COATS PRODDING HIM ALONG ALL DAY--
--AND VANESSA HERE, IN YOUR OWN HOME, LIVING LIKE A NORMAL FIVE-YEAR-OLD GIRL.
NATURE VERSUS NURTURE IN ACTION, ISN'T IT? AS FAR AS EXPERIMENTS GO, I COULD THINK OF WORSE.
TREAT ONE LIKE A TEST SUBJECT, TREAT THE OTHER LIKE SHE WAS YOUR OWN DAUGH--
SHE IS MY DAUGHTER.
SORRY?
I SAID SHE IS MY DAUGHTER.

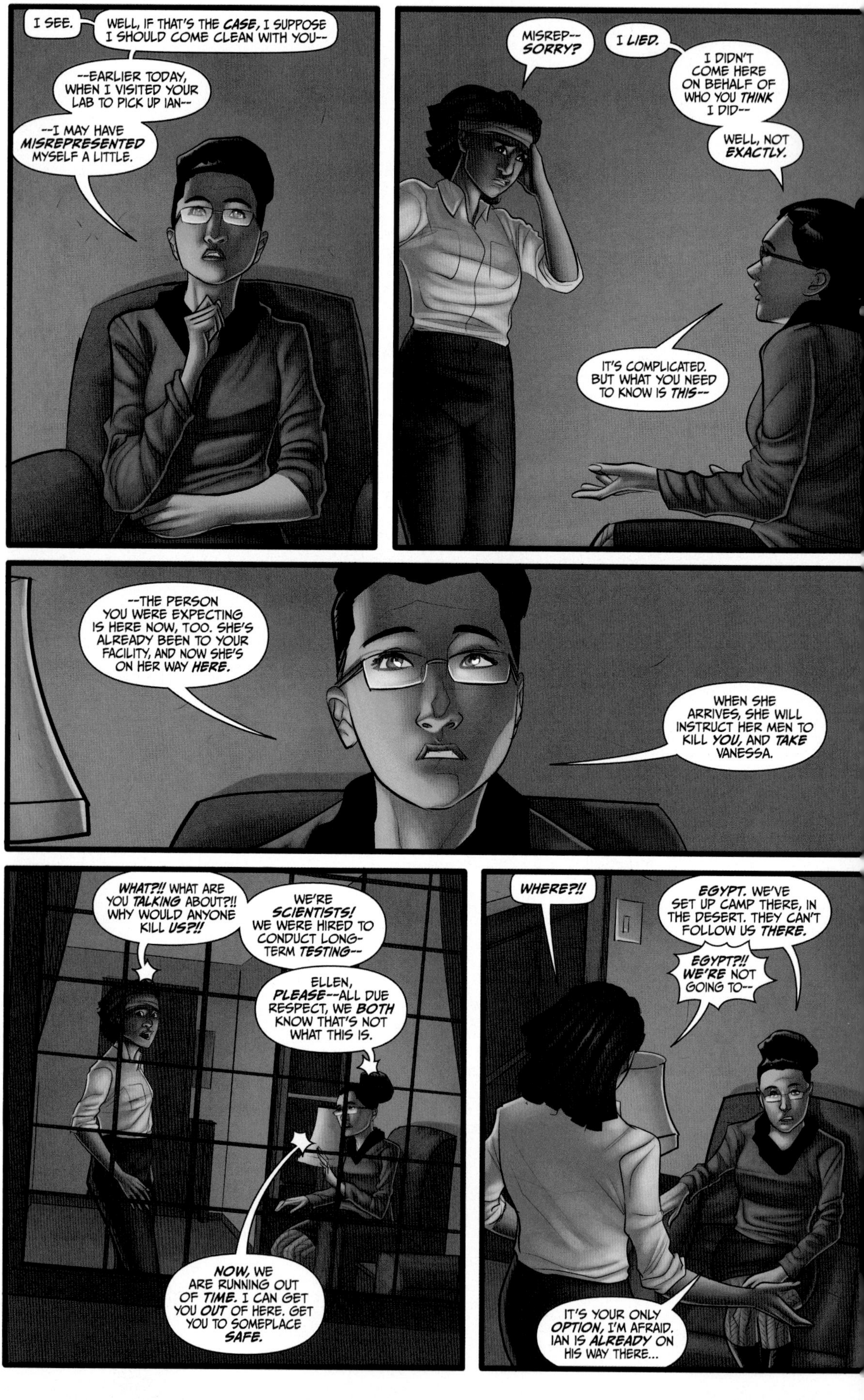
I SEE.
WELL, IF THAT'S THE CASE, I SUPPOSE I SHOULD COME CLEAN WITH YOU--
--EARLIER TODAY, WHEN I VISITED YOUR LAB TO PICK UP IAN--
--I MAY HAVE MISREPRESENTED MYSELF A LITTLE.
MISREP-- SORRY?
I LIED.
I DIDN'T COME HERE ON BEHALF OF WHO YOU THINK I DID--
WELL, NOT EXACTLY.
IT'S COMPLICATED. BUT WHAT YOU NEED TO KNOW IS THIS--
--THE PERSON YOU WERE EXPECTING IS HERE NOW, TOO. SHE'S ALREADY BEEN TO YOUR FACILITY, AND NOW SHE'S ON HER WAY HERE.
WHEN SHE ARRIVES, SHE WILL INSTRUCT HER MEN TO KILL YOU, AND TAKE VANESSA.
WHAT?!! WHAT ARE YOU TALKING ABOUT?!! WHY WOULD ANYONE KILL US?!!
WE'RE SCIENTISTS! WE WERE HIRED TO CONDUCT LONG-TERM TESTING--
ELLEN, PLEASE--ALL DUE RESPECT, WE BOTH KNOW THAT'S NOT WHAT THIS IS.
NOW, WE ARE RUNNING OUT OF TIME. I CAN GET YOU OUT OF HERE. GET YOU TO SOMEPLACE SAFE.
WHERE?!!
EGYPT. WE'VE SET UP CAMP THERE, IN THE DESERT. THEY CAN'T FOLLOW US THERE.
EGYPT?!! WE'RE NOT GOING TO--
IT'S YOUR ONLY OPTION, I'M AFRAID. IAN IS ALREADY ON HIS WAY THERE...

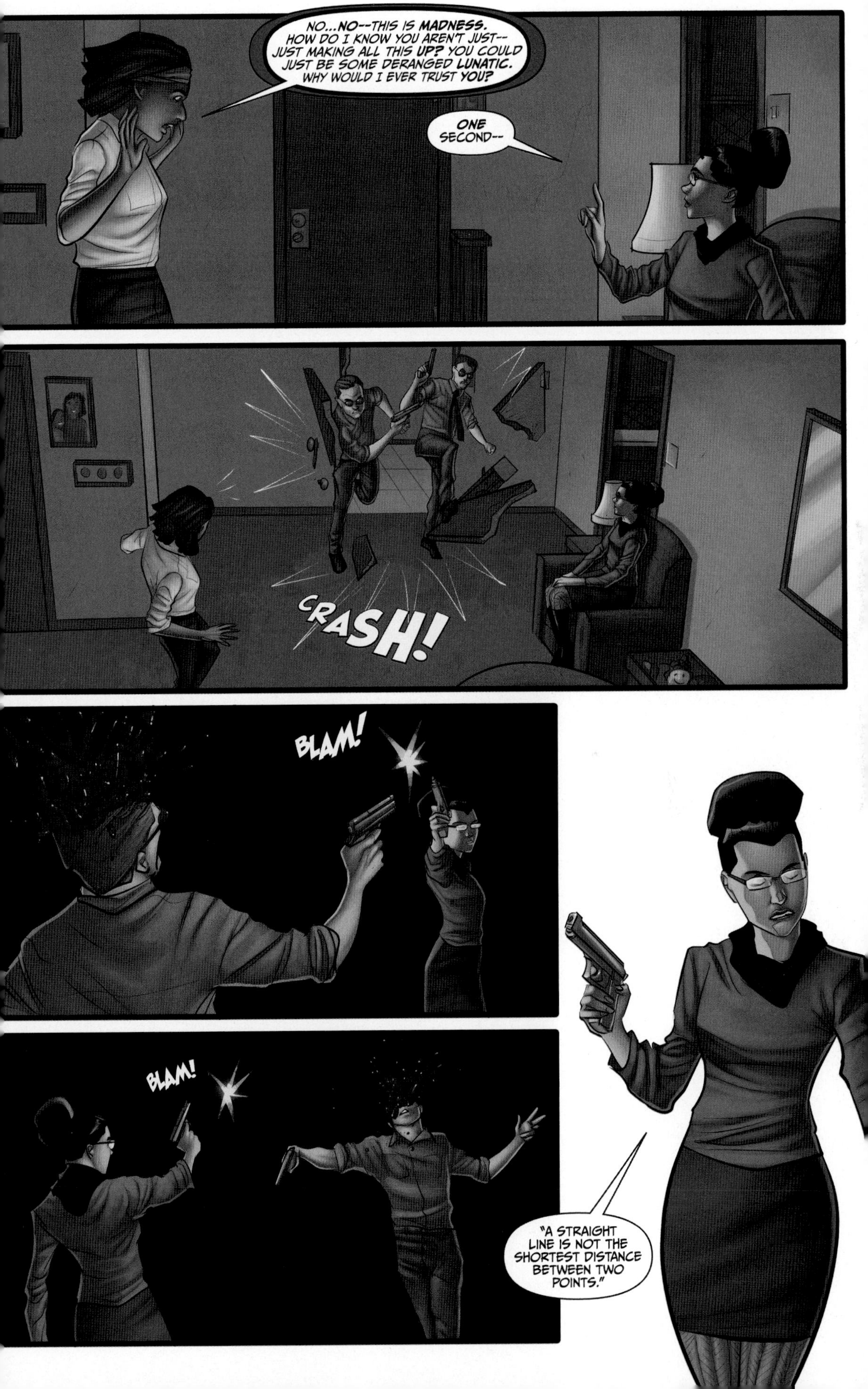
NO...NO--THIS IS MADNESS. HOW DO I KNOW YOU AREN'T JUST-- JUST MAKING ALL THIS UP? YOU COULD JUST BE SOME DERANGED LUNATIC. WHY WOULD I EVER TRUST YOU?
ONE SECOND--
CRASH!
BLAM!
BLAM!
"A STRAIGHT LINE IS NOT THE SHORTEST DISTANCE BETWEEN TWO POINTS."

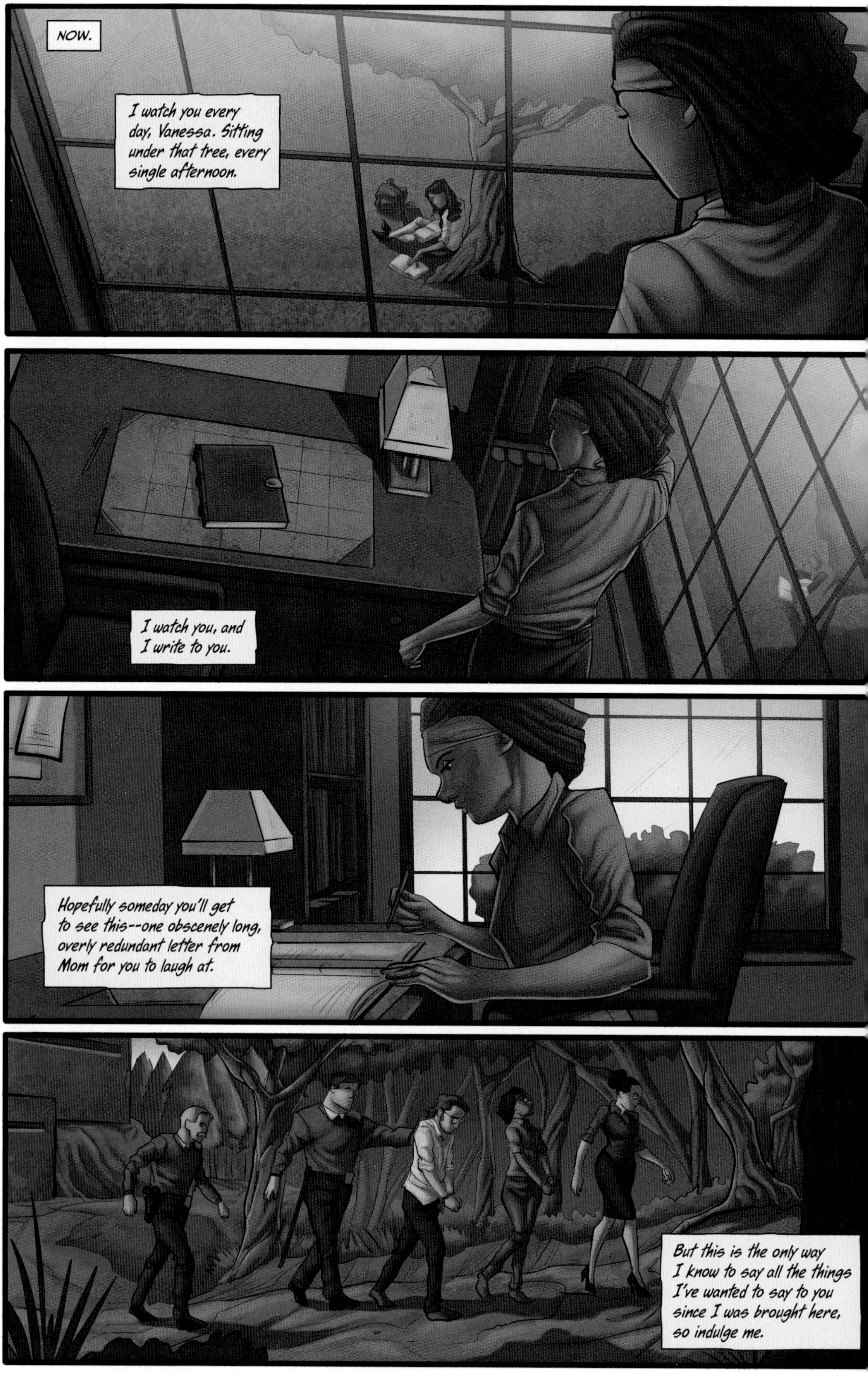
NOW.
I watch you every day, Vanessa. Sitting under that tree, every single afternoon.
I watch you, and I write to you.
Hopefully someday you'll get to see this--one obscenely long, overly redundant letter from Mom for you to laugh at.
But this is the only way I know to say all the things I've wanted to say to you since I was brought here, so indulge me.

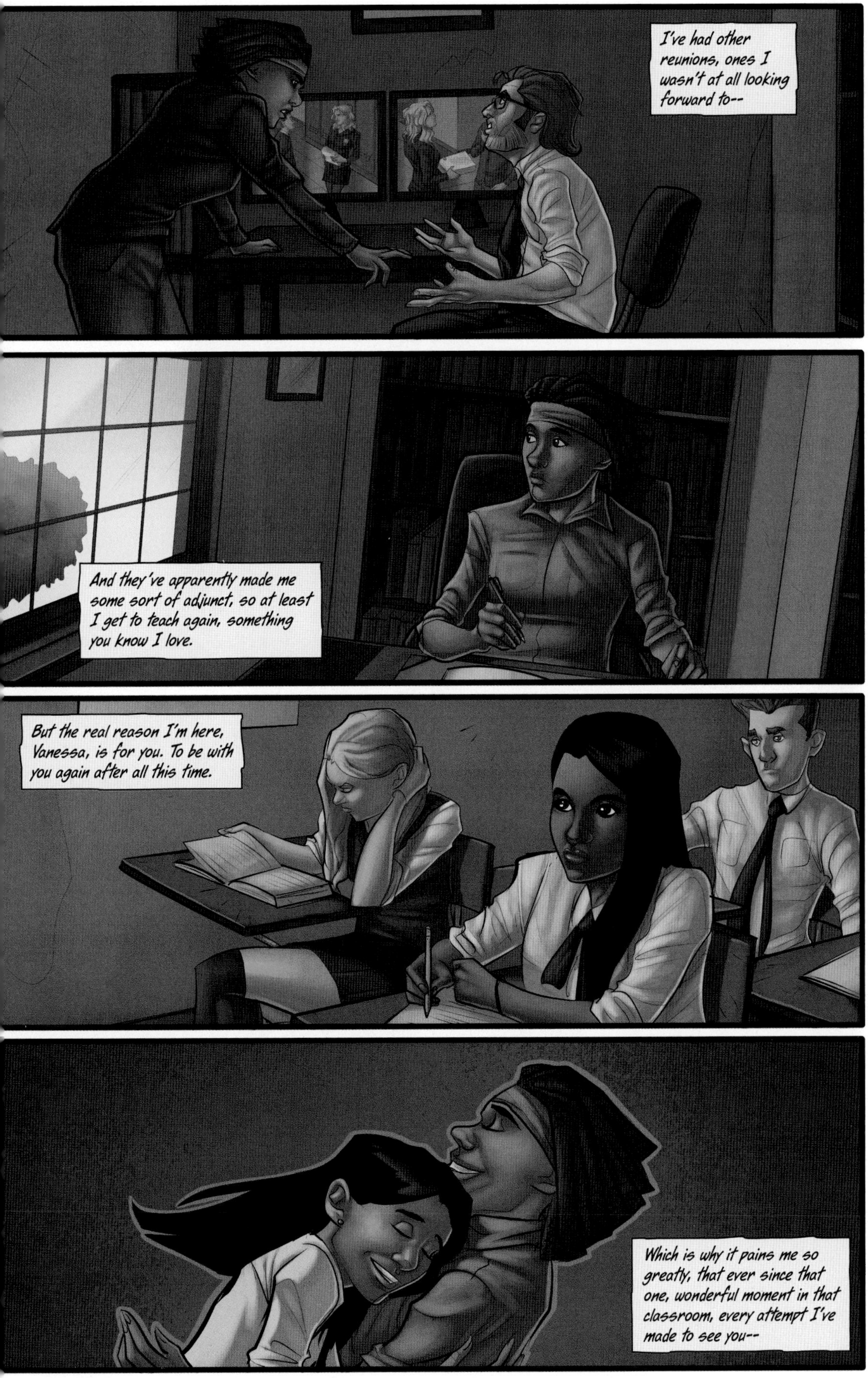
I've had other reunions, ones I wasn't at all looking forward to--
And they've apparently made me some sort of adjunct, so at least I get to teach again, something you know I love.
But the real reason I'm here, Vanessa, is for you. To be with you again after all this time.
Which is why it pains me so greatly, that ever since that one, wonderful moment in that classroom, every attempt I've made to see you--

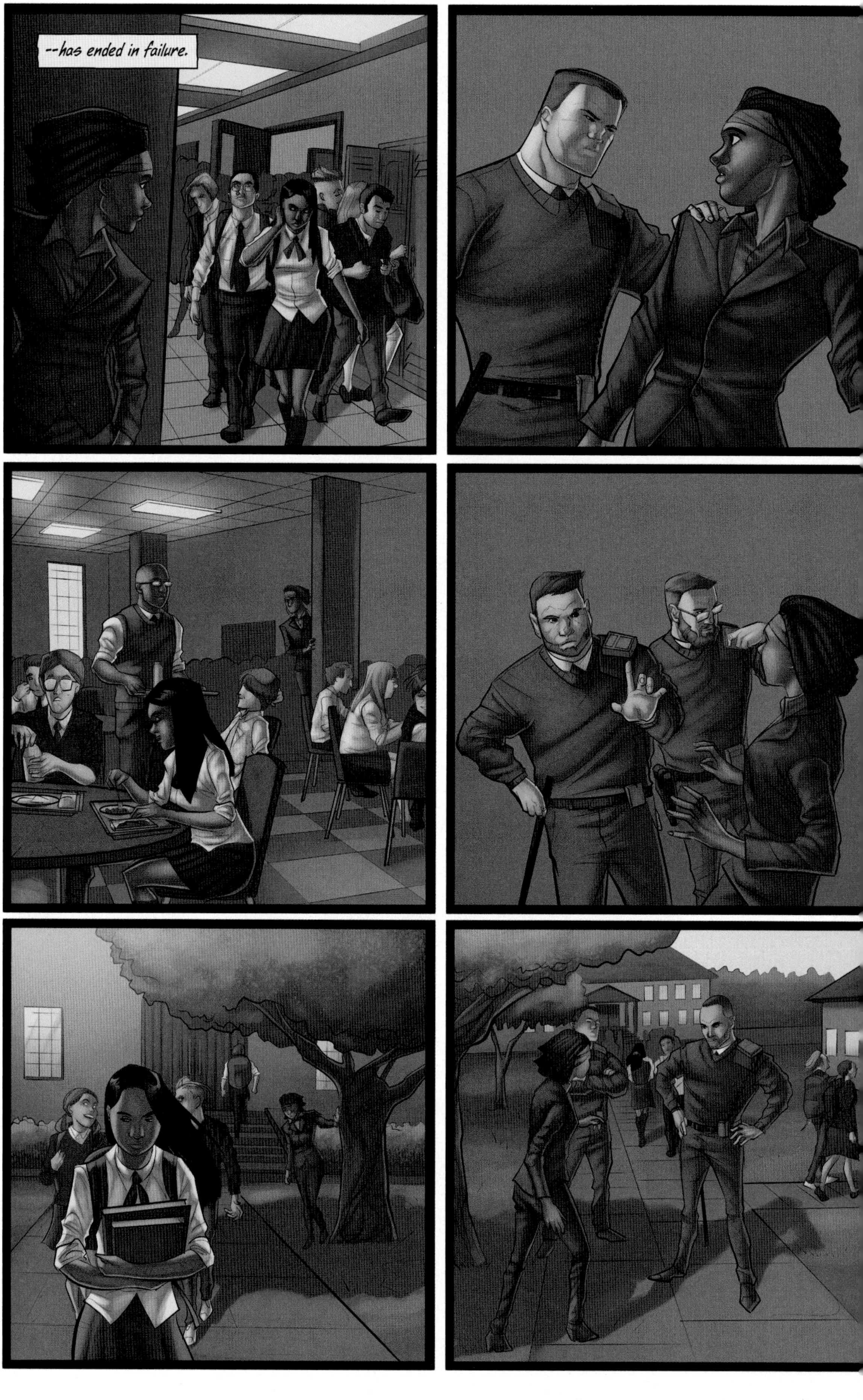
--has ended in failure.

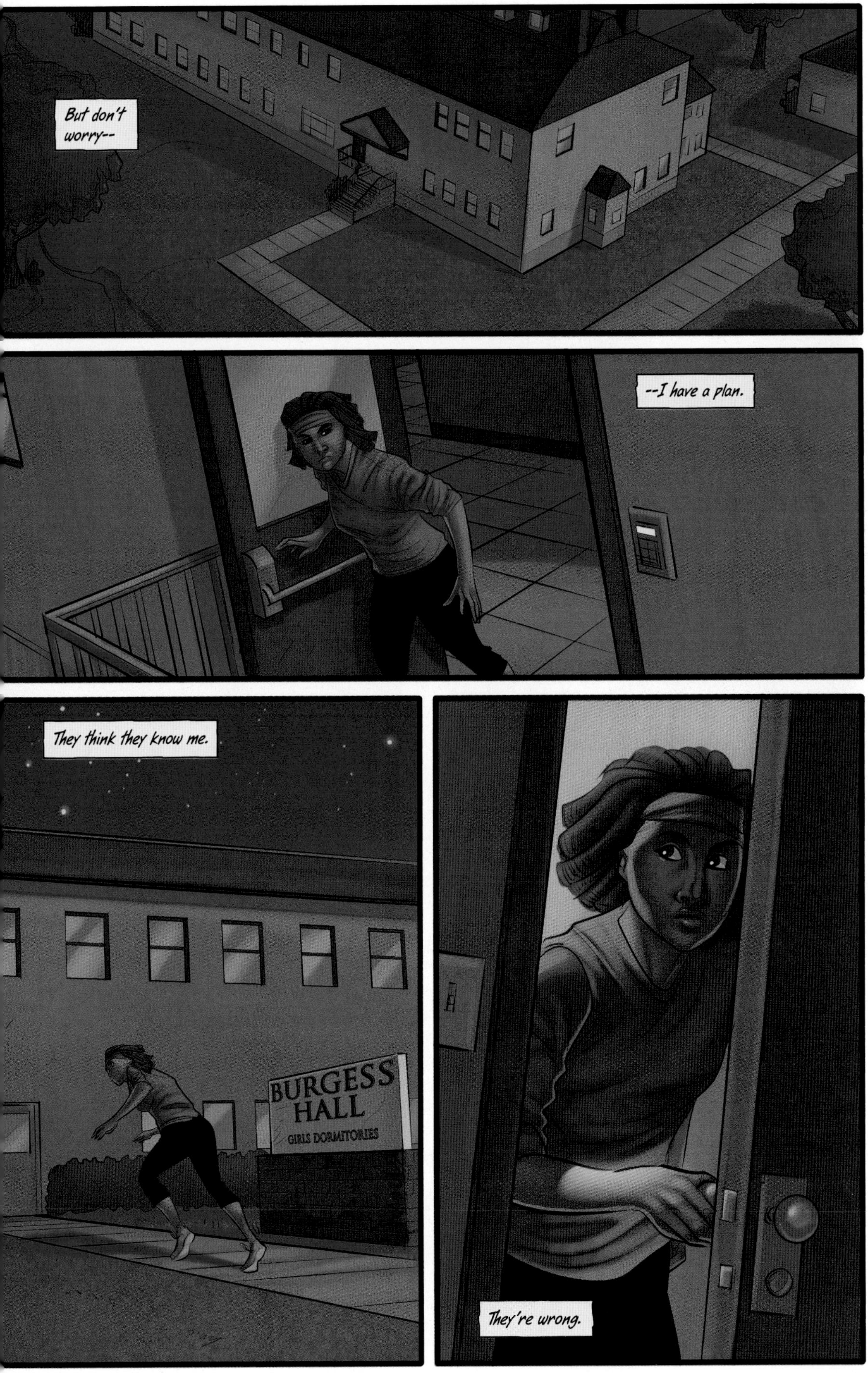
But don't worry--
--I have a plan.
They think they know me.
BURGESS HALL
GIRLS DORMITORIES
They're wrong.

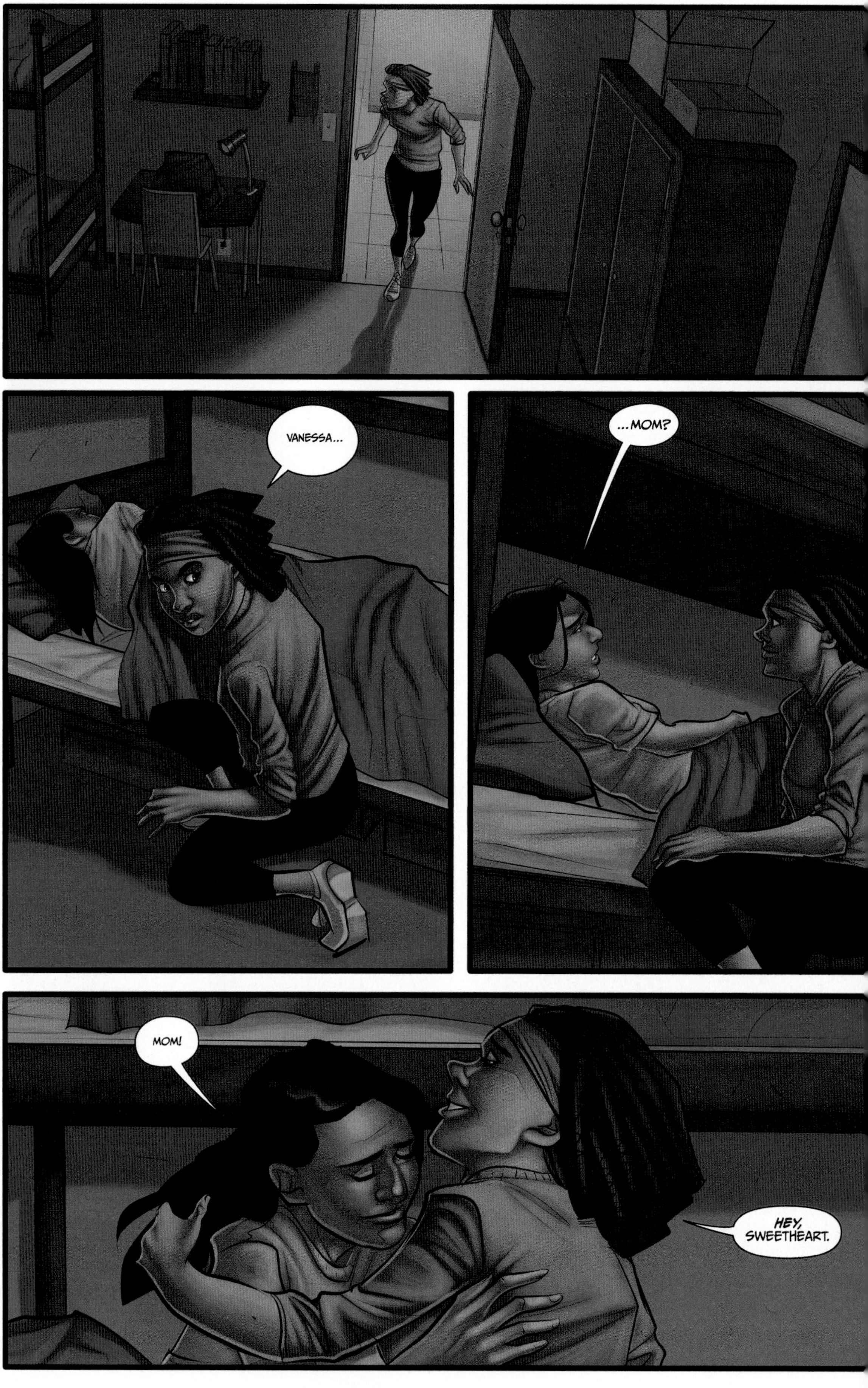
VANESSA...
...MOM?
MOM!
HEY, SWEETHEART.

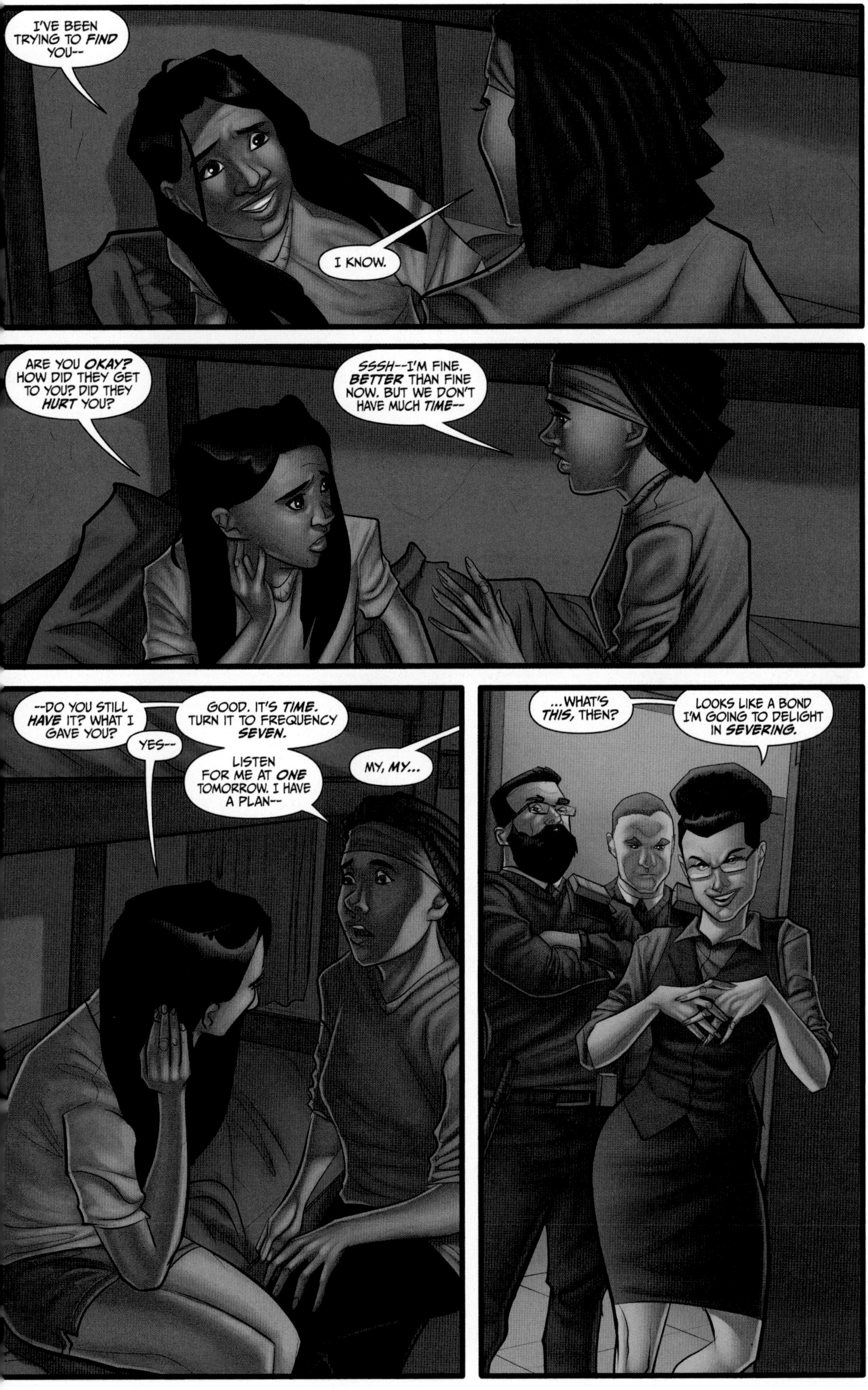
I'VE BEEN TRYING TO *FIND* YOU--
I KNOW.
ARE YOU *OKAY?* HOW DID THEY GET TO YOU? DID THEY *HURT* YOU?
SSSH--I'M FINE. *BETTER* THAN FINE NOW. BUT WE DON'T HAVE MUCH *TIME*--
--DO YOU STILL *HAVE* IT? WHAT I GAVE YOU?
YES--
GOOD. IT'S *TIME.* TURN IT TO FREQUENCY *SEVEN.*
LISTEN FOR ME AT *ONE* TOMORROW. I HAVE A PLAN--
MY, *MY*...
...WHAT'S *THIS,* THEN?
LOOKS LIKE A BOND I'M GOING TO DELIGHT IN *SEVERING.*

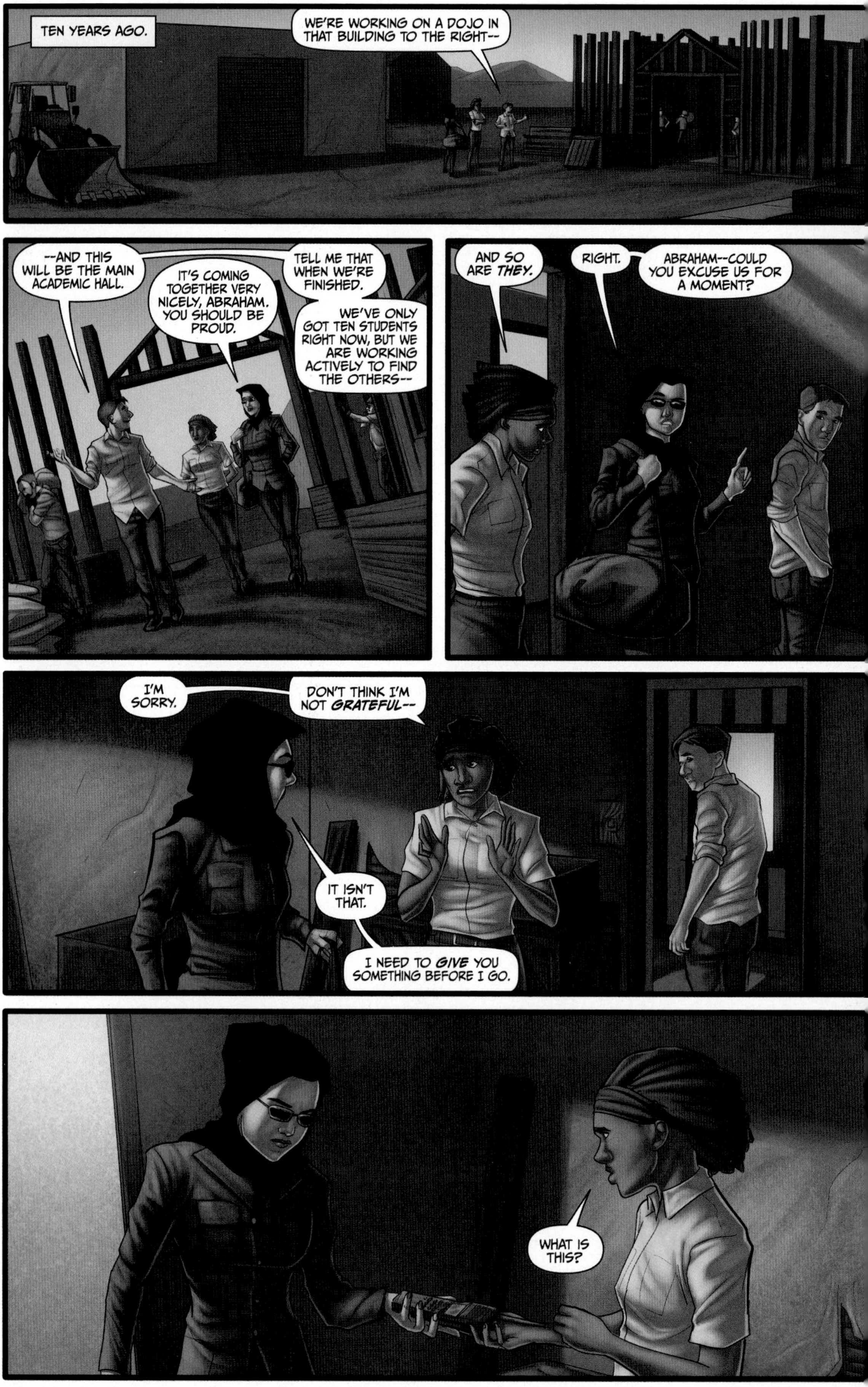
TEN YEARS AGO.
WE'RE WORKING ON A DOJO IN THAT BUILDING TO THE RIGHT--
--AND THIS WILL BE THE MAIN ACADEMIC HALL.
IT'S COMING TOGETHER VERY NICELY, ABRAHAM. YOU SHOULD BE PROUD.
TELL ME THAT WHEN WE'RE FINISHED.
WE'VE ONLY GOT TEN STUDENTS RIGHT NOW, BUT WE ARE WORKING ACTIVELY TO FIND THE OTHERS--
AND SO ARE *THEY.*
RIGHT.
ABRAHAM--COULD YOU EXCUSE US FOR A MOMENT?
I'M SORRY.
DON'T THINK I'M NOT *GRATEFUL*--
IT ISN'T THAT.
I NEED TO *GIVE* YOU SOMETHING BEFORE I GO.
WHAT IS THIS?

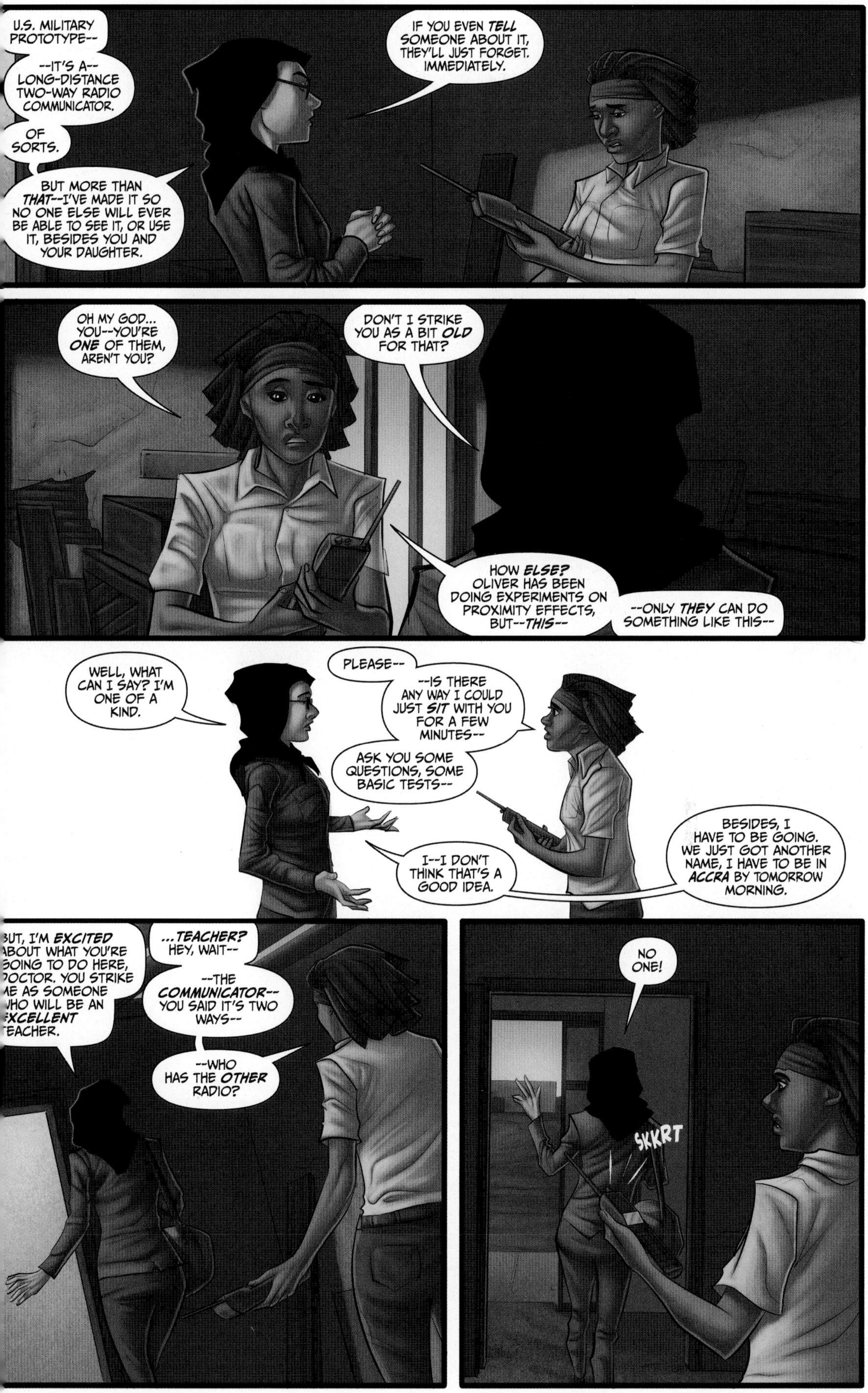
U.S. MILITARY PROTOTYPE--
--IT'S A-- LONG-DISTANCE TWO-WAY RADIO COMMUNICATOR.
OF SORTS.
BUT MORE THAN THAT--I'VE MADE IT SO NO ONE ELSE WILL EVER BE ABLE TO SEE IT, OR USE IT, BESIDES YOU AND YOUR DAUGHTER.
IF YOU EVEN TELL SOMEONE ABOUT IT, THEY'LL JUST FORGET. IMMEDIATELY.
OH MY GOD... YOU--YOU'RE ONE OF THEM, AREN'T YOU?
DON'T I STRIKE YOU AS A BIT OLD FOR THAT?
HOW ELSE? OLIVER HAS BEEN DOING EXPERIMENTS ON PROXIMITY EFFECTS, BUT--THIS--
--ONLY THEY CAN DO SOMETHING LIKE THIS--
WELL, WHAT CAN I SAY? I'M ONE OF A KIND.
PLEASE--
--IS THERE ANY WAY I COULD JUST SIT WITH YOU FOR A FEW MINUTES--
ASK YOU SOME QUESTIONS, SOME BASIC TESTS--
I--I DON'T THINK THAT'S A GOOD IDEA.
BESIDES, I HAVE TO BE GOING. WE JUST GOT ANOTHER NAME, I HAVE TO BE IN ACCRA BY TOMORROW MORNING.
BUT, I'M EXCITED ABOUT WHAT YOU'RE GOING TO DO HERE, DOCTOR. YOU STRIKE ME AS SOMEONE WHO WILL BE AN EXCELLENT TEACHER.
...TEACHER? HEY, WAIT--
--THE COMMUNICATOR-- YOU SAID IT'S TWO WAYS--
--WHO HAS THE OTHER RADIO?
NO ONE!
SKKRT

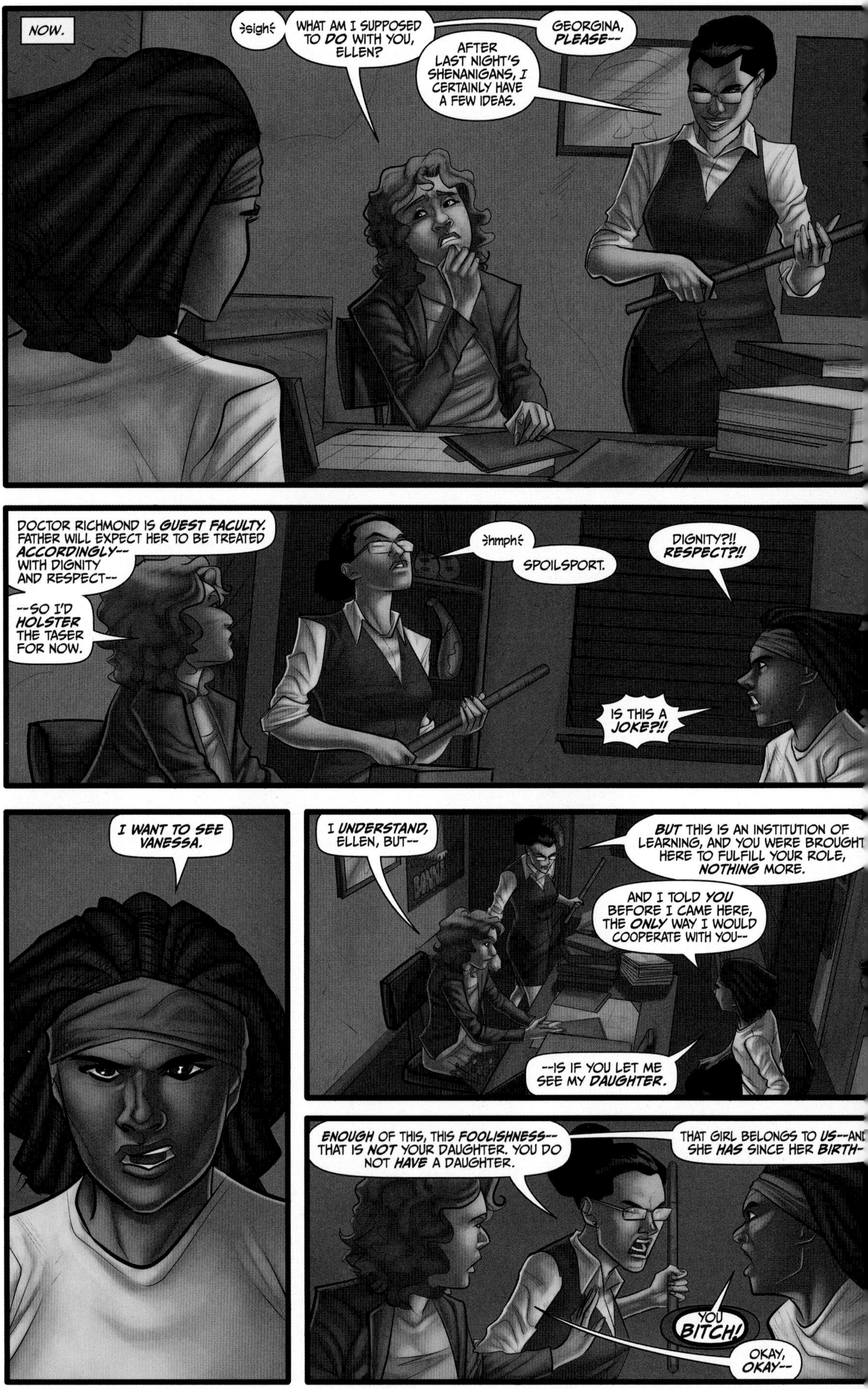
NOW.
⋟sigh⋞
WHAT AM I SUPPOSED TO DO WITH YOU, ELLEN?
GEORGINA, PLEASE--
AFTER LAST NIGHT'S SHENANIGANS, I CERTAINLY HAVE A FEW IDEAS.
DOCTOR RICHMOND IS GUEST FACULTY. FATHER WILL EXPECT HER TO BE TREATED ACCORDINGLY-- WITH DIGNITY AND RESPECT--
--SO I'D HOLSTER THE TASER FOR NOW.
⋟hmph⋞
SPOILSPORT.
DIGNITY?!! RESPECT?!!
IS THIS A JOKE?!!
I WANT TO SEE VANESSA.
I UNDERSTAND, ELLEN, BUT--
BUT THIS IS AN INSTITUTION OF LEARNING, AND YOU WERE BROUGHT HERE TO FULFILL YOUR ROLE, NOTHING MORE.
AND I TOLD YOU BEFORE I CAME HERE, THE ONLY WAY I WOULD COOPERATE WITH YOU--
--IS IF YOU LET ME SEE MY DAUGHTER.
ENOUGH OF THIS, THIS FOOLISHNESS-- THAT IS NOT YOUR DAUGHTER. YOU DO NOT HAVE A DAUGHTER.
THAT GIRL BELONGS TO US--AND SHE HAS SINCE HER BIRTH-
YOU BITCH!
OKAY, OKAY--

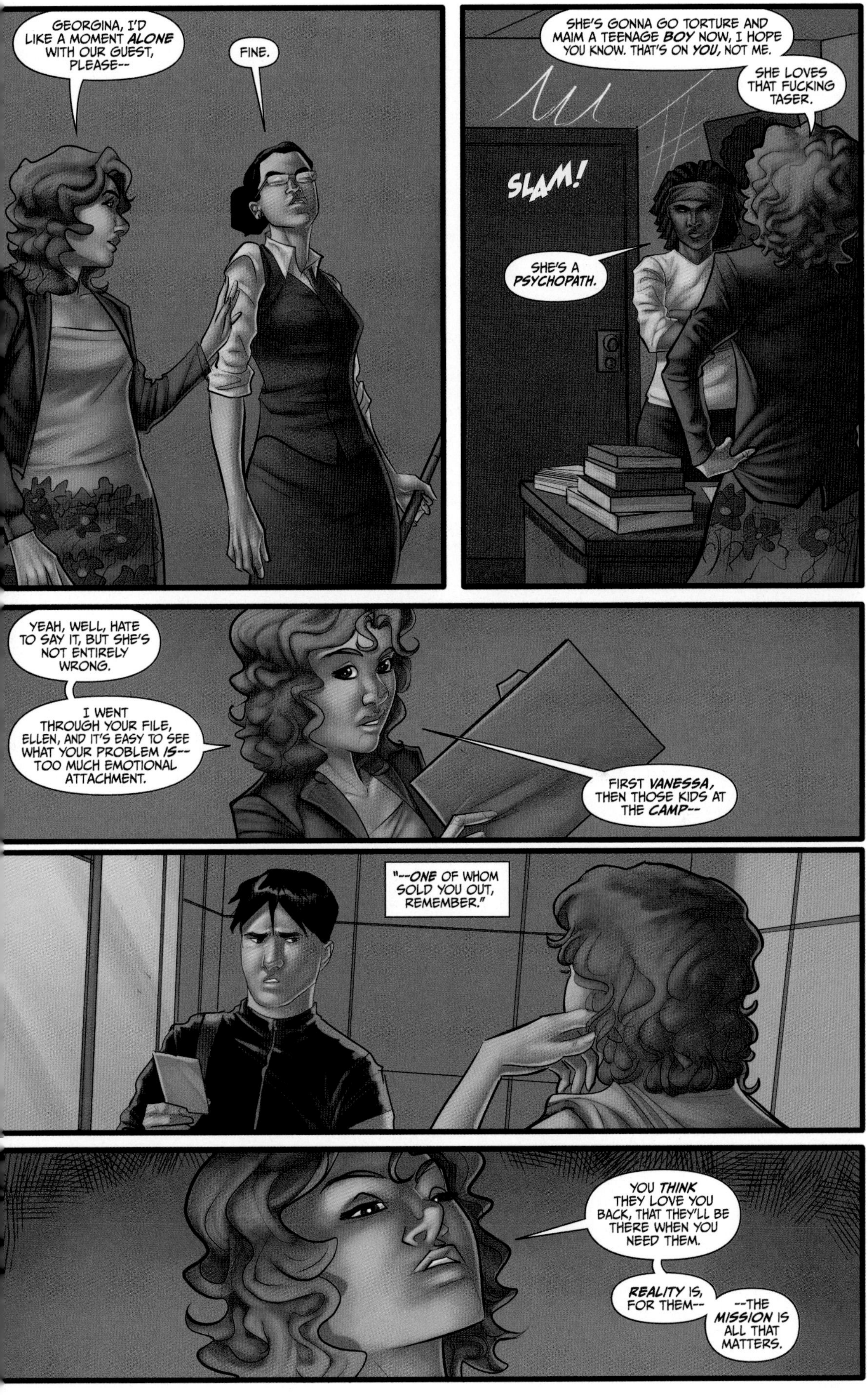
GEORGINA, I'D LIKE A MOMENT ALONE WITH OUR GUEST, PLEASE--
FINE.
SHE'S GONNA GO TORTURE AND MAIM A TEENAGE BOY NOW, I HOPE YOU KNOW. THAT'S ON YOU, NOT ME.
SHE LOVES THAT FUCKING TASER.
SLAM!
SHE'S A PSYCHOPATH.
YEAH, WELL, HATE TO SAY IT, BUT SHE'S NOT ENTIRELY WRONG.
I WENT THROUGH YOUR FILE, ELLEN, AND IT'S EASY TO SEE WHAT YOUR PROBLEM IS-- TOO MUCH EMOTIONAL ATTACHMENT.
FIRST VANESSA, THEN THOSE KIDS AT THE CAMP--
"--ONE OF WHOM SOLD YOU OUT, REMEMBER."
YOU THINK THEY LOVE YOU BACK, THAT THEY'LL BE THERE WHEN YOU NEED THEM.
REALITY IS, FOR THEM--
--THE MISSION IS ALL THAT MATTERS.

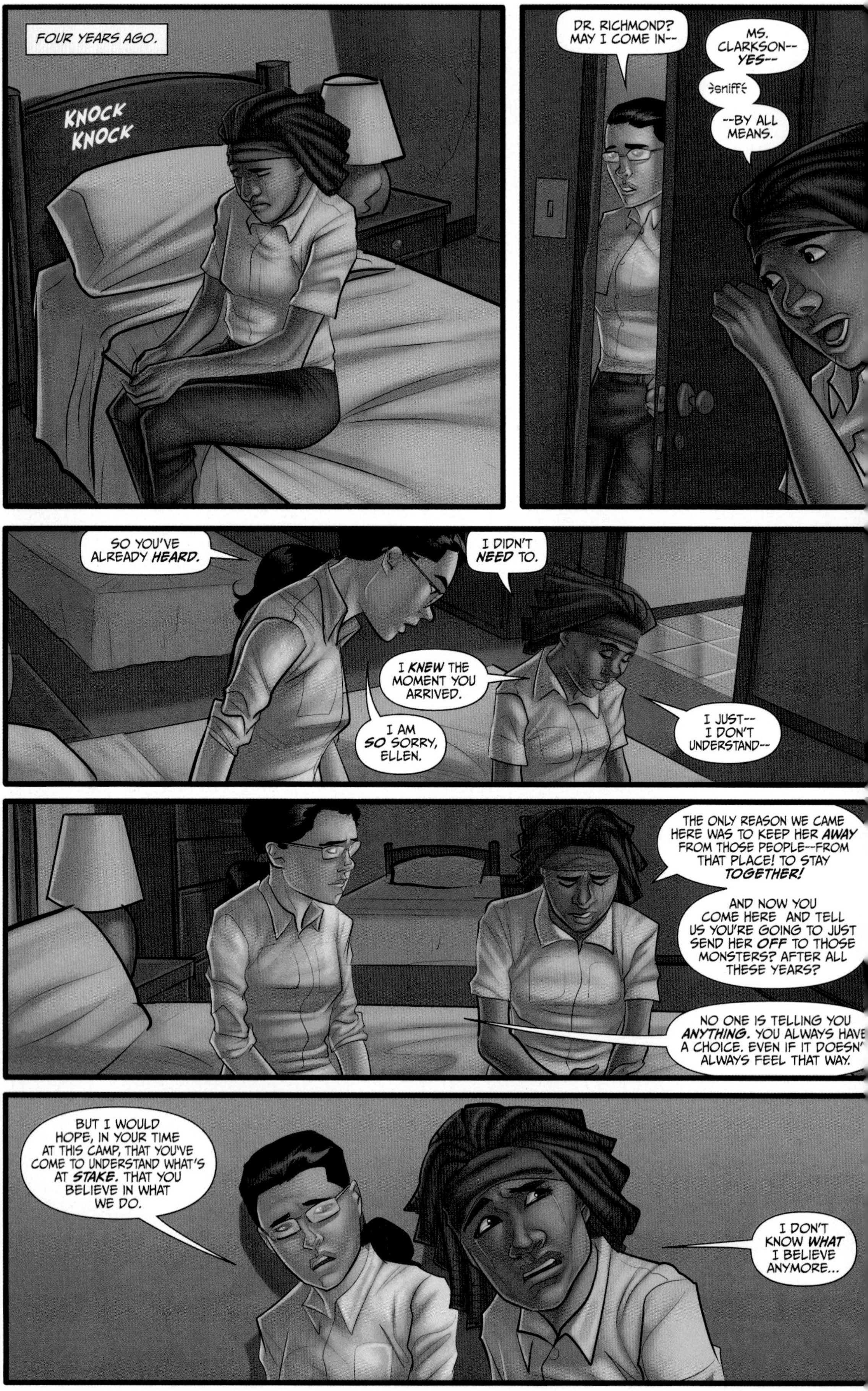
FOUR YEARS AGO.
KNOCK KNOCK
DR. RICHMOND? MAY I COME IN--
MS. CLARKSON-- YES--
sniff
--BY ALL MEANS.
SO YOU'VE ALREADY HEARD.
I DIDN'T NEED TO.
I KNEW THE MOMENT YOU ARRIVED.
I AM SO SORRY, ELLEN.
I JUST-- I DON'T UNDERSTAND--
THE ONLY REASON WE CAME HERE WAS TO KEEP HER AWAY FROM THOSE PEOPLE--FROM THAT PLACE! TO STAY TOGETHER!
AND NOW YOU COME HERE AND TELL US YOU'RE GOING TO JUST SEND HER OFF TO THOSE MONSTERS? AFTER ALL THESE YEARS?
NO ONE IS TELLING YOU ANYTHING. YOU ALWAYS HAVE A CHOICE. EVEN IF IT DOESN'T ALWAYS FEEL THAT WAY.
BUT I WOULD HOPE, IN YOUR TIME AT THIS CAMP, THAT YOU'VE COME TO UNDERSTAND WHAT'S AT STAKE. THAT YOU BELIEVE IN WHAT WE DO.
I DON'T KNOW WHAT I BELIEVE ANYMORE...

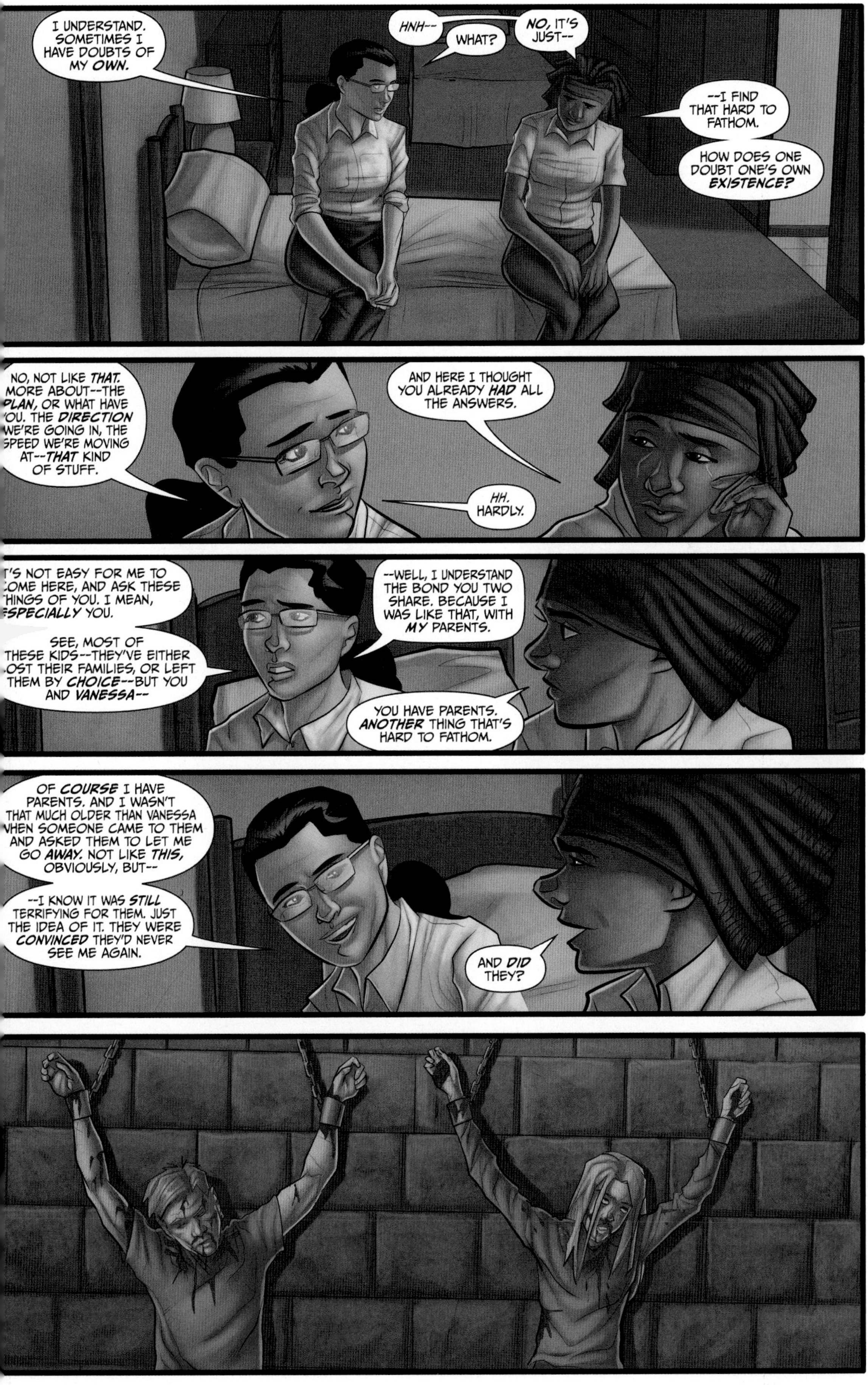

I UNDERSTAND. SOMETIMES I HAVE DOUBTS OF MY OWN.
HNH--
WHAT?
NO, IT'S JUST--
--I FIND THAT HARD TO FATHOM.
HOW DOES ONE DOUBT ONE'S OWN EXISTENCE?
NO, NOT LIKE THAT. MORE ABOUT--THE PLAN, OR WHAT HAVE OU. THE DIRECTION WE'RE GOING IN, THE SPEED WE'RE MOVING AT--THAT KIND OF STUFF.
AND HERE I THOUGHT YOU ALREADY HAD ALL THE ANSWERS.
HH. HARDLY.
T'S NOT EASY FOR ME TO OME HERE, AND ASK THESE HINGS OF YOU. I MEAN, SPECIALLY YOU.
SEE, MOST OF THESE KIDS--THEY'VE EITHER OST THEIR FAMILIES, OR LEFT THEM BY CHOICE--BUT YOU AND VANESSA--
--WELL, I UNDERSTAND THE BOND YOU TWO SHARE. BECAUSE I WAS LIKE THAT, WITH MY PARENTS.
YOU HAVE PARENTS. ANOTHER THING THAT'S HARD TO FATHOM.
OF COURSE I HAVE PARENTS. AND I WASN'T THAT MUCH OLDER THAN VANESSA HEN SOMEONE CAME TO THEM AND ASKED THEM TO LET ME GO AWAY. NOT LIKE THIS, OBVIOUSLY, BUT--
--I KNOW IT WAS STILL TERRIFYING FOR THEM. JUST THE IDEA OF IT. THEY WERE CONVINCED THEY'D NEVER SEE ME AGAIN.
AND DID THEY?

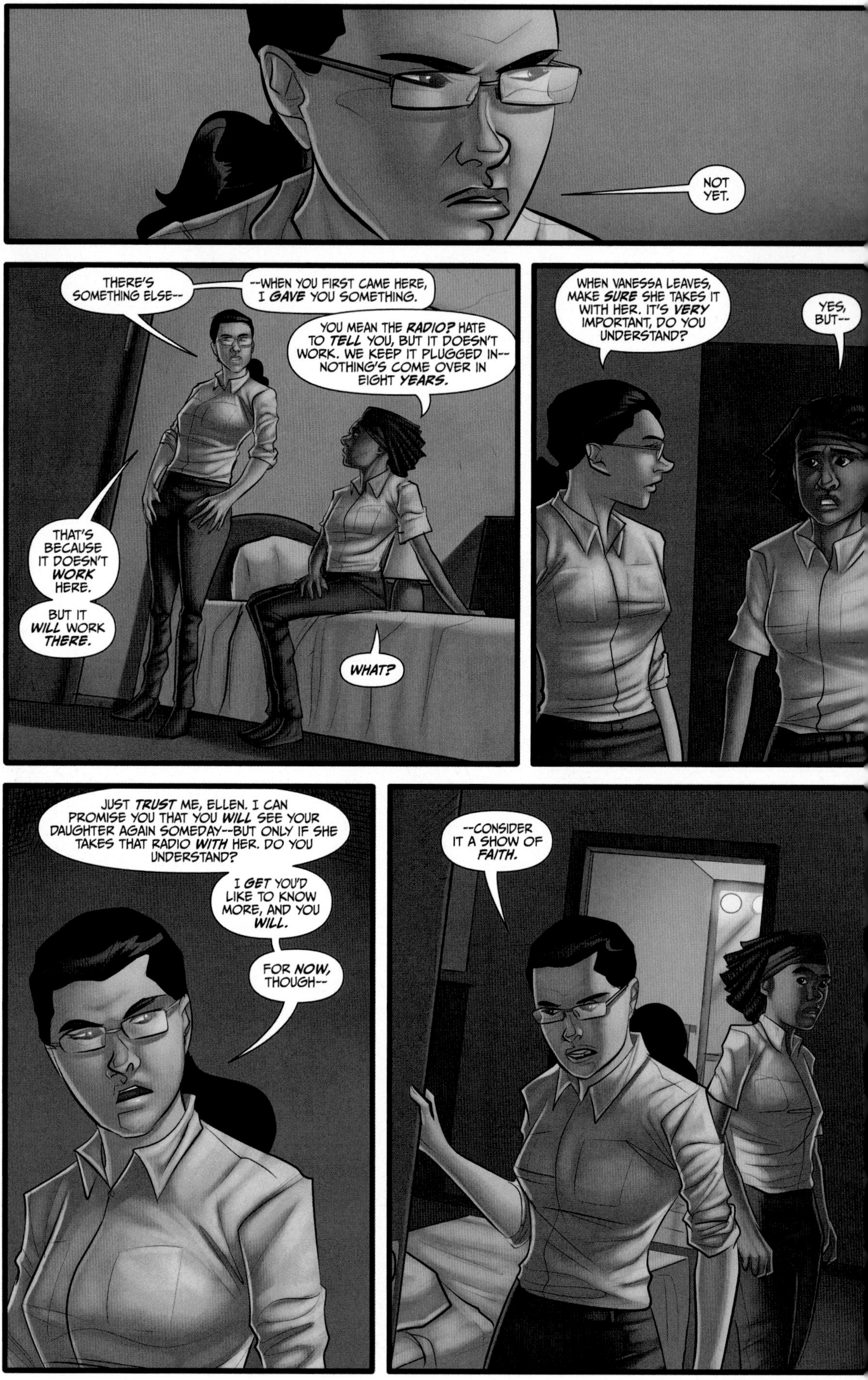
NOT YET.
THERE'S SOMETHING ELSE--
--WHEN YOU FIRST CAME HERE, I GAVE YOU SOMETHING.
YOU MEAN THE RADIO? HATE TO TELL YOU, BUT IT DOESN'T WORK. WE KEEP IT PLUGGED IN--NOTHING'S COME OVER IN EIGHT YEARS.
THAT'S BECAUSE IT DOESN'T WORK HERE.
BUT IT WILL WORK THERE.
WHAT?
WHEN VANESSA LEAVES, MAKE SURE SHE TAKES IT WITH HER. IT'S VERY IMPORTANT, DO YOU UNDERSTAND?
YES, BUT--
JUST TRUST ME, ELLEN. I CAN PROMISE YOU THAT YOU WILL SEE YOUR DAUGHTER AGAIN SOMEDAY--BUT ONLY IF SHE TAKES THAT RADIO WITH HER. DO YOU UNDERSTAND?
I GET YOU'D LIKE TO KNOW MORE, AND YOU WILL.
FOR NOW, THOUGH--
--CONSIDER IT A SHOW OF FAITH.

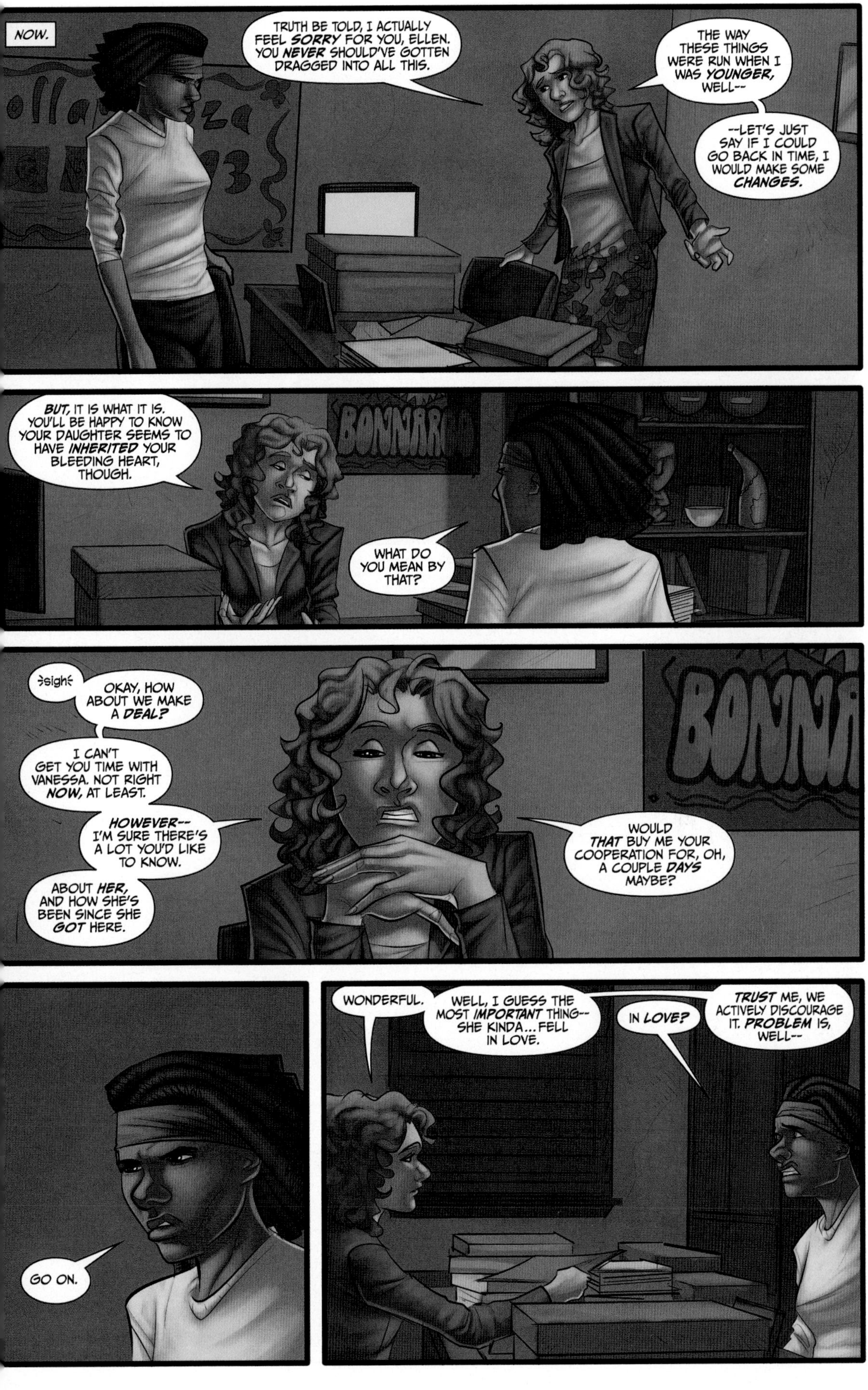
NOW.
TRUTH BE TOLD, I ACTUALLY FEEL SORRY FOR YOU, ELLEN. YOU NEVER SHOULD'VE GOTTEN DRAGGED INTO ALL THIS.
THE WAY THESE THINGS WERE RUN WHEN I WAS YOUNGER, WELL--
--LET'S JUST SAY IF I COULD GO BACK IN TIME, I WOULD MAKE SOME CHANGES.
BUT, IT IS WHAT IT IS. YOU'LL BE HAPPY TO KNOW YOUR DAUGHTER SEEMS TO HAVE INHERITED YOUR BLEEDING HEART, THOUGH.
WHAT DO YOU MEAN BY THAT?
BONNAR
sigh
OKAY, HOW ABOUT WE MAKE A DEAL?
I CAN'T GET YOU TIME WITH VANESSA. NOT RIGHT NOW, AT LEAST.
HOWEVER-- I'M SURE THERE'S A LOT YOU'D LIKE TO KNOW.
ABOUT HER, AND HOW SHE'S BEEN SINCE SHE GOT HERE.
WOULD THAT BUY ME YOUR COOPERATION FOR, OH, A COUPLE DAYS MAYBE?
GO ON.
WONDERFUL.
WELL, I GUESS THE MOST IMPORTANT THING-- SHE KINDA... FELL IN LOVE.
IN LOVE?
TRUST ME, WE ACTIVELY DISCOURAGE IT. PROBLEM IS, WELL--

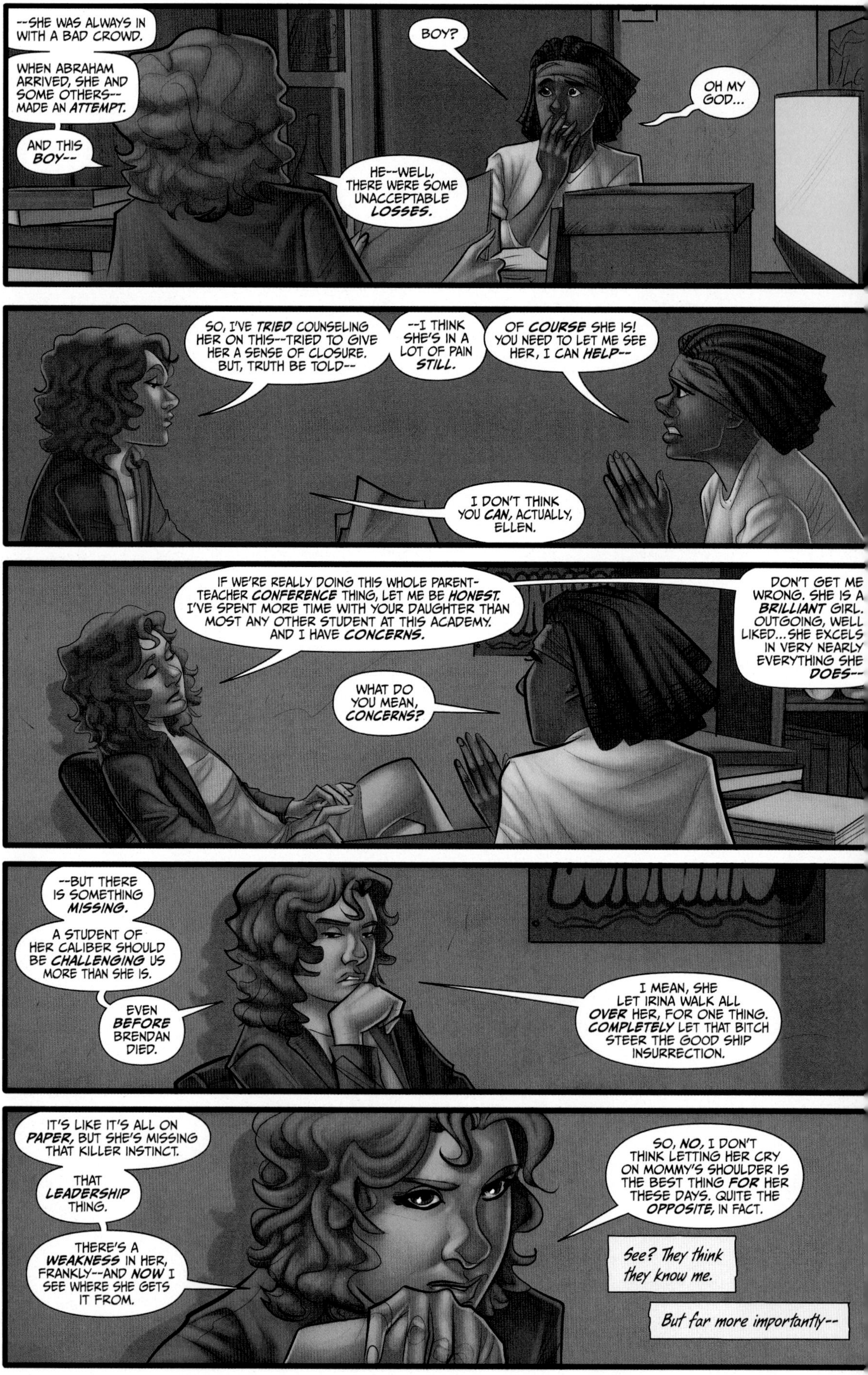
--SHE WAS ALWAYS IN WITH A BAD CROWD.
WHEN ABRAHAM ARRIVED, SHE AND SOME OTHERS--MADE AN ATTEMPT.
AND THIS BOY--
BOY?
HE--WELL, THERE WERE SOME UNACCEPTABLE LOSSES.
OH MY GOD...
SO, I'VE TRIED COUNSELING HER ON THIS--TRIED TO GIVE HER A SENSE OF CLOSURE. BUT, TRUTH BE TOLD--
--I THINK SHE'S IN A LOT OF PAIN STILL.
OF COURSE SHE IS! YOU NEED TO LET ME SEE HER, I CAN HELP--
I DON'T THINK YOU CAN, ACTUALLY, ELLEN.
IF WE'RE REALLY DOING THIS WHOLE PARENT-TEACHER CONFERENCE THING, LET ME BE HONEST. I'VE SPENT MORE TIME WITH YOUR DAUGHTER THAN MOST ANY OTHER STUDENT AT THIS ACADEMY. AND I HAVE CONCERNS.
WHAT DO YOU MEAN, CONCERNS?
DON'T GET ME WRONG. SHE IS A BRILLIANT GIRL. OUTGOING, WELL LIKED...SHE EXCELS IN VERY NEARLY EVERYTHING SHE DOES--
--BUT THERE IS SOMETHING MISSING.
A STUDENT OF HER CALIBER SHOULD BE CHALLENGING US MORE THAN SHE IS.
EVEN BEFORE BRENDAN DIED.
I MEAN, SHE LET IRINA WALK ALL OVER HER, FOR ONE THING. COMPLETELY LET THAT BITCH STEER THE GOOD SHIP INSURRECTION.
IT'S LIKE IT'S ALL ON PAPER, BUT SHE'S MISSING THAT KILLER INSTINCT.
THAT LEADERSHIP THING.
THERE'S A WEAKNESS IN HER, FRANKLY--AND NOW I SEE WHERE SHE GETS IT FROM.
SO, NO, I DON'T THINK LETTING HER CRY ON MOMMY'S SHOULDER IS THE BEST THING FOR HER THESE DAYS. QUITE THE OPPOSITE, IN FACT.
See? They think they know me.
But far more importantly--

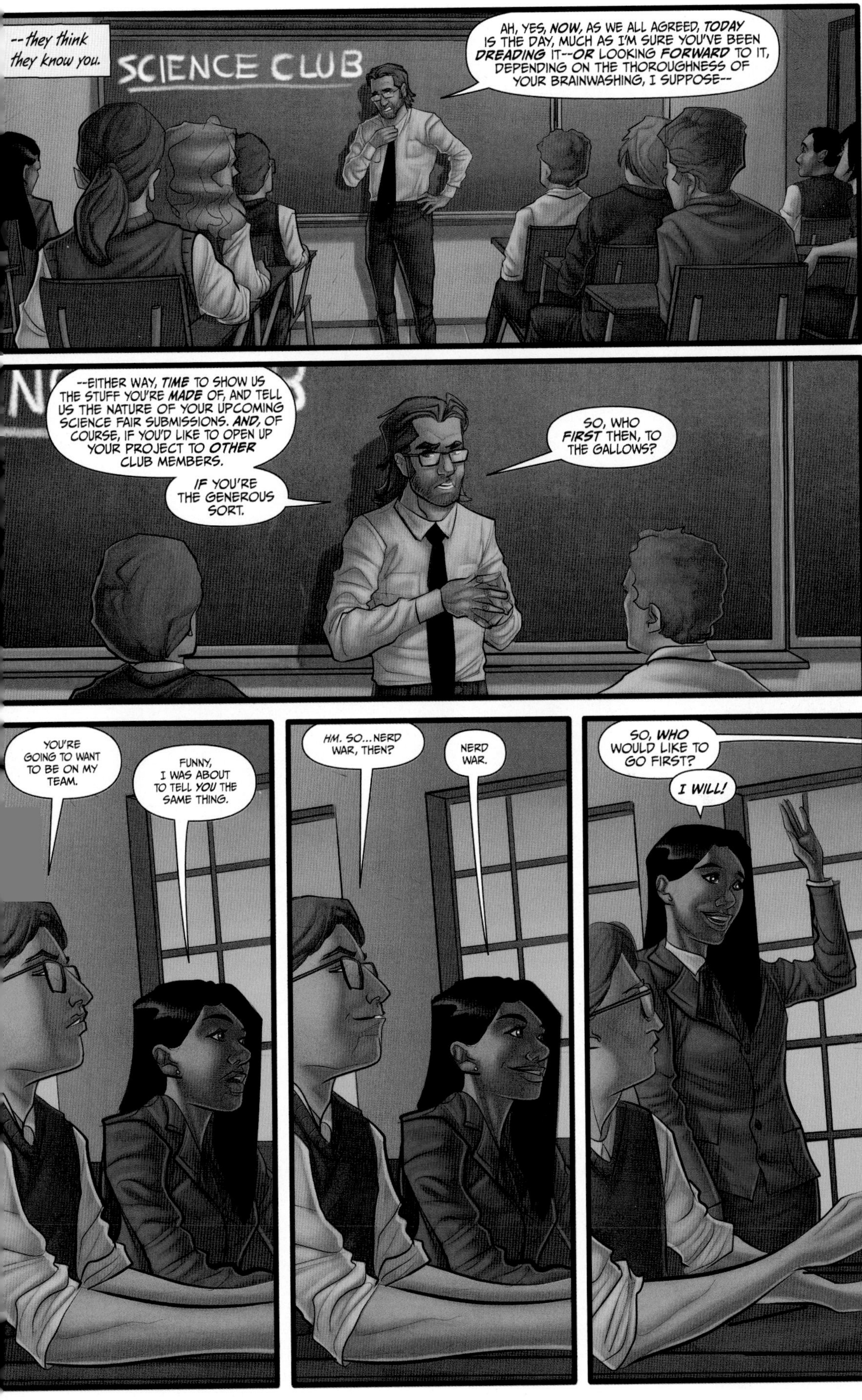
--they think they know you.
SCIENCE CLUB
AH, YES, NOW, AS WE ALL AGREED, TODAY IS THE DAY, MUCH AS I'M SURE YOU'VE BEEN DREADING IT--OR LOOKING FORWARD TO IT, DEPENDING ON THE THOROUGHNESS OF YOUR BRAINWASHING, I SUPPOSE--
--EITHER WAY, TIME TO SHOW US THE STUFF YOU'RE MADE OF, AND TELL US THE NATURE OF YOUR UPCOMING SCIENCE FAIR SUBMISSIONS. AND, OF COURSE, IF YOU'D LIKE TO OPEN UP YOUR PROJECT TO OTHER CLUB MEMBERS.
IF YOU'RE THE GENEROUS SORT.
SO, WHO FIRST THEN, TO THE GALLOWS?
YOU'RE GOING TO WANT TO BE ON MY TEAM.
FUNNY, I WAS ABOUT TO TELL YOU THE SAME THING.
HM. SO... NERD WAR, THEN?
NERD WAR.
SO, WHO WOULD LIKE TO GO FIRST?
I WILL!

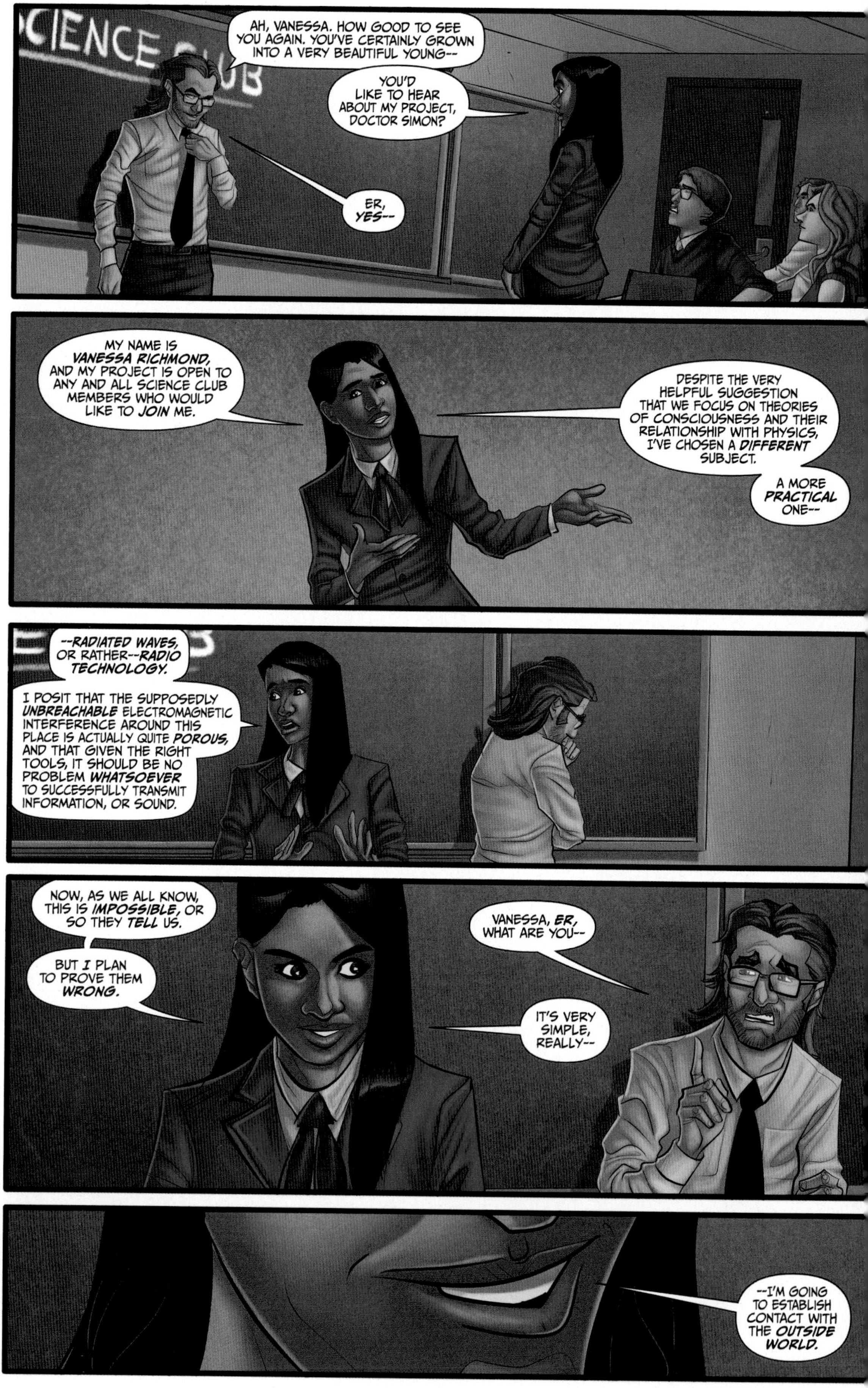

SCIENCE CLUB
AH, VANESSA. HOW GOOD TO SEE YOU AGAIN. YOU'VE CERTAINLY GROWN INTO A VERY BEAUTIFUL YOUNG--
YOU'D LIKE TO HEAR ABOUT MY PROJECT, DOCTOR SIMON?
ER, *YES*--
MY NAME IS *VANESSA RICHMOND,* AND MY PROJECT IS OPEN TO ANY AND ALL SCIENCE CLUB MEMBERS WHO WOULD LIKE TO *JOIN* ME.
DESPITE THE VERY HELPFUL SUGGESTION THAT WE FOCUS ON THEORIES OF CONSCIOUSNESS AND THEIR RELATIONSHIP WITH PHYSICS, I'VE CHOSEN A *DIFFERENT* SUBJECT.
A MORE *PRACTICAL* ONE--
--*RADIATED WAVES,* OR RATHER--*RADIO TECHNOLOGY.*
I POSIT THAT THE SUPPOSEDLY *UNBREACHABLE* ELECTROMAGNETIC INTERFERENCE AROUND THIS PLACE IS ACTUALLY QUITE *POROUS,* AND THAT GIVEN THE RIGHT TOOLS, IT SHOULD BE NO PROBLEM *WHATSOEVER* TO SUCCESSFULLY TRANSMIT INFORMATION, OR SOUND.
NOW, AS WE ALL KNOW, THIS IS *IMPOSSIBLE,* OR SO THEY *TELL* US.
BUT *I* PLAN TO PROVE THEM *WRONG.*
VANESSA, *ER,* WHAT ARE YOU--
IT'S VERY SIMPLE, REALLY--
--I'M GOING TO ESTABLISH CONTACT WITH THE *OUTSIDE WORLD.*

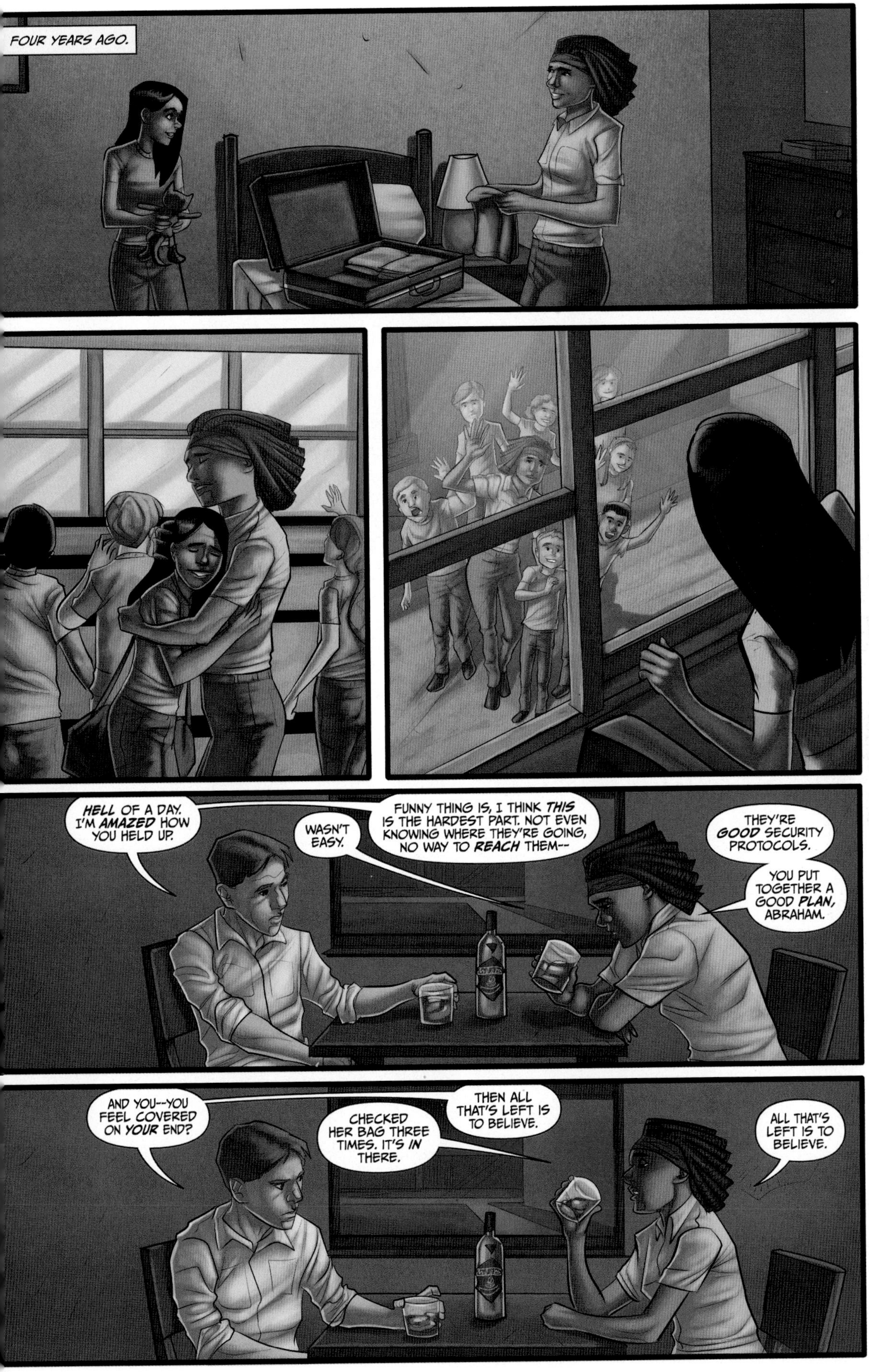
FOUR YEARS AGO.
HELL OF A DAY. I'M AMAZED HOW YOU HELD UP.
WASN'T EASY.
FUNNY THING IS, I THINK THIS IS THE HARDEST PART. NOT EVEN KNOWING WHERE THEY'RE GOING, NO WAY TO REACH THEM--
THEY'RE GOOD SECURITY PROTOCOLS.
YOU PUT TOGETHER A GOOD PLAN, ABRAHAM.
AND YOU--YOU FEEL COVERED ON YOUR END?
CHECKED HER BAG THREE TIMES. IT'S IN THERE.
THEN ALL THAT'S LEFT IS TO BELIEVE.
ALL THAT'S LEFT IS TO BELIEVE.

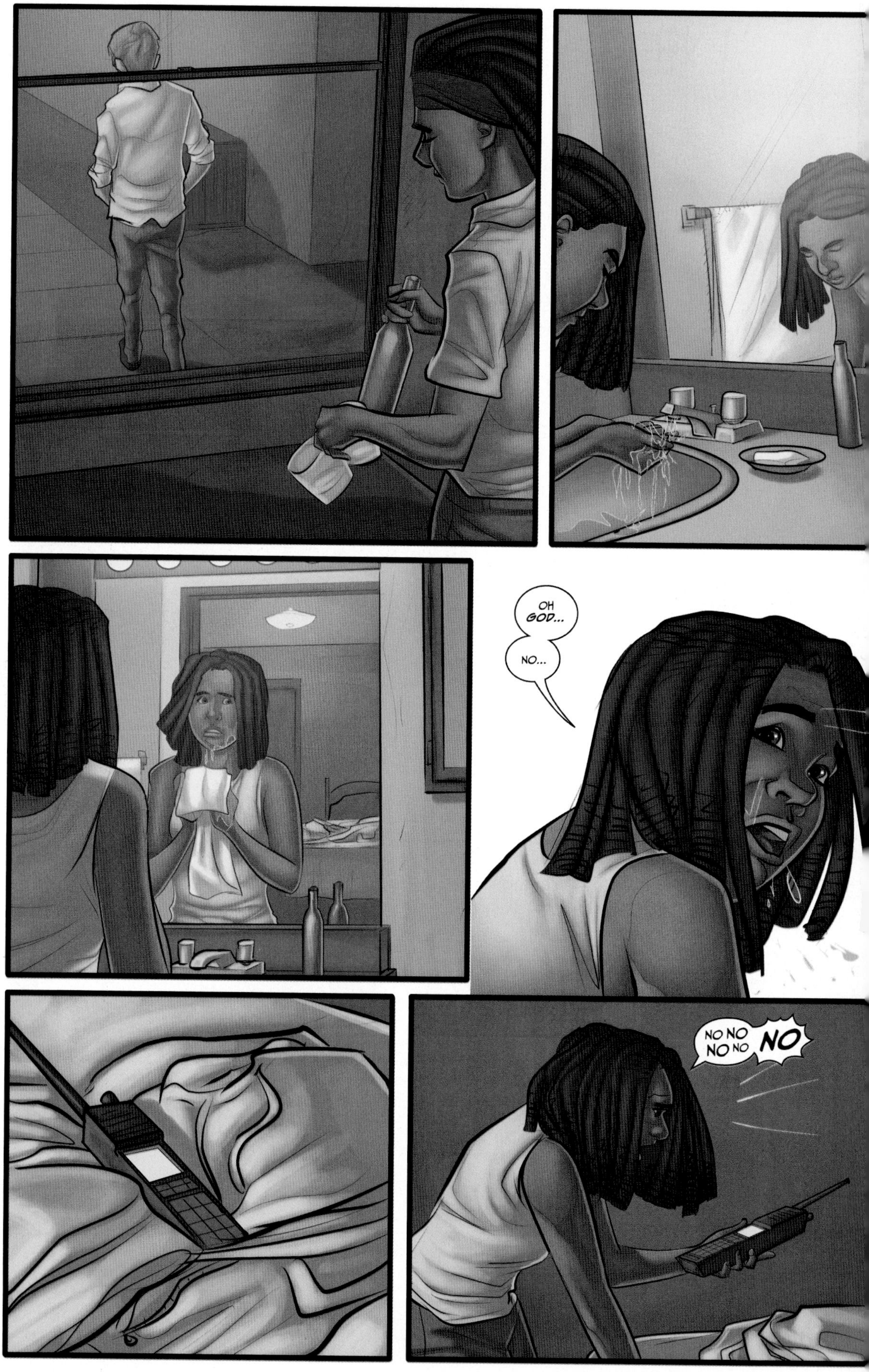
OH GOD...
NO...
NO NO NO NO NO

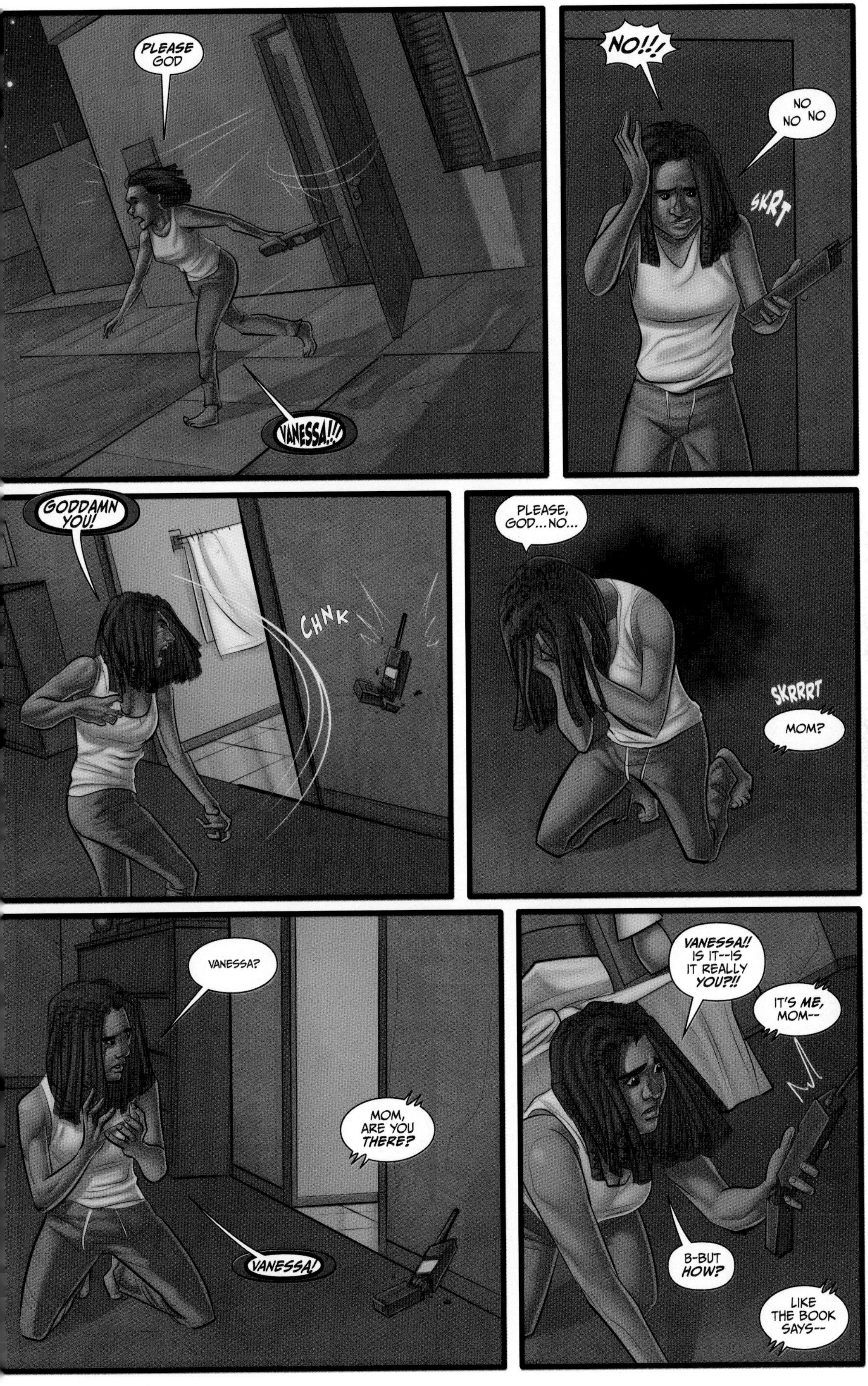
PLEASE GOD
VANESSA!!!
NO!!!
NO NO NO
SKRT
GODDAMN YOU!
CHNK
PLEASE, GOD...NO...
SKRRRT
MOM?
VANESSA?
MOM, ARE YOU THERE?
VANESSA!
VANESSA!! IS IT--IS IT REALLY YOU?!!
IT'S ME, MOM--
B-BUT HOW?
LIKE THE BOOK SAYS--

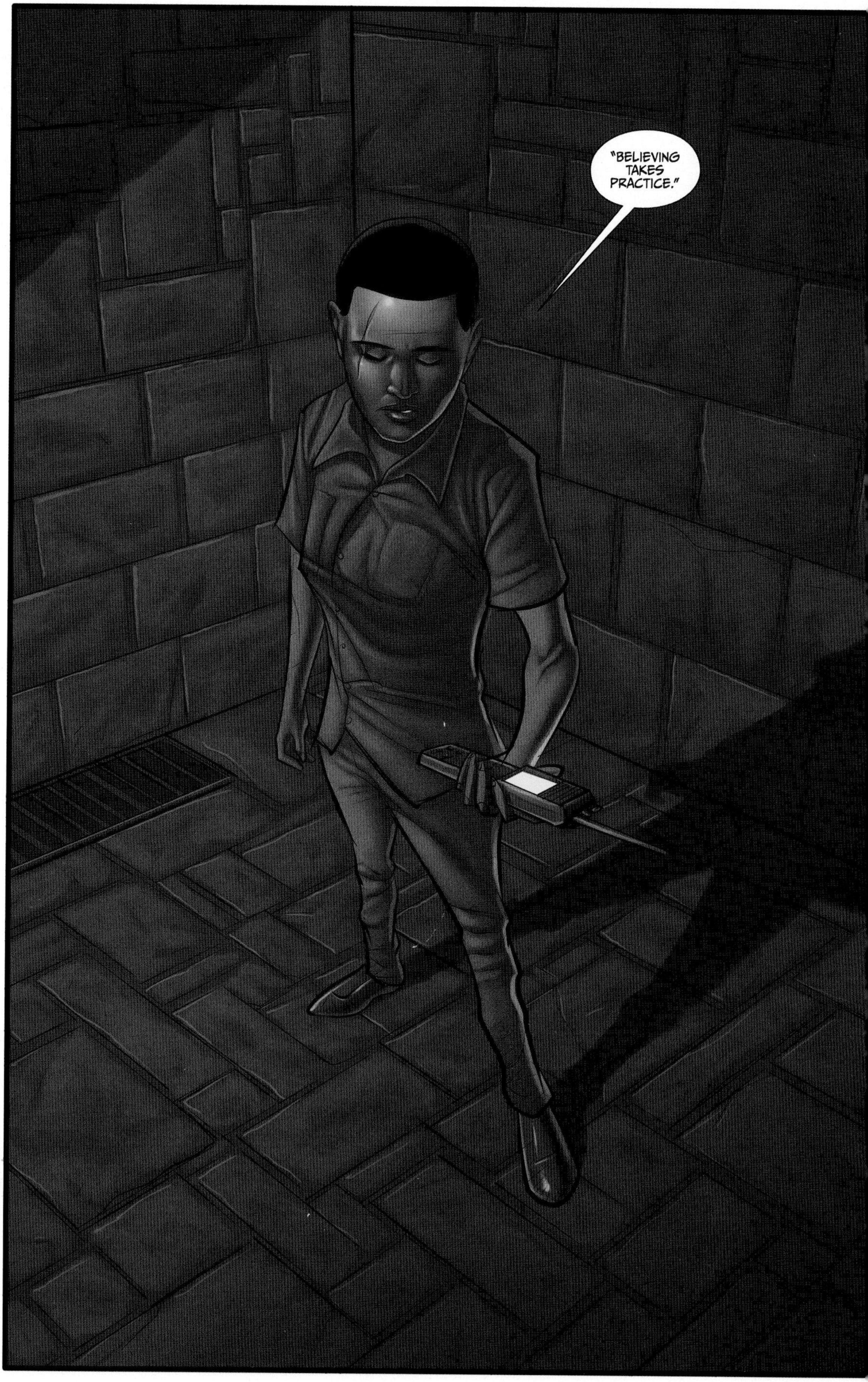
"BELIEVING TAKES PRACTICE."

forty**five**

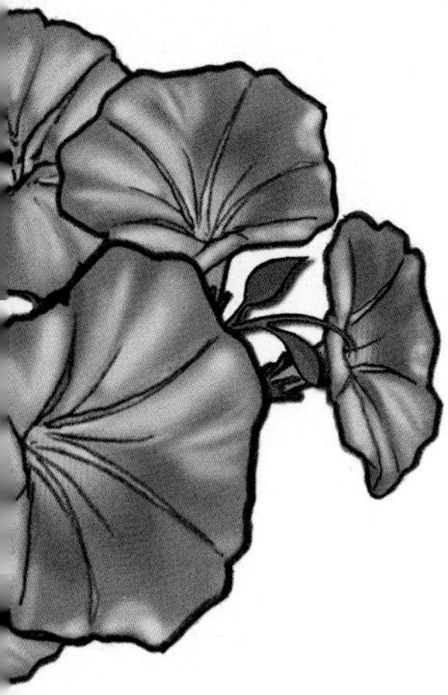

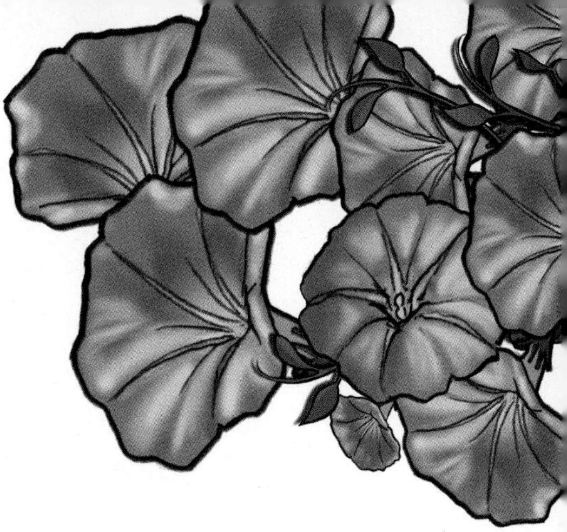

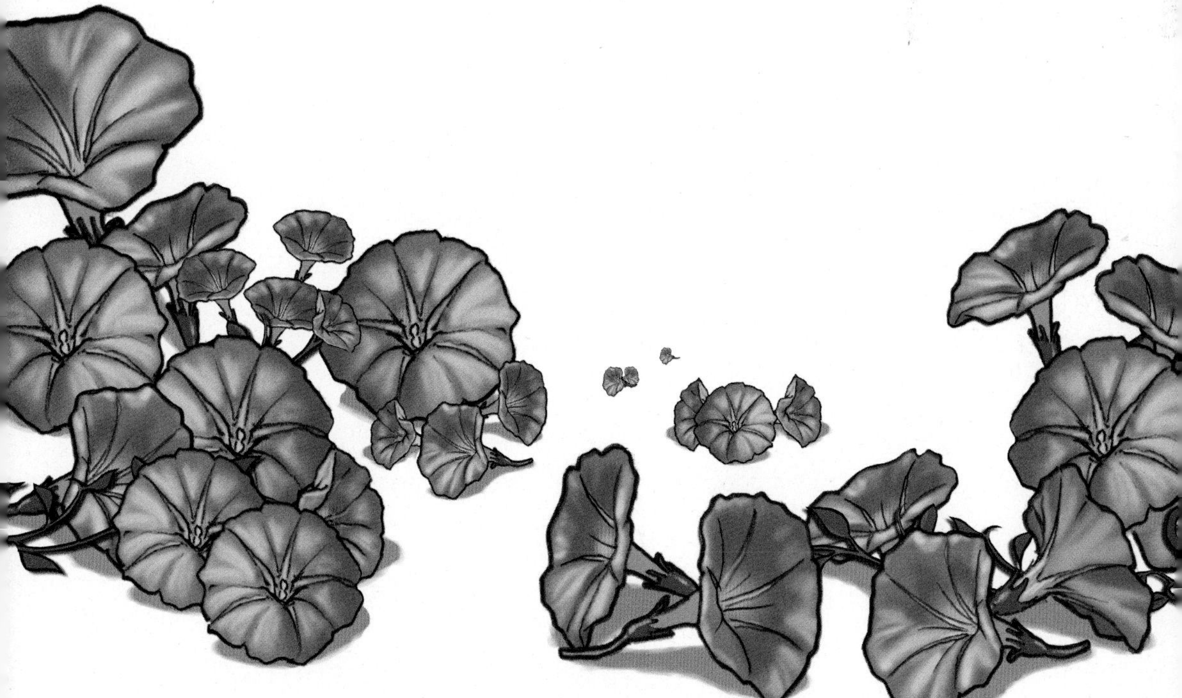

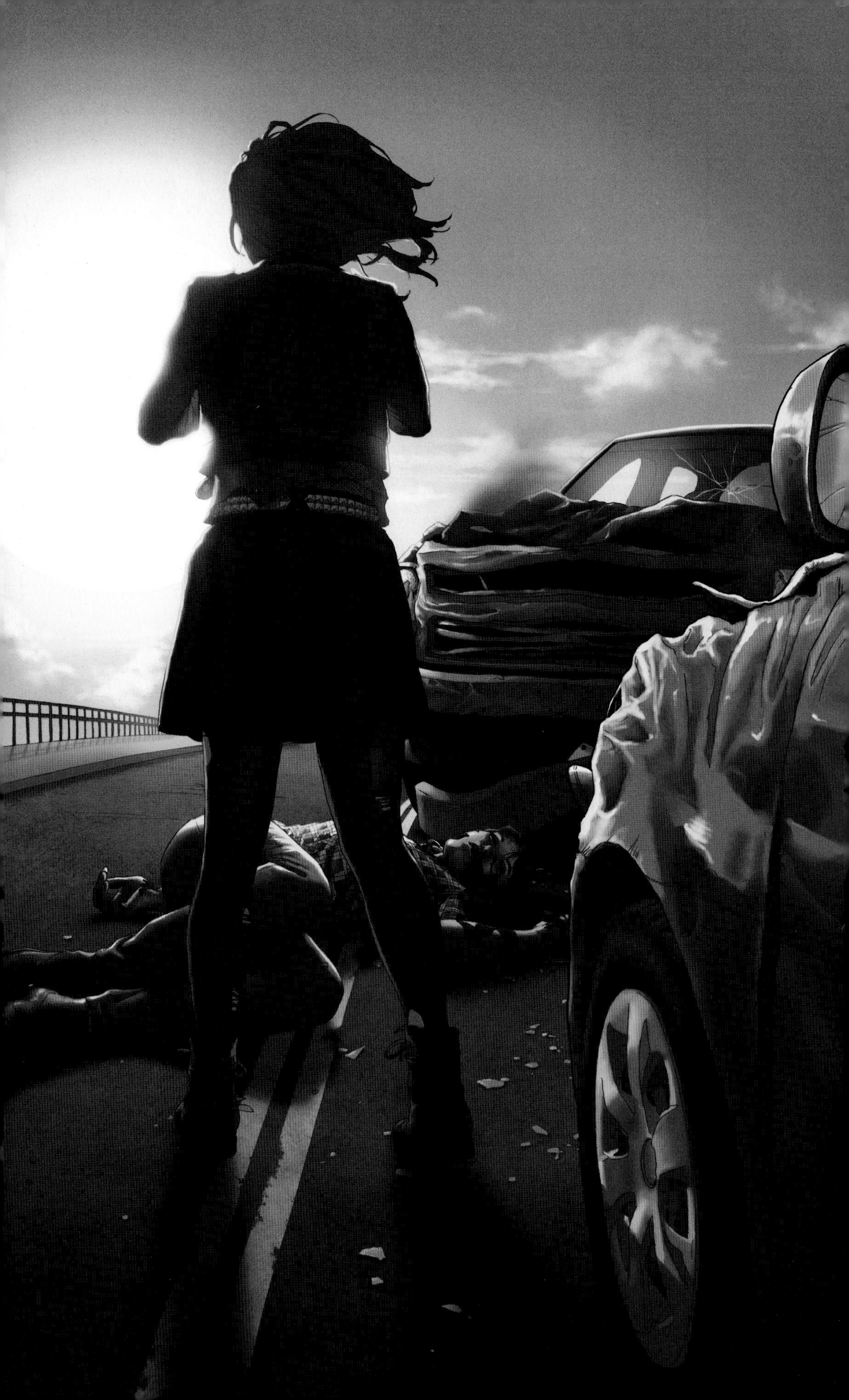

THREE YEARS AGO.

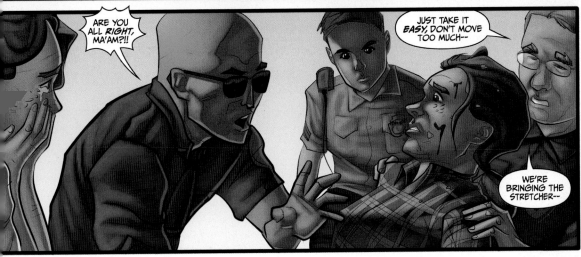

ARE YOU ALL *RIGHT,* MA'AM?!!

JUST TAKE IT *EASY,* DON'T MOVE TOO MUCH--

WE'RE BRINGING THE STRETCHER--

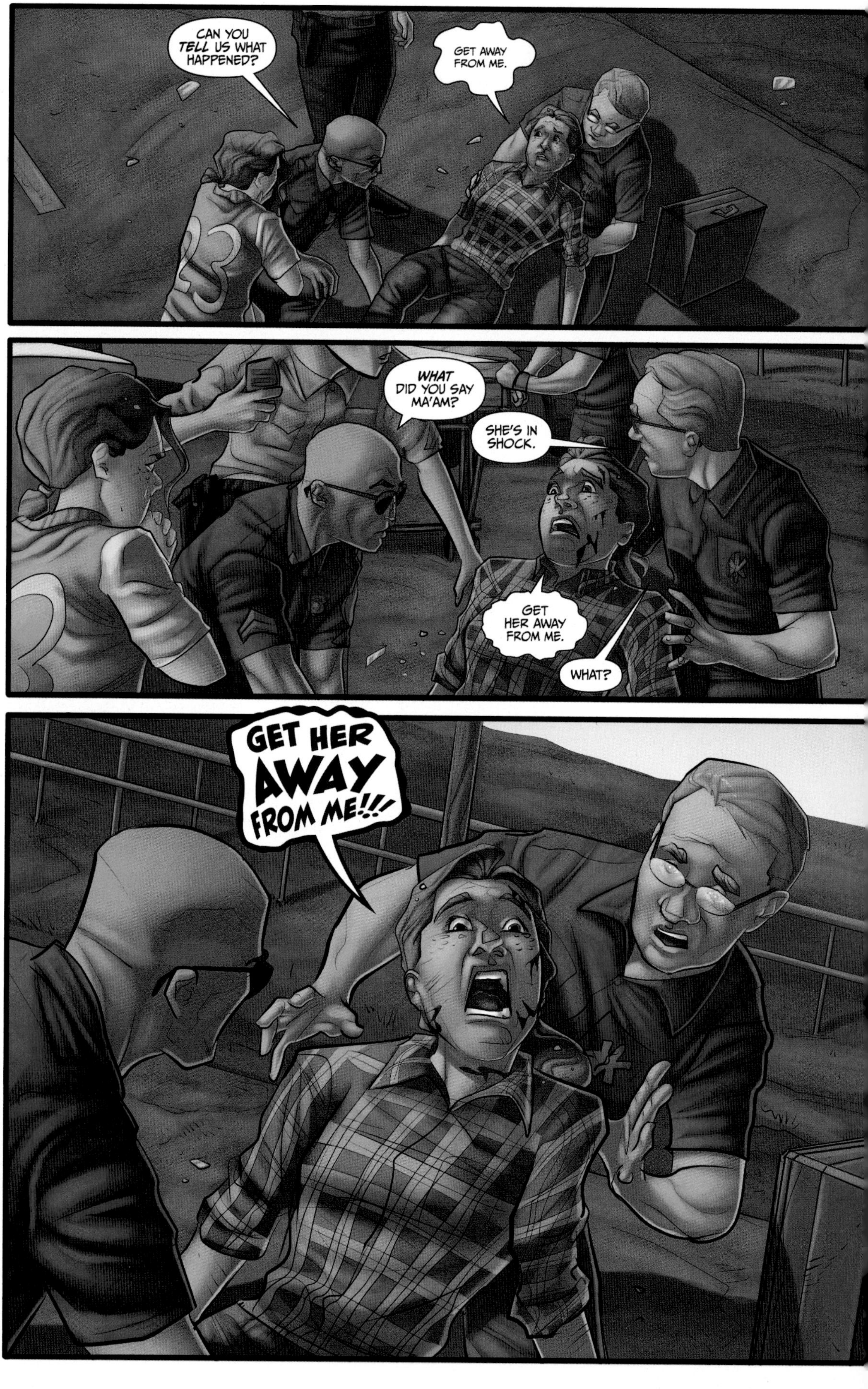
CAN YOU TELL US WHAT HAPPENED?
GET AWAY FROM ME.
WHAT DID YOU SAY MA'AM?
SHE'S IN SHOCK.
GET HER AWAY FROM ME.
WHAT?
GET HER AWAY FROM ME!!!

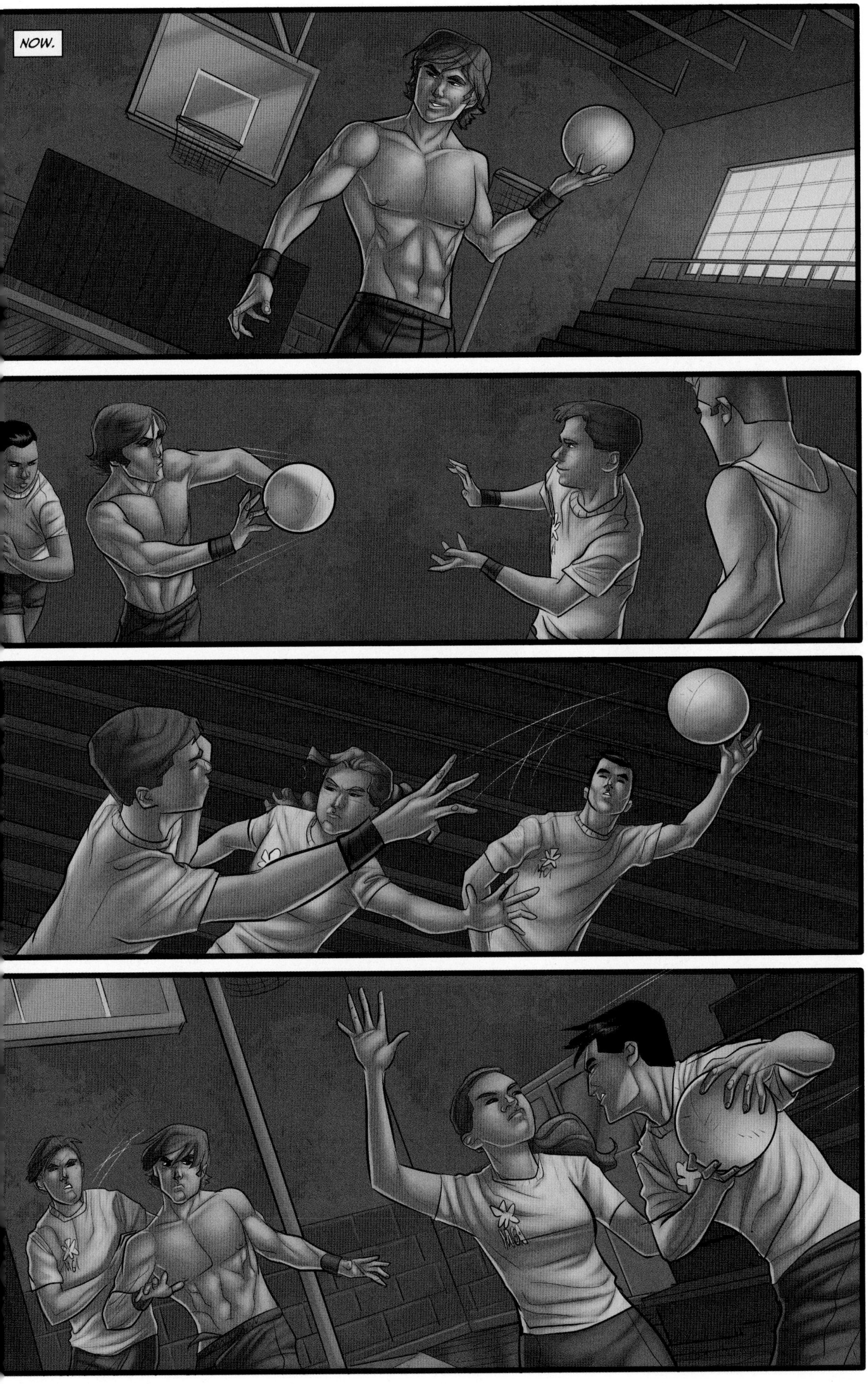
NOW.

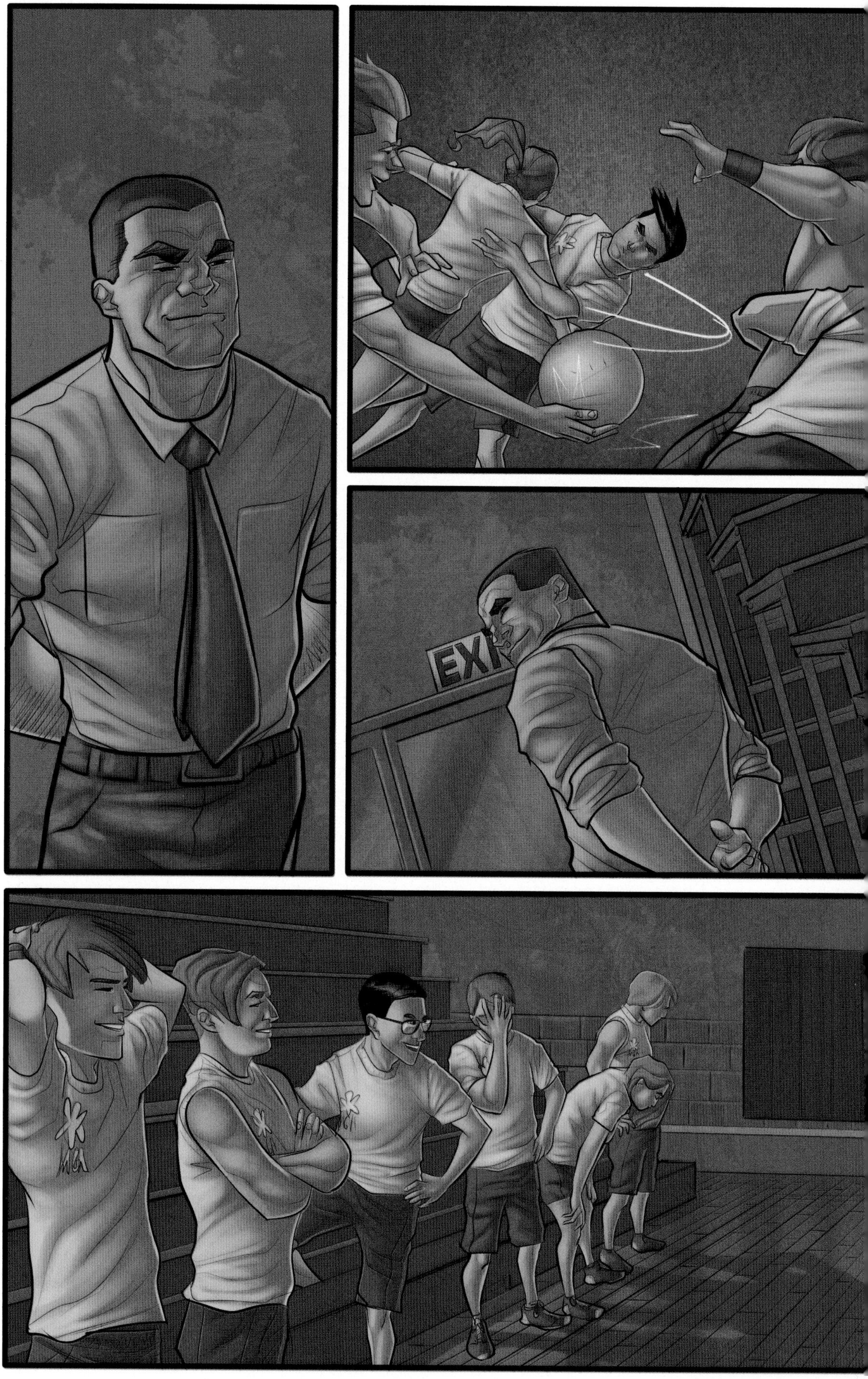

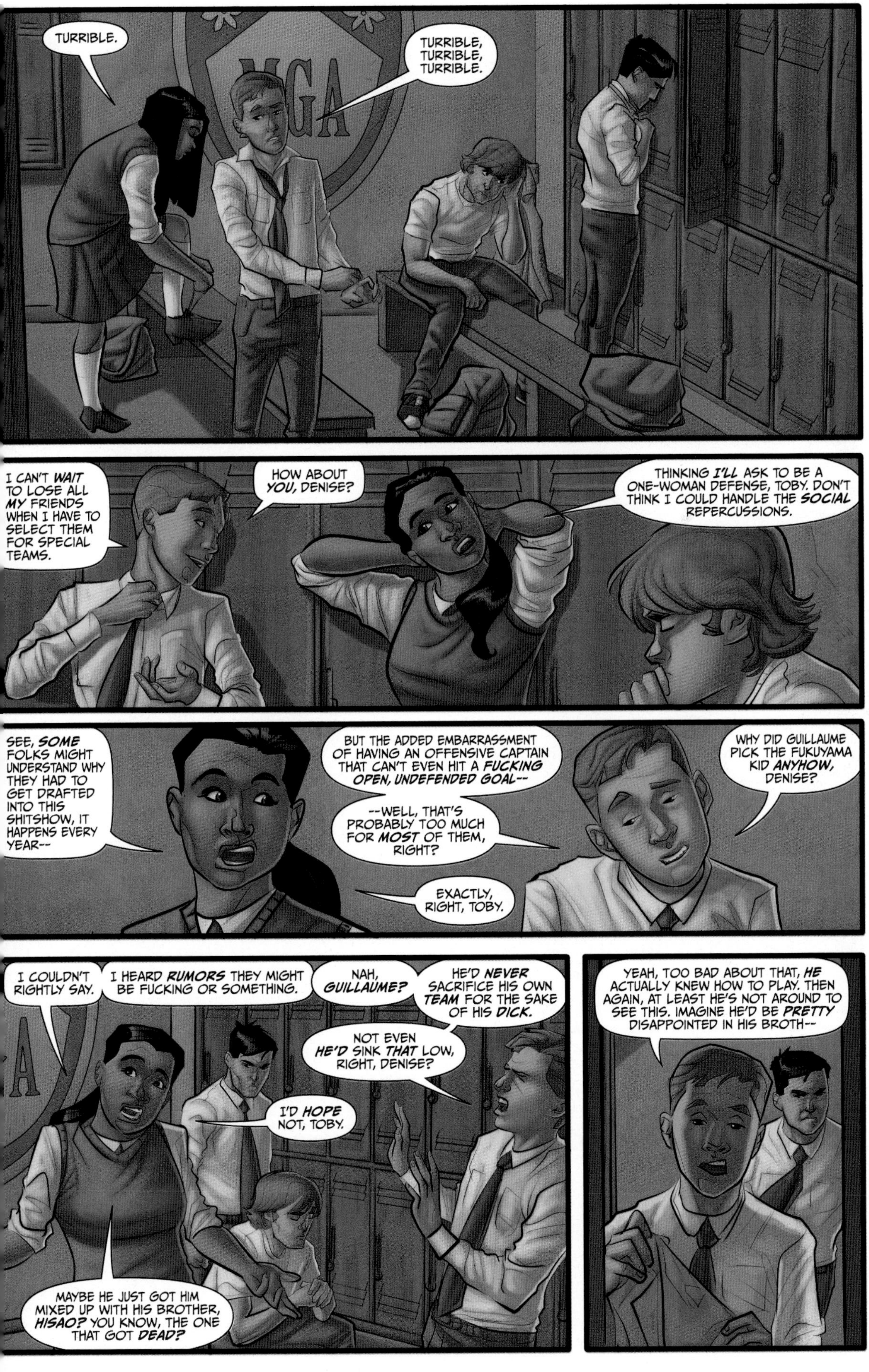
TURRIBLE.
TURRIBLE, TURRIBLE, TURRIBLE.
I CAN'T WAIT TO LOSE ALL MY FRIENDS WHEN I HAVE TO SELECT THEM FOR SPECIAL TEAMS.
HOW ABOUT YOU, DENISE?
THINKING I'LL ASK TO BE A ONE-WOMAN DEFENSE, TOBY. DON'T THINK I COULD HANDLE THE SOCIAL REPERCUSSIONS.
SEE, SOME FOLKS MIGHT UNDERSTAND WHY THEY HAD TO GET DRAFTED INTO THIS SHITSHOW, IT HAPPENS EVERY YEAR--
BUT THE ADDED EMBARRASSMENT OF HAVING AN OFFENSIVE CAPTAIN THAT CAN'T EVEN HIT A FUCKING OPEN, UNDEFENDED GOAL--
--WELL, THAT'S PROBABLY TOO MUCH FOR MOST OF THEM, RIGHT?
EXACTLY, RIGHT, TOBY.
WHY DID GUILLAUME PICK THE FUKUYAMA KID ANYHOW, DENISE?
I COULDN'T RIGHTLY SAY.
I HEARD RUMORS THEY MIGHT BE FUCKING OR SOMETHING.
NAH, GUILLAUME?
HE'D NEVER SACRIFICE HIS OWN TEAM FOR THE SAKE OF HIS DICK.
NOT EVEN HE'D SINK THAT LOW, RIGHT, DENISE?
I'D HOPE NOT, TOBY.
MAYBE HE JUST GOT HIM MIXED UP WITH HIS BROTHER, HISAO? YOU KNOW, THE ONE THAT GOT DEAD?
YEAH, TOO BAD ABOUT THAT, HE ACTUALLY KNEW HOW TO PLAY. THEN AGAIN, AT LEAST HE'S NOT AROUND TO SEE THIS. IMAGINE HE'D BE PRETTY DISAPPOINTED IN HIS BROTH--

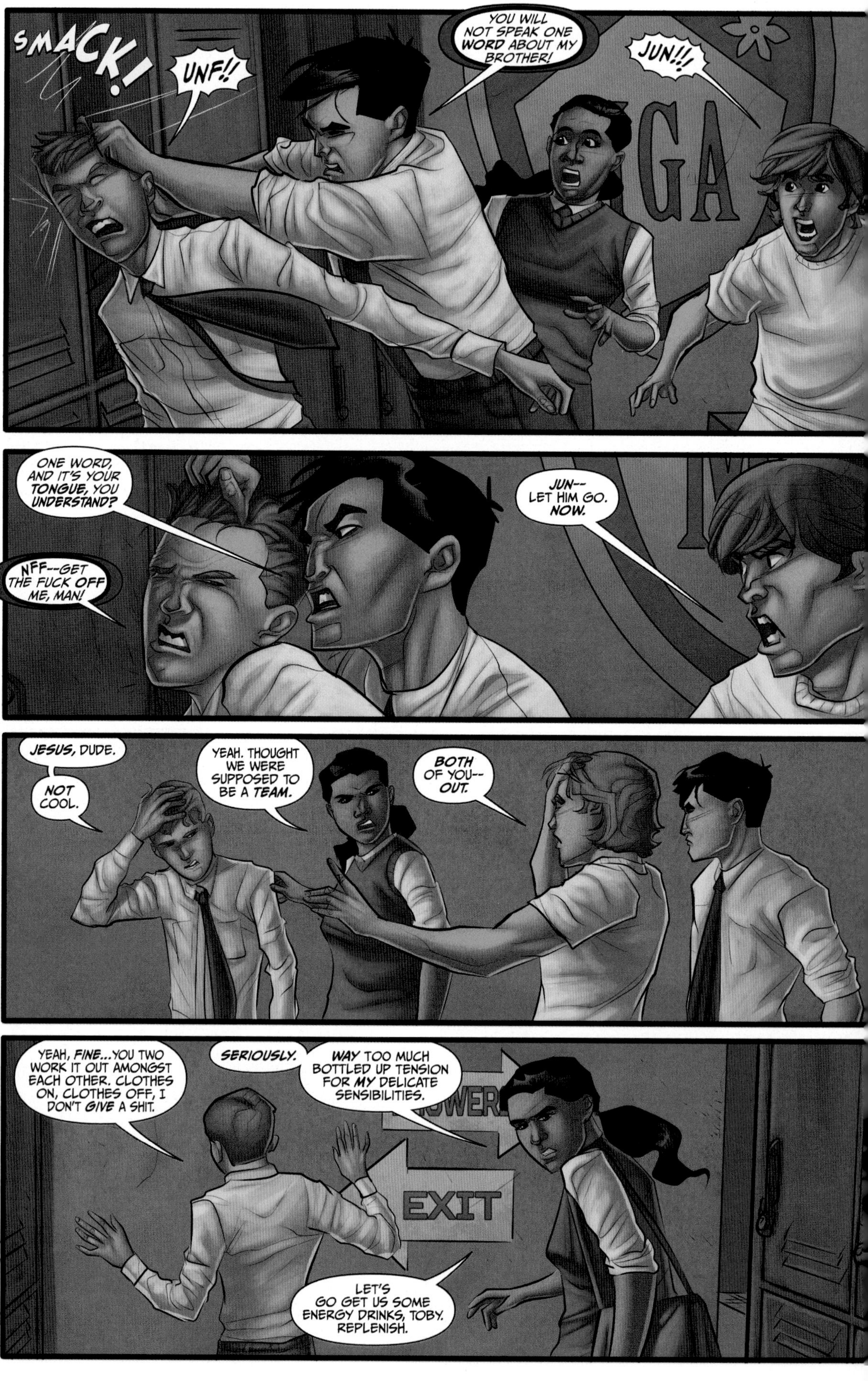
SMACK!
UNF!!
YOU WILL NOT SPEAK ONE WORD ABOUT MY BROTHER!
JUN!!!
GA
ONE WORD, AND IT'S YOUR TONGUE, YOU UNDERSTAND?
NFF--GET THE FUCK OFF ME, MAN!
JUN-- LET HIM GO. NOW.
JESUS, DUDE.
NOT COOL.
YEAH. THOUGHT WE WERE SUPPOSED TO BE A TEAM.
BOTH OF YOU-- OUT.
YEAH, FINE...YOU TWO WORK IT OUT AMONGST EACH OTHER. CLOTHES ON, CLOTHES OFF, I DON'T GIVE A SHIT.
SERIOUSLY.
WAY TOO MUCH BOTTLED UP TENSION FOR MY DELICATE SENSIBILITIES.
EXIT
LET'S GO GET US SOME ENERGY DRINKS, TOBY. REPLENISH.

ARE YOU OUT OF YOUR MIND?!!

WHAT?!!

WE *NEED* THEM!

THEY ARE BOTH *SUBPAR* ATHLETES.

NO, THEY'RE *NOT*. THEY'RE FRUSTRATED, SO THEY'RE NOT *TRYING*.

BECAUSE THEY THINK I AM-- BECAUSE YOU MAKE ME *FAIL!*

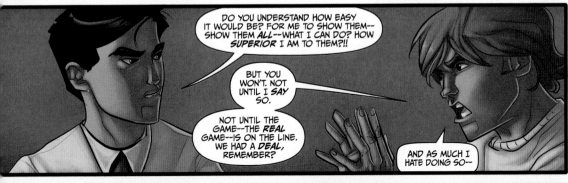

DO YOU UNDERSTAND HOW EASY IT WOULD BE? FOR ME TO SHOW THEM-- SHOW THEM *ALL*--WHAT I CAN DO? HOW *SUPERIOR* I AM TO THEM?!!

BUT YOU WON'T. NOT UNTIL I *SAY* SO.

NOT UNTIL THE GAME--THE *REAL* GAME--IS ON THE LINE. WE HAD A *DEAL*, REMEMBER?

AND AS MUCH I HATE DOING SO--

"--I HAVE HELD UP *MY* END."

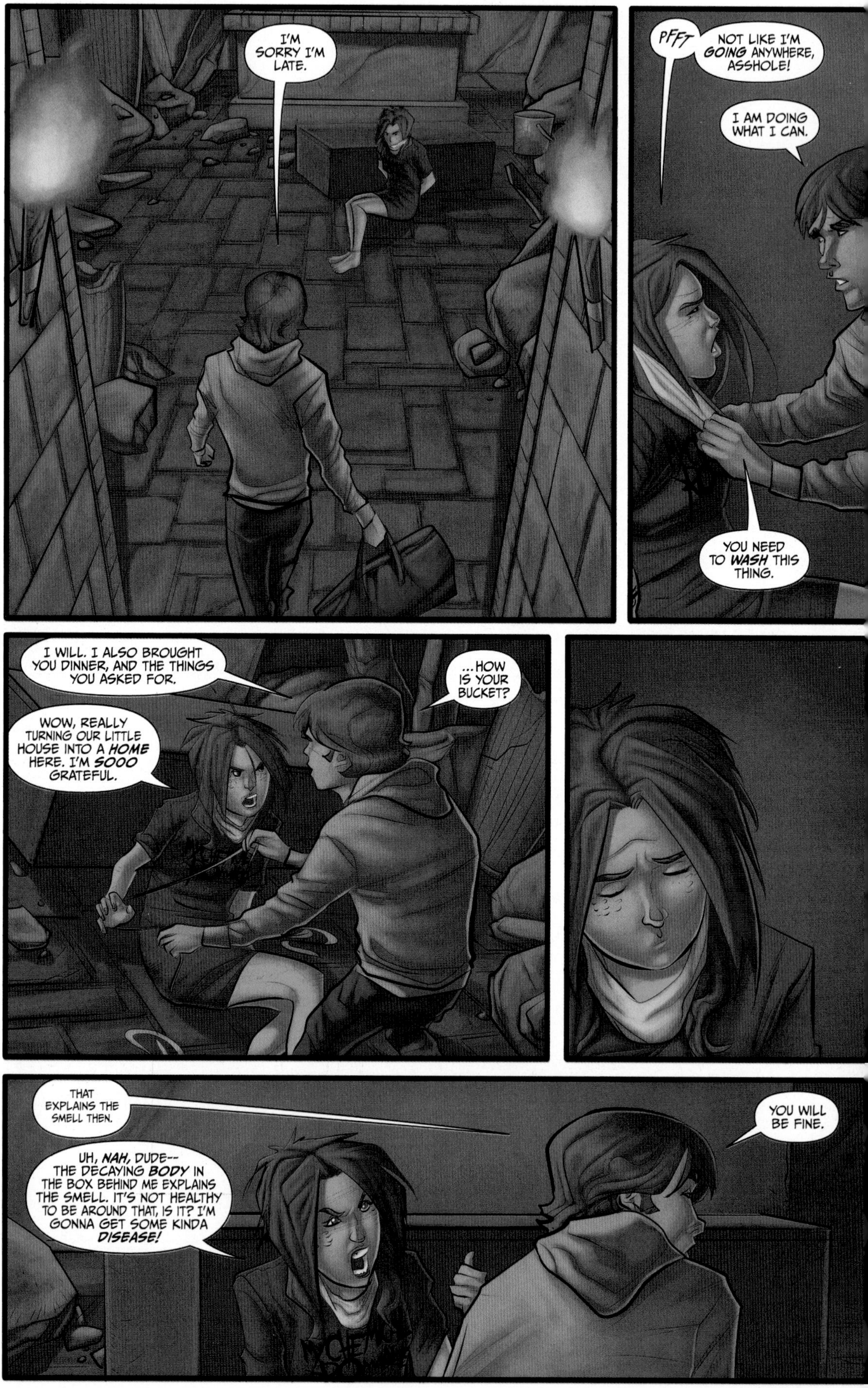
I'M SORRY I'M LATE.
PFFT
NOT LIKE I'M GOING ANYWHERE, ASSHOLE!
I AM DOING WHAT I CAN.
YOU NEED TO WASH THIS THING.
I WILL. I ALSO BROUGHT YOU DINNER, AND THE THINGS YOU ASKED FOR.
WOW, REALLY TURNING OUR LITTLE HOUSE INTO A HOME HERE. I'M SOOO GRATEFUL.
...HOW IS YOUR BUCKET?
THAT EXPLAINS THE SMELL THEN.
UH, NAH, DUDE-- THE DECAYING BODY IN THE BOX BEHIND ME EXPLAINS THE SMELL. IT'S NOT HEALTHY TO BE AROUND THAT, IS IT? I'M GONNA GET SOME KINDA DISEASE!
YOU WILL BE FINE.

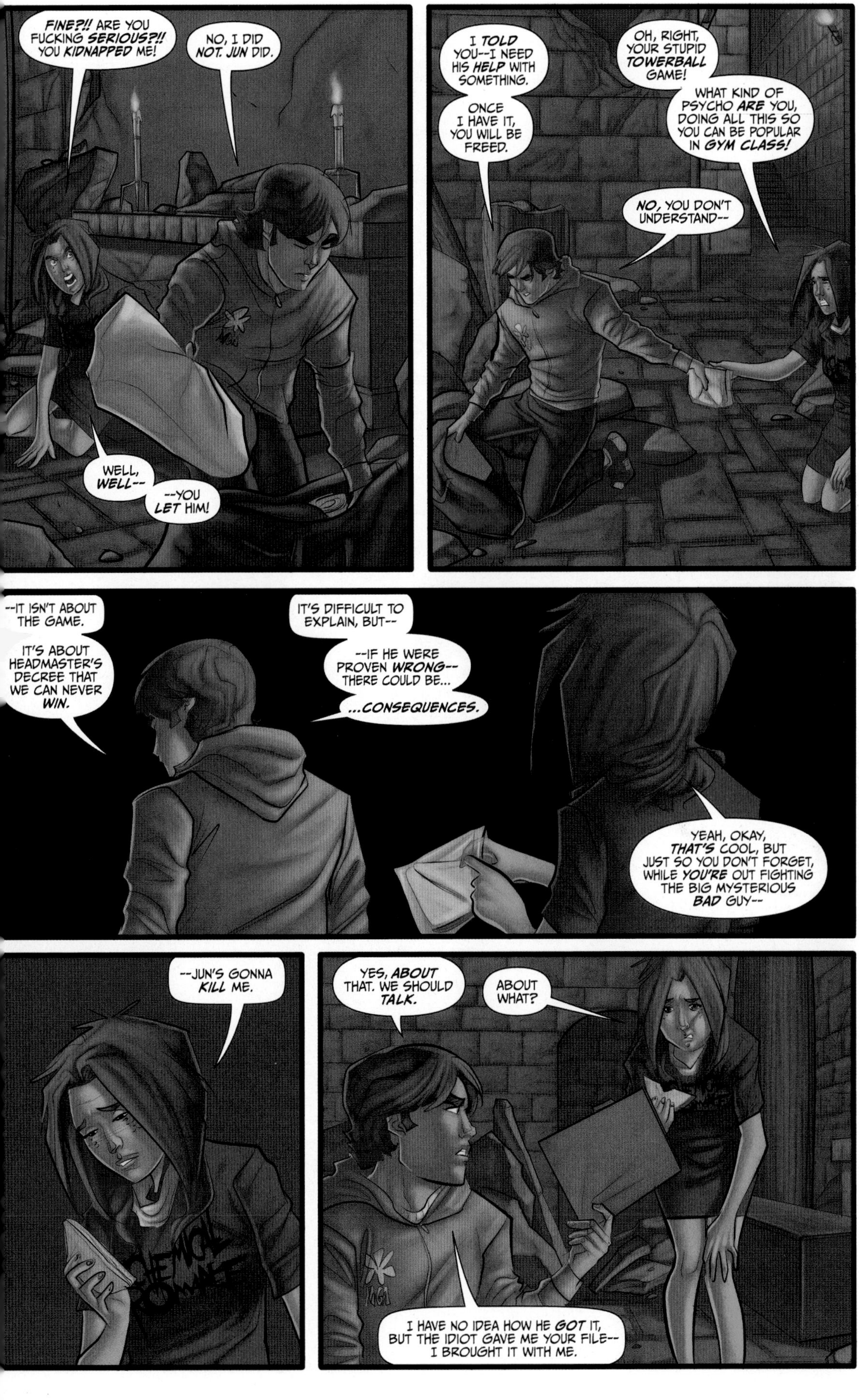
FINE?!! ARE YOU FUCKING SERIOUS?!! YOU KIDNAPPED ME!
NO, I DID NOT. JUN DID.
WELL, WELL--
--YOU LET HIM!
I TOLD YOU--I NEED HIS HELP WITH SOMETHING.
ONCE I HAVE IT, YOU WILL BE FREED.
OH, RIGHT, YOUR STUPID TOWERBALL GAME!
WHAT KIND OF PSYCHO ARE YOU, DOING ALL THIS SO YOU CAN BE POPULAR IN GYM CLASS!
NO, YOU DON'T UNDERSTAND--
--IT ISN'T ABOUT THE GAME.
IT'S ABOUT HEADMASTER'S DECREE THAT WE CAN NEVER WIN.
IT'S DIFFICULT TO EXPLAIN, BUT--
--IF HE WERE PROVEN WRONG--THERE COULD BE...
...CONSEQUENCES.
YEAH, OKAY, THAT'S COOL, BUT JUST SO YOU DON'T FORGET, WHILE YOU'RE OUT FIGHTING THE BIG MYSTERIOUS BAD GUY--
--JUN'S GONNA KILL ME.
YES, ABOUT THAT. WE SHOULD TALK.
ABOUT WHAT?
I HAVE NO IDEA HOW HE GOT IT, BUT THE IDIOT GAVE ME YOUR FILE--I BROUGHT IT WITH ME.

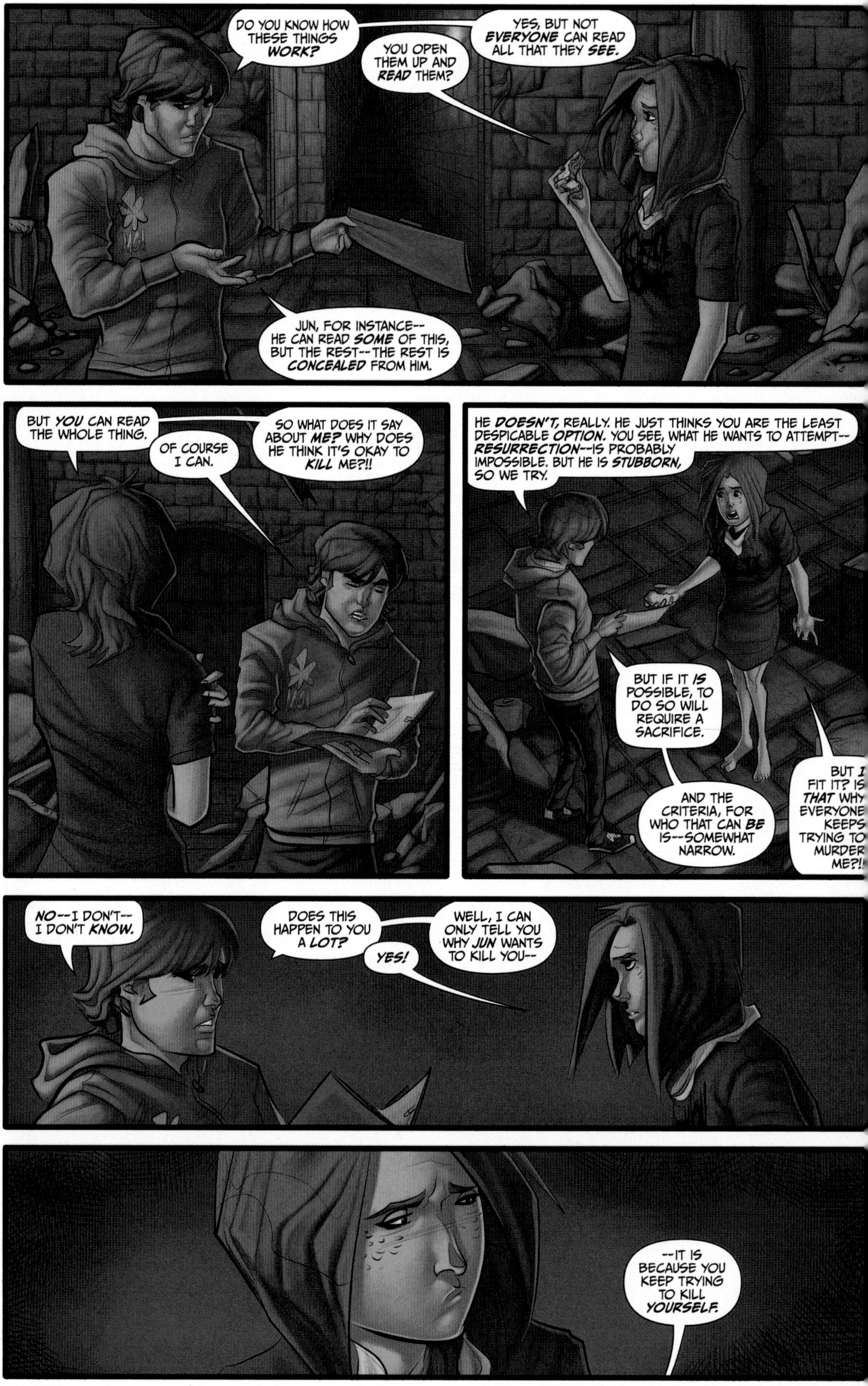

DO YOU KNOW HOW THESE THINGS ***WORK?***
YOU OPEN THEM UP AND ***READ*** THEM?
YES, BUT NOT ***EVERYONE*** CAN READ ALL THAT THEY ***SEE.***
JUN, FOR INSTANCE-- HE CAN READ ***SOME*** OF THIS, BUT THE REST--THE REST IS ***CONCEALED*** FROM HIM.
BUT ***YOU*** CAN READ THE WHOLE THING.
OF COURSE I CAN.
SO WHAT DOES IT SAY ABOUT ***ME?*** WHY DOES HE THINK IT'S OKAY TO ***KILL*** ME?!!
HE ***DOESN'T,*** REALLY. HE JUST THINKS YOU ARE THE LEAST DESPICABLE ***OPTION.*** YOU SEE, WHAT HE WANTS TO ATTEMPT-- ***RESURRECTION***--IS PROBABLY IMPOSSIBLE. BUT HE IS ***STUBBORN,*** SO WE TRY.
BUT IF IT ***IS*** POSSIBLE, TO DO SO WILL REQUIRE A SACRIFICE.
AND THE CRITERIA, FOR WHO THAT CAN ***BE*** IS--SOMEWHAT NARROW.
BUT ***I*** FIT IT? IS ***THAT*** WHY EVERYONE KEEPS TRYING TO MURDER ME?!!
NO--I DON'T-- I DON'T ***KNOW.***
DOES THIS HAPPEN TO YOU A ***LOT?***
YES!
WELL, I CAN ONLY TELL YOU WHY ***JUN*** WANTS TO KILL YOU--
--IT IS BECAUSE YOU KEEP TRYING TO KILL ***YOURSELF.***

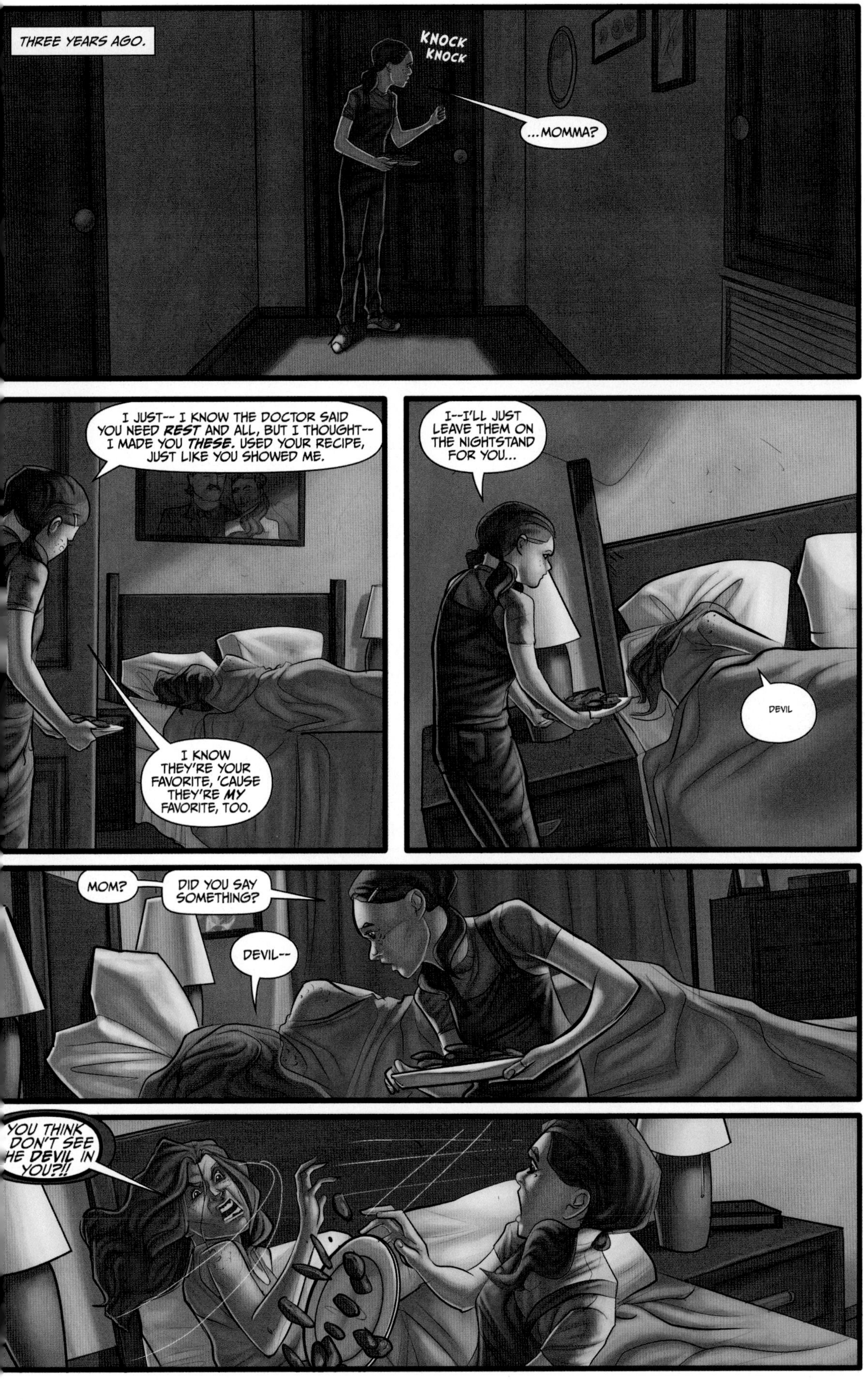
THREE YEARS AGO.
KNOCK KNOCK
...MOMMA?
I JUST-- I KNOW THE DOCTOR SAID YOU NEED REST AND ALL, BUT I THOUGHT-- I MADE YOU THESE. USED YOUR RECIPE, JUST LIKE YOU SHOWED ME.
I KNOW THEY'RE YOUR FAVORITE, 'CAUSE THEY'RE MY FAVORITE, TOO.
I--I'LL JUST LEAVE THEM ON THE NIGHTSTAND FOR YOU...
DEVIL
MOM?
DID YOU SAY SOMETHING?
DEVIL--
YOU THINK DON'T SEE HE DEVIL IN YOU?!!

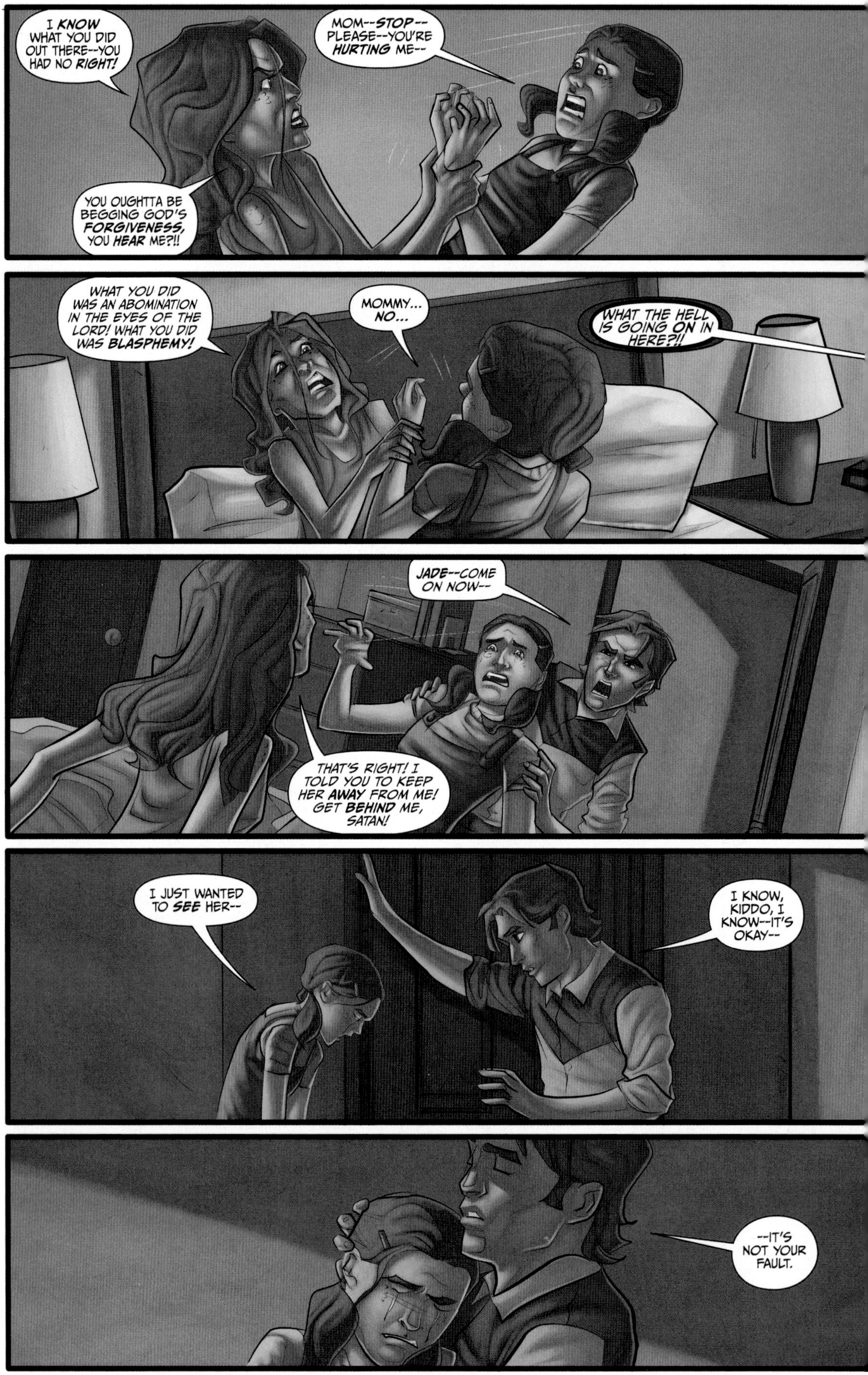
I KNOW WHAT YOU DID OUT THERE--YOU HAD NO RIGHT!
MOM--STOP--PLEASE--YOU'RE HURTING ME--
YOU OUGHTTA BE BEGGING GOD'S FORGIVENESS, YOU HEAR ME?!!
WHAT YOU DID WAS AN ABOMINATION IN THE EYES OF THE LORD! WHAT YOU DID WAS BLASPHEMY!
MOMMY... NO...
WHAT THE HELL IS GOING ON IN HERE?!!
JADE--COME ON NOW--
THAT'S RIGHT! I TOLD YOU TO KEEP HER AWAY FROM ME! GET BEHIND ME, SATAN!
I JUST WANTED TO SEE HER--
I KNOW, KIDDO, I KNOW--IT'S OKAY--
--IT'S NOT YOUR FAULT.

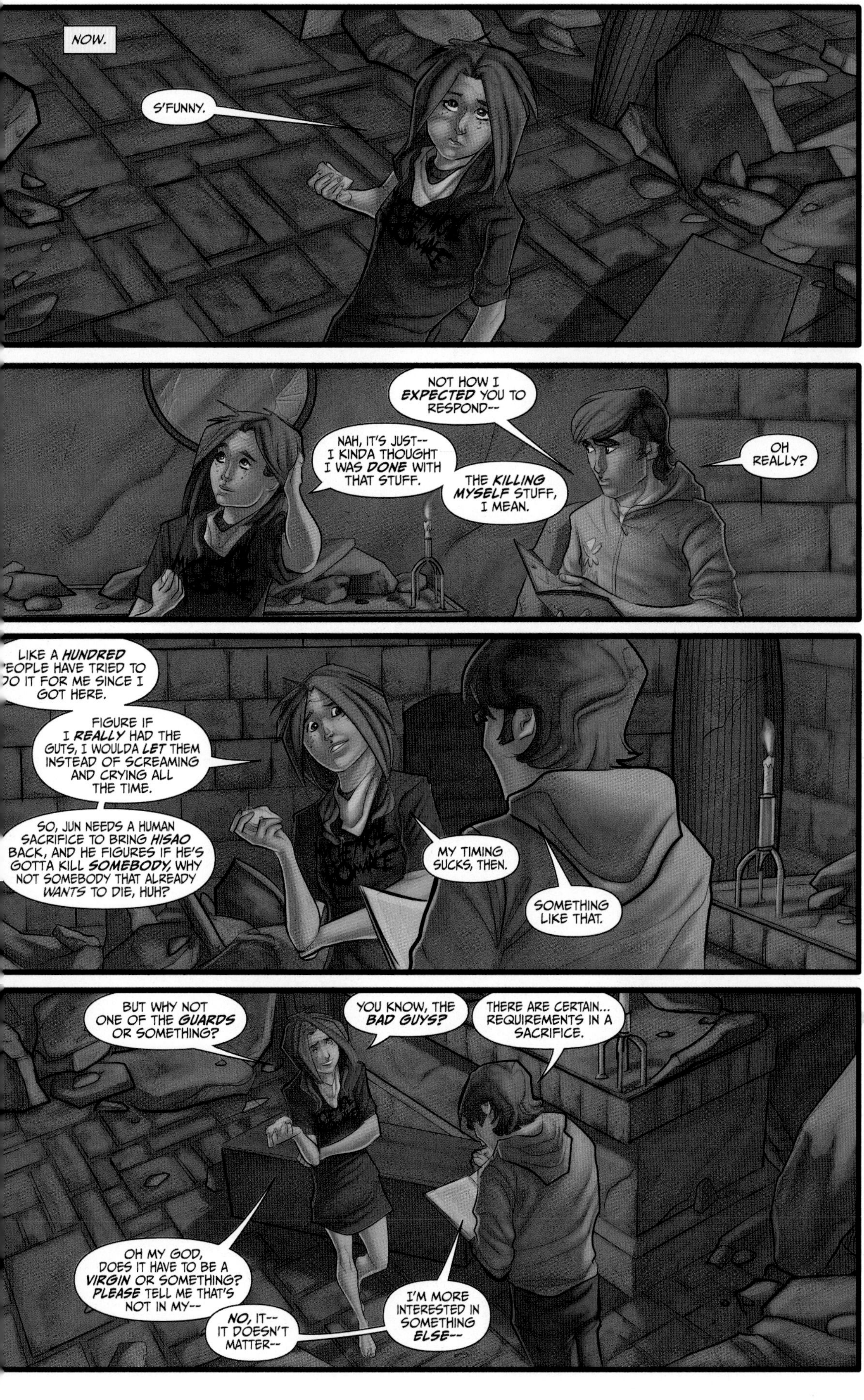
NOW.
S'FUNNY.
NOT HOW I EXPECTED YOU TO RESPOND--
NAH, IT'S JUST-- I KINDA THOUGHT I WAS DONE WITH THAT STUFF.
THE KILLING MYSELF STUFF, I MEAN.
OH REALLY?
LIKE A HUNDRED PEOPLE HAVE TRIED TO DO IT FOR ME SINCE I GOT HERE.
FIGURE IF I REALLY HAD THE GUTS, I WOULDA LET THEM INSTEAD OF SCREAMING AND CRYING ALL THE TIME.
SO, JUN NEEDS A HUMAN SACRIFICE TO BRING HISAO BACK, AND HE FIGURES IF HE'S GOTTA KILL SOMEBODY, WHY NOT SOMEBODY THAT ALREADY WANTS TO DIE, HUH?
MY TIMING SUCKS, THEN.
SOMETHING LIKE THAT.
BUT WHY NOT ONE OF THE GUARDS OR SOMETHING?
YOU KNOW, THE BAD GUYS?
THERE ARE CERTAIN... REQUIREMENTS IN A SACRIFICE.
OH MY GOD, DOES IT HAVE TO BE A VIRGIN OR SOMETHING? PLEASE TELL ME THAT'S NOT IN MY--
NO, IT-- IT DOESN'T MATTER--
I'M MORE INTERESTED IN SOMETHING ELSE--

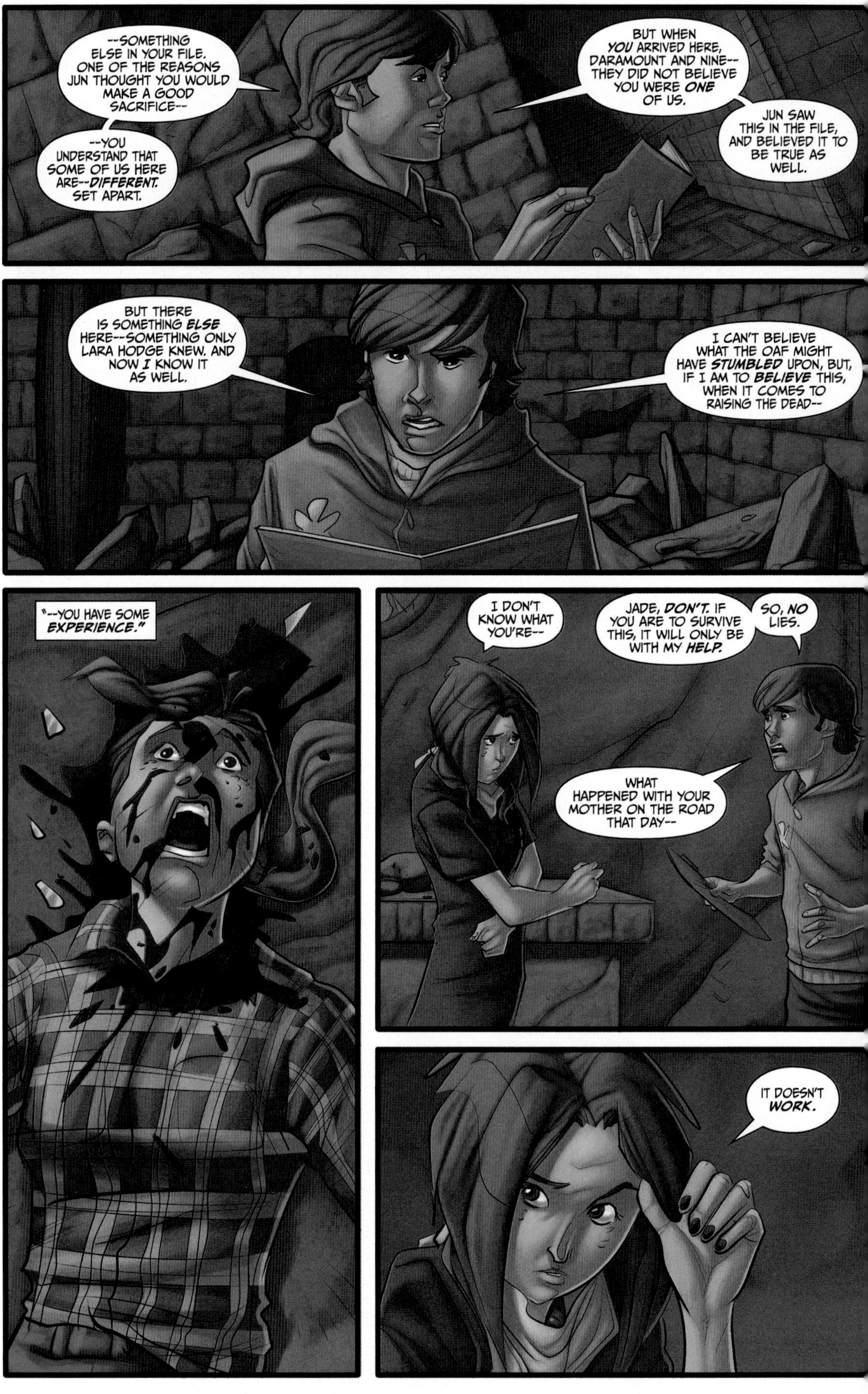
--SOMETHING ELSE IN YOUR FILE. ONE OF THE REASONS JUN THOUGHT YOU WOULD MAKE A GOOD SACRIFICE--
--YOU UNDERSTAND THAT SOME OF US HERE ARE--*DIFFERENT.* SET APART.
BUT WHEN *YOU* ARRIVED HERE, DARAMOUNT AND NINE--THEY DID NOT BELIEVE YOU WERE *ONE* OF US.
JUN SAW THIS IN THE FILE, AND BELIEVED IT TO BE TRUE AS WELL.
BUT THERE IS SOMETHING *ELSE* HERE--SOMETHING ONLY LARA HODGE KNEW. AND NOW *I* KNOW IT AS WELL.
I CAN'T BELIEVE WHAT THE OAF MIGHT HAVE *STUMBLED* UPON, BUT, IF I AM TO *BELIEVE* THIS, WHEN IT COMES TO RAISING THE DEAD--
"--YOU HAVE SOME *EXPERIENCE.*"
I DON'T KNOW WHAT YOU'RE--
JADE, *DON'T.* IF YOU ARE TO SURVIVE THIS, IT WILL ONLY BE WITH MY *HELP.*
SO, *NO* LIES.
WHAT HAPPENED WITH YOUR MOTHER ON THE ROAD THAT DAY--
IT DOESN'T *WORK.*

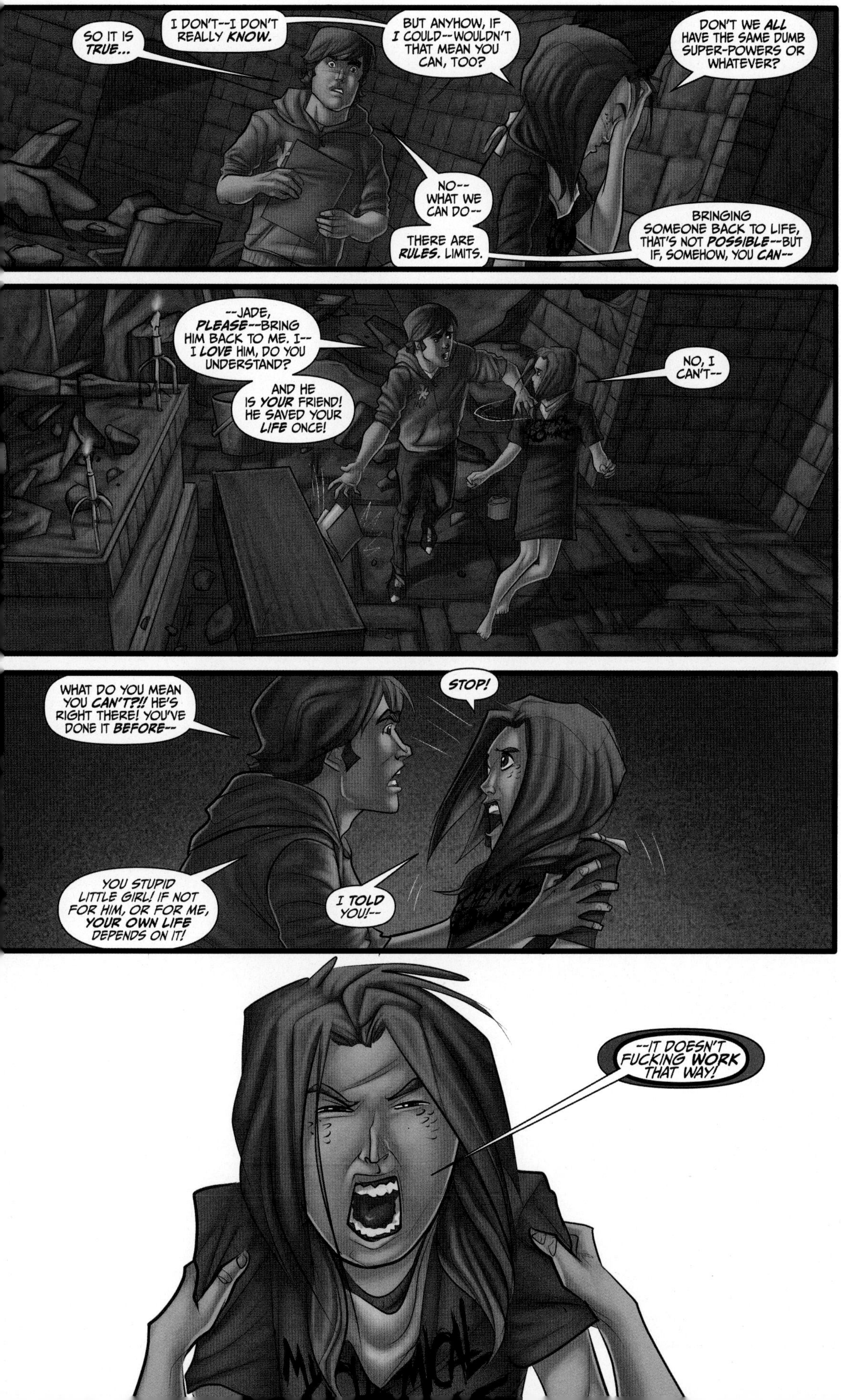
SO IT IS TRUE...
I DON'T--I DON'T REALLY KNOW.
BUT ANYHOW, IF I COULD--WOULDN'T THAT MEAN YOU CAN, TOO?
DON'T WE ALL HAVE THE SAME DUMB SUPER-POWERS OR WHATEVER?
NO-- WHAT WE CAN DO--
THERE ARE RULES. LIMITS.
BRINGING SOMEONE BACK TO LIFE, THAT'S NOT POSSIBLE--BUT IF, SOMEHOW, YOU CAN--
--JADE, PLEASE--BRING HIM BACK TO ME. I-- I LOVE HIM, DO YOU UNDERSTAND?
AND HE IS YOUR FRIEND! HE SAVED YOUR LIFE ONCE!
NO, I CAN'T--
WHAT DO YOU MEAN YOU CAN'T?!! HE'S RIGHT THERE! YOU'VE DONE IT BEFORE--
STOP!
YOU STUPID LITTLE GIRL! IF NOT FOR HIM, OR FOR ME, YOUR OWN LIFE DEPENDS ON IT!
I TOLD YOU!--
--IT DOESN'T FUCKING WORK THAT WAY!

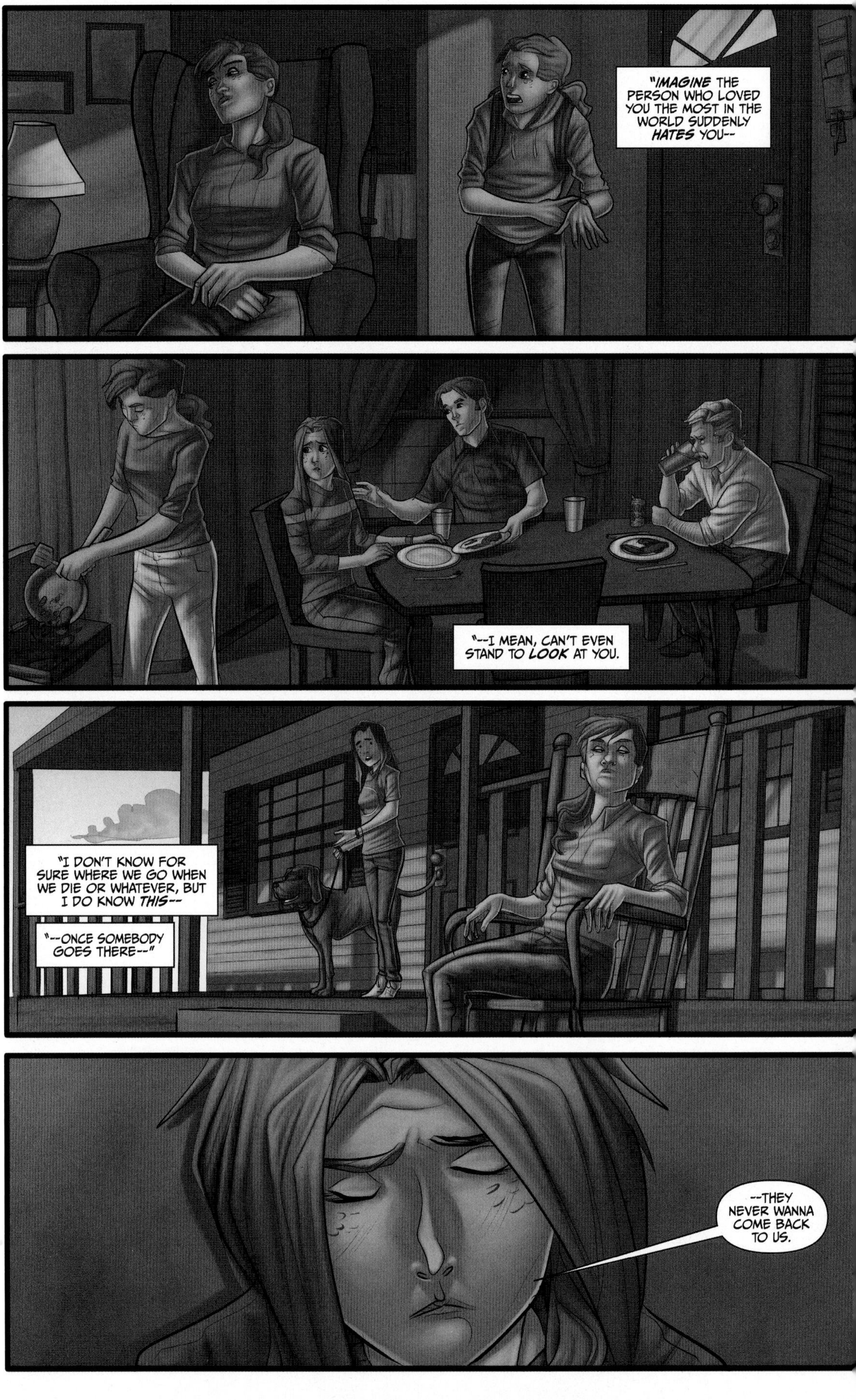
"IMAGINE THE PERSON WHO LOVED YOU THE MOST IN THE WORLD SUDDENLY HATES YOU--
"--I MEAN, CAN'T EVEN STAND TO LOOK AT YOU.
"I DON'T KNOW FOR SURE WHERE WE GO WHEN WE DIE OR WHATEVER, BUT I DO KNOW THIS--
"--ONCE SOMEBODY GOES THERE--"
--THEY NEVER WANNA COME BACK TO US.

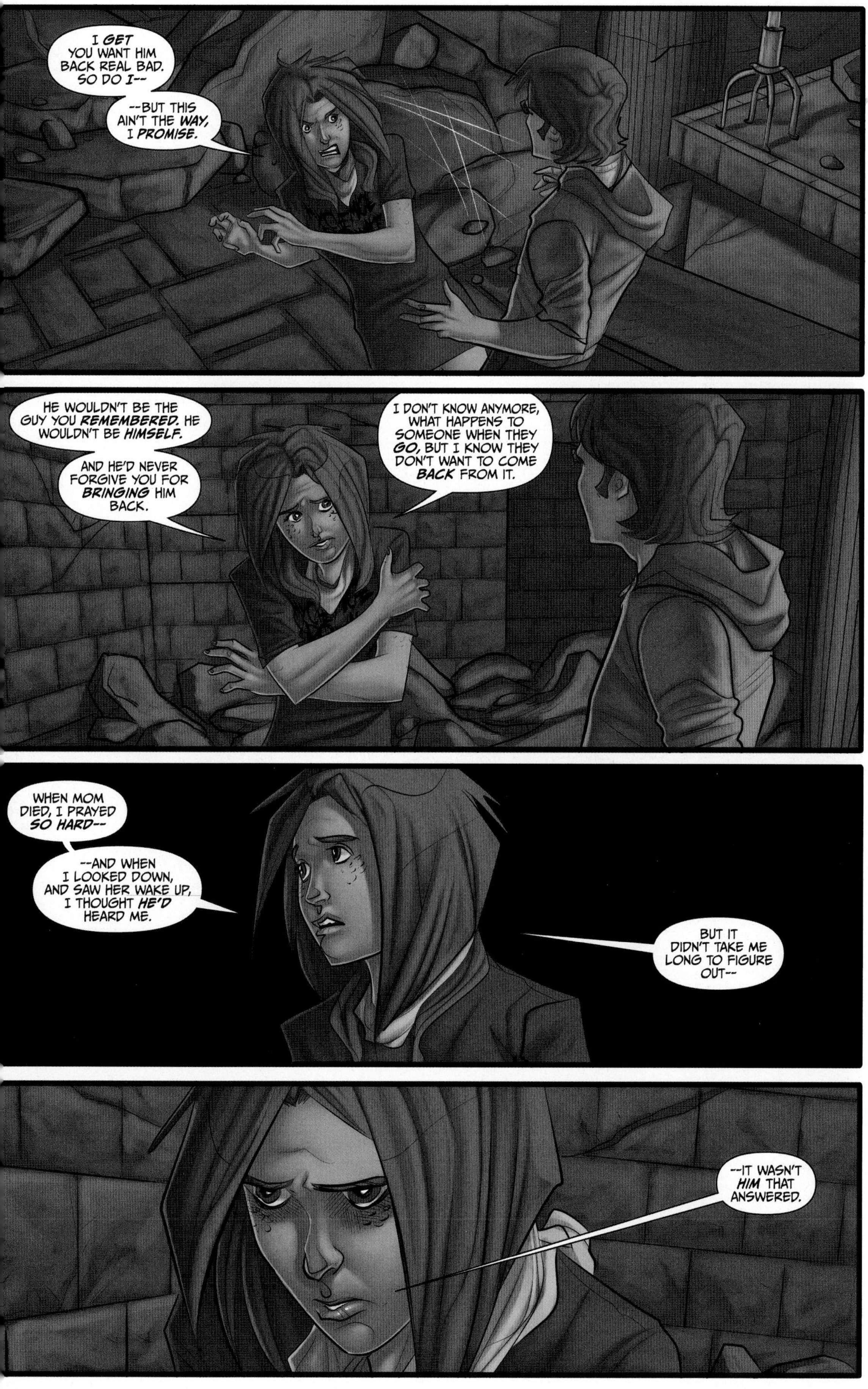

I GET YOU WANT HIM BACK REAL BAD. SO DO I--
--BUT THIS AIN'T THE WAY, I PROMISE.
HE WOULDN'T BE THE GUY YOU REMEMBERED. HE WOULDN'T BE HIMSELF.
AND HE'D NEVER FORGIVE YOU FOR BRINGING HIM BACK.
I DON'T KNOW ANYMORE, WHAT HAPPENS TO SOMEONE WHEN THEY GO, BUT I KNOW THEY DON'T WANT TO COME BACK FROM IT.
WHEN MOM DIED, I PRAYED SO HARD--
--AND WHEN I LOOKED DOWN, AND SAW HER WAKE UP, I THOUGHT HE'D HEARD ME.
BUT IT DIDN'T TAKE ME LONG TO FIGURE OUT--
--IT WASN'T HIM THAT ANSWERED.

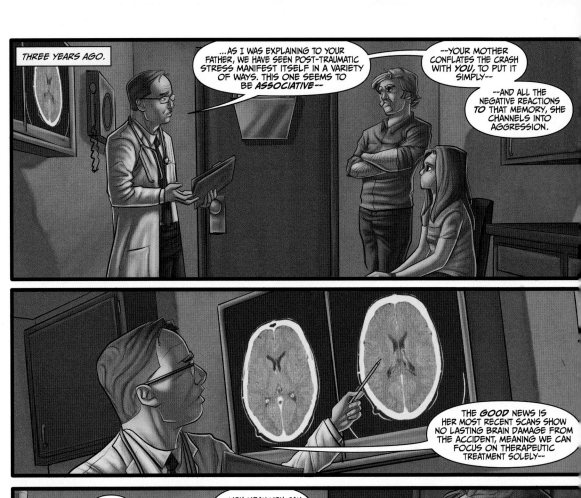

THREE YEARS AGO.

...AS I WAS EXPLAINING TO YOUR FATHER, WE HAVE SEEN POST-TRAUMATIC STRESS MANIFEST ITSELF IN A VARIETY OF WAYS. THIS ONE SEEMS TO BE *ASSOCIATIVE*--

--YOUR MOTHER CONFLATES THE CRASH WITH *YOU*, TO PUT IT SIMPLY--

--AND ALL THE NEGATIVE REACTIONS *TO* THAT MEMORY, SHE CHANNELS INTO AGGRESSION.

THE *GOOD* NEWS IS HER MOST RECENT SCANS SHOW NO LASTING BRAIN DAMAGE FROM THE ACCIDENT, MEANING WE CAN FOCUS ON THERAPEUTIC TREATMENT SOLELY--

SO, WAIT--

--YOU MEAN YOU CAN *HELP* HER? YOU CAN MAKE HER *LOVE* ME AGAIN?

ER, JADE-- I SHOULD WARN YOU--

--THERE'S A LOT WE *STILL* DON'T UNDERSTAND ABOUT HOW TO TREAT CONDITIONS LIKE YOUR MOTHER'S--THIS COULD TAKE *YEARS*.

BOTTOM LINE--

--I WOULDN'T GET YOUR HOPES UP *TOO* MUCH.

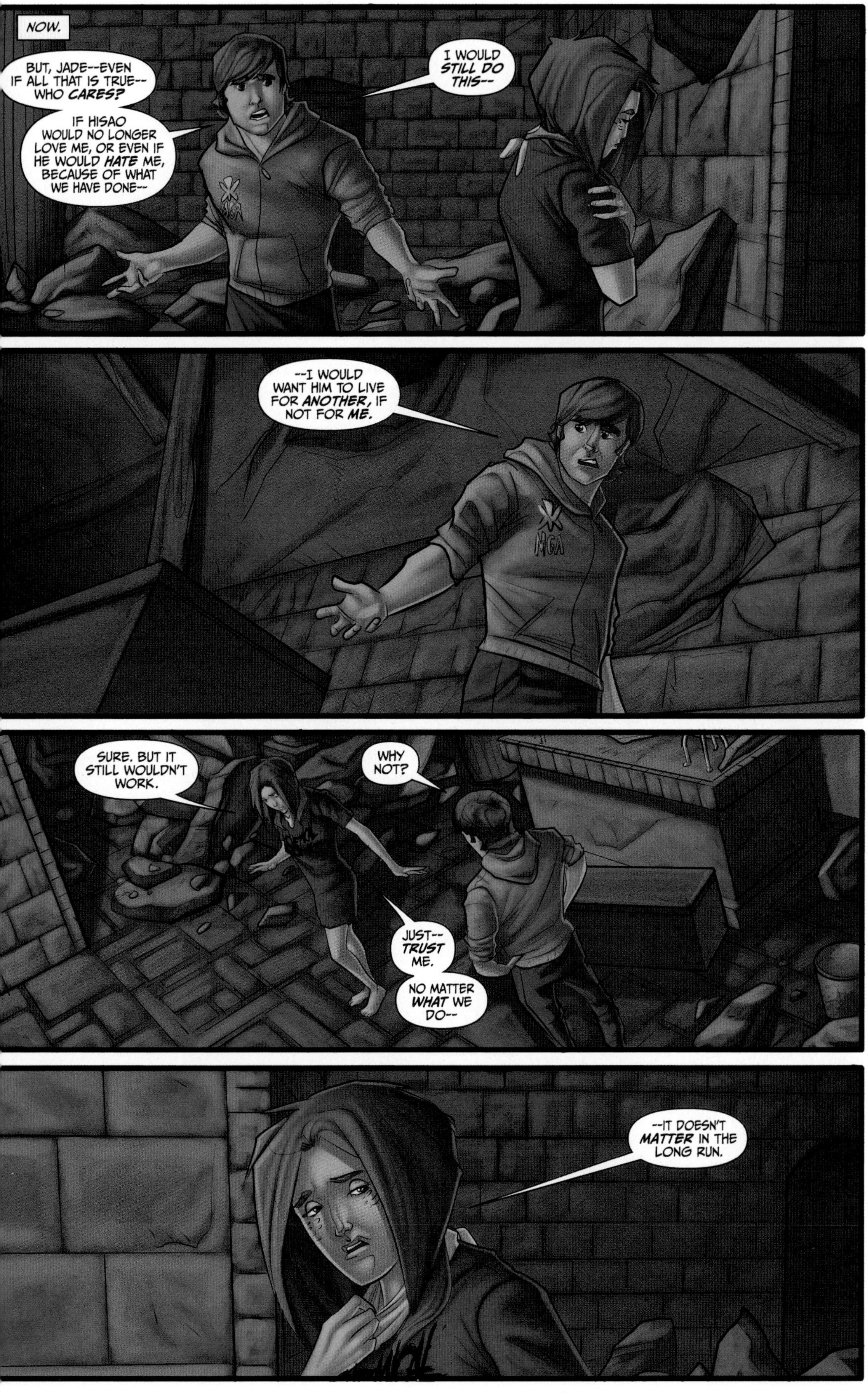
NOW.
BUT, JADE--EVEN IF ALL THAT IS TRUE-- WHO CARES?
IF HISAO WOULD NO LONGER LOVE ME, OR EVEN IF HE WOULD HATE ME, BECAUSE OF WHAT WE HAVE DONE--
I WOULD STILL DO THIS--
--I WOULD WANT HIM TO LIVE FOR ANOTHER, IF NOT FOR ME.
SURE. BUT IT STILL WOULDN'T WORK.
WHY NOT?
JUST-- TRUST ME.
NO MATTER WHAT WE DO--
--IT DOESN'T MATTER IN THE LONG RUN.

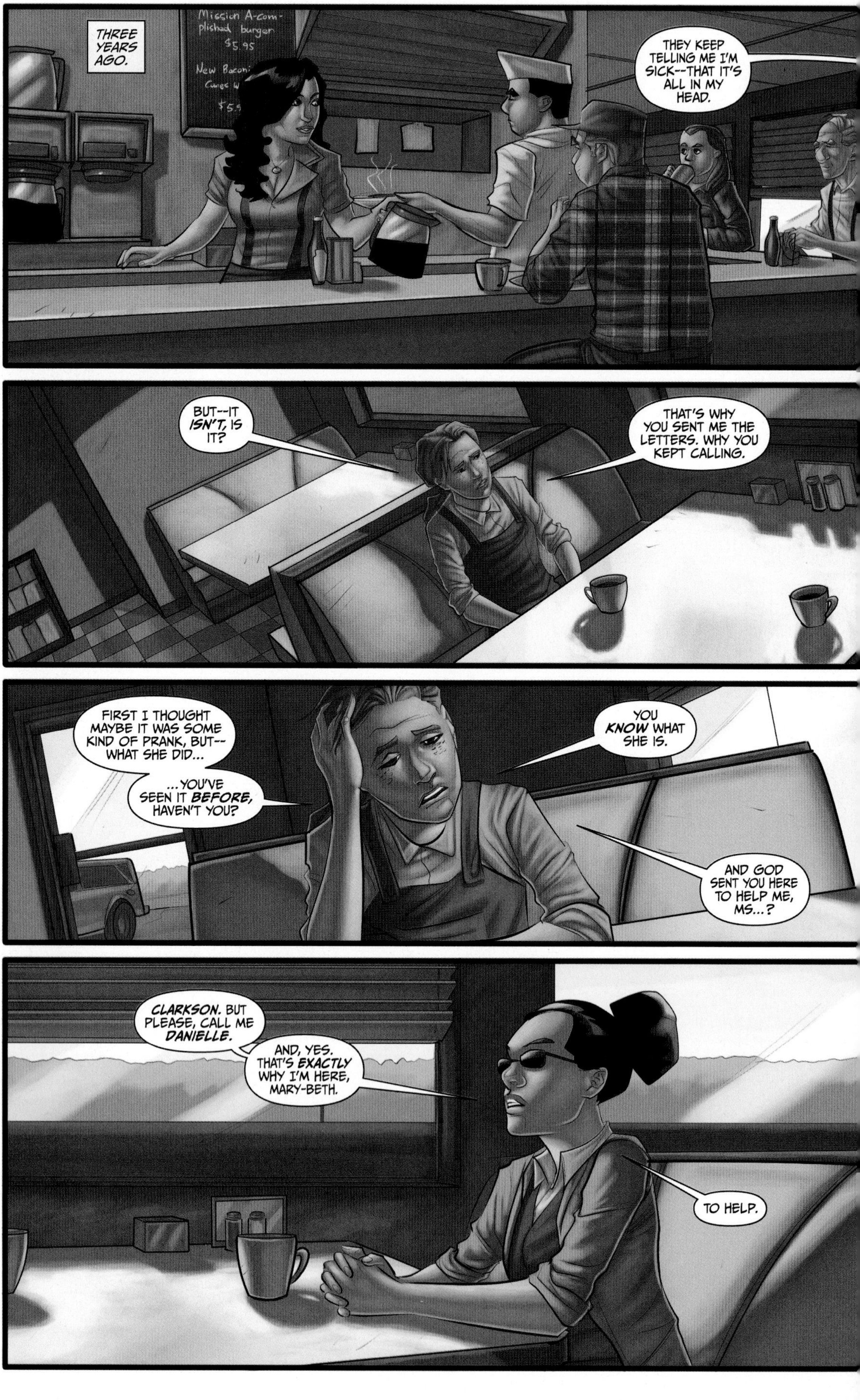
THREE YEARS AGO.
Mission A-complished burger $5.95
THEY KEEP TELLING ME I'M SICK--THAT IT'S ALL IN MY HEAD.
BUT--IT ISN'T, IS IT?
THAT'S WHY YOU SENT ME THE LETTERS. WHY YOU KEPT CALLING.
FIRST I THOUGHT MAYBE IT WAS SOME KIND OF PRANK, BUT-- WHAT SHE DID...
...YOU'VE SEEN IT BEFORE, HAVEN'T YOU?
YOU KNOW WHAT SHE IS.
AND GOD SENT YOU HERE TO HELP ME, MS...?
CLARKSON. BUT PLEASE, CALL ME DANIELLE.
AND, YES. THAT'S EXACTLY WHY I'M HERE, MARY-BETH.
TO HELP.

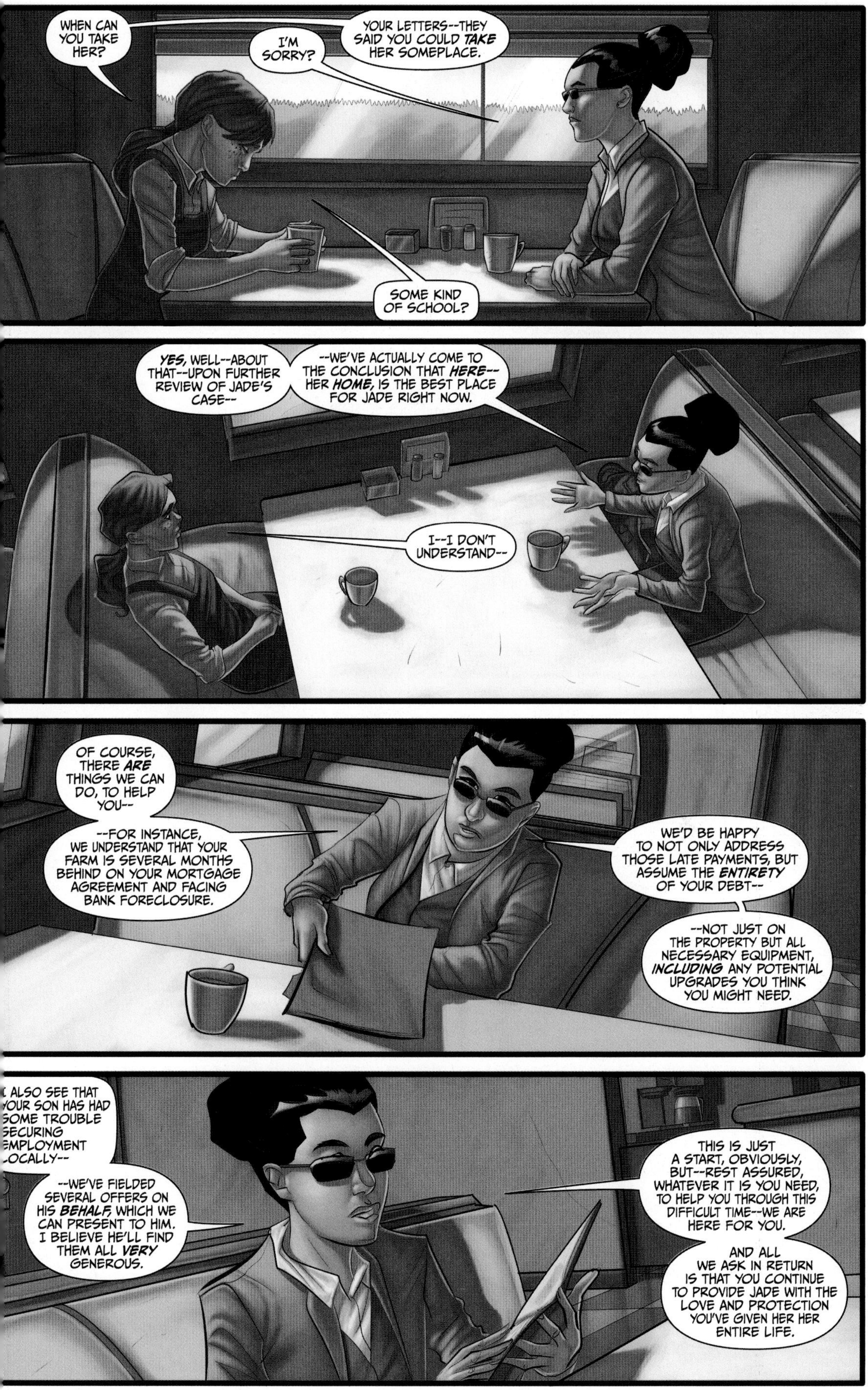

WHEN CAN YOU TAKE HER?
I'M SORRY?
YOUR LETTERS--THEY SAID YOU COULD *TAKE* HER SOMEPLACE.
SOME KIND OF SCHOOL?
YES, WELL--ABOUT THAT--UPON FURTHER REVIEW OF JADE'S CASE--
--WE'VE ACTUALLY COME TO THE CONCLUSION THAT *HERE*--HER *HOME,* IS THE BEST PLACE FOR JADE RIGHT NOW.
I--I DON'T UNDERSTAND--
OF COURSE, THERE *ARE* THINGS WE CAN DO, TO HELP YOU--
--FOR INSTANCE, WE UNDERSTAND THAT YOUR FARM IS SEVERAL MONTHS BEHIND ON YOUR MORTGAGE AGREEMENT AND FACING BANK FORECLOSURE.
WE'D BE HAPPY TO NOT ONLY ADDRESS THOSE LATE PAYMENTS, BUT ASSUME THE *ENTIRETY* OF YOUR DEBT--
--NOT JUST ON THE PROPERTY BUT ALL NECESSARY EQUIPMENT, *INCLUDING* ANY POTENTIAL UPGRADES YOU THINK YOU MIGHT NEED.
I ALSO SEE THAT YOUR SON HAS HAD SOME TROUBLE SECURING EMPLOYMENT LOCALLY--
--WE'VE FIELDED SEVERAL OFFERS ON HIS *BEHALF,* WHICH WE CAN PRESENT TO HIM. I BELIEVE HE'LL FIND THEM ALL *VERY* GENEROUS.
THIS IS JUST A START, OBVIOUSLY, BUT--REST ASSURED, WHATEVER IT IS YOU NEED, TO HELP YOU THROUGH THIS DIFFICULT TIME--WE ARE HERE FOR YOU.
AND ALL WE ASK IN RETURN IS THAT YOU CONTINUE TO PROVIDE JADE WITH THE LOVE AND PROTECTION YOU'VE GIVEN HER HER ENTIRE LIFE.

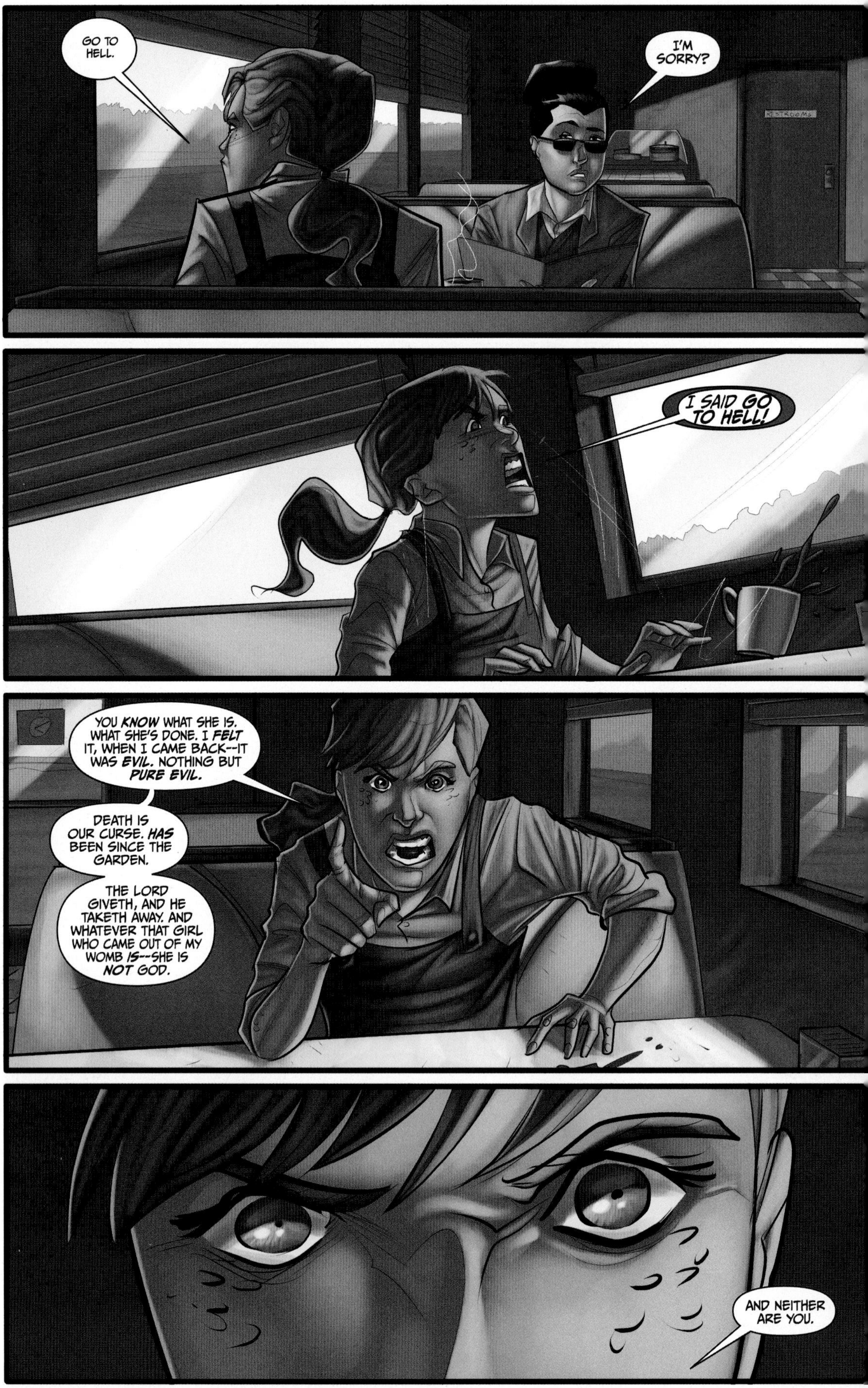
GO TO HELL.
I'M SORRY?
I SAID GO TO HELL!
YOU KNOW WHAT SHE IS. WHAT SHE'S DONE. I FELT IT, WHEN I CAME BACK--IT WAS EVIL. NOTHING BUT PURE EVIL.
DEATH IS OUR CURSE. HAS BEEN SINCE THE GARDEN.
THE LORD GIVETH, AND HE TAKETH AWAY. AND WHATEVER THAT GIRL WHO CAME OUT OF MY WOMB IS--SHE IS NOT GOD.
AND NEITHER ARE YOU.

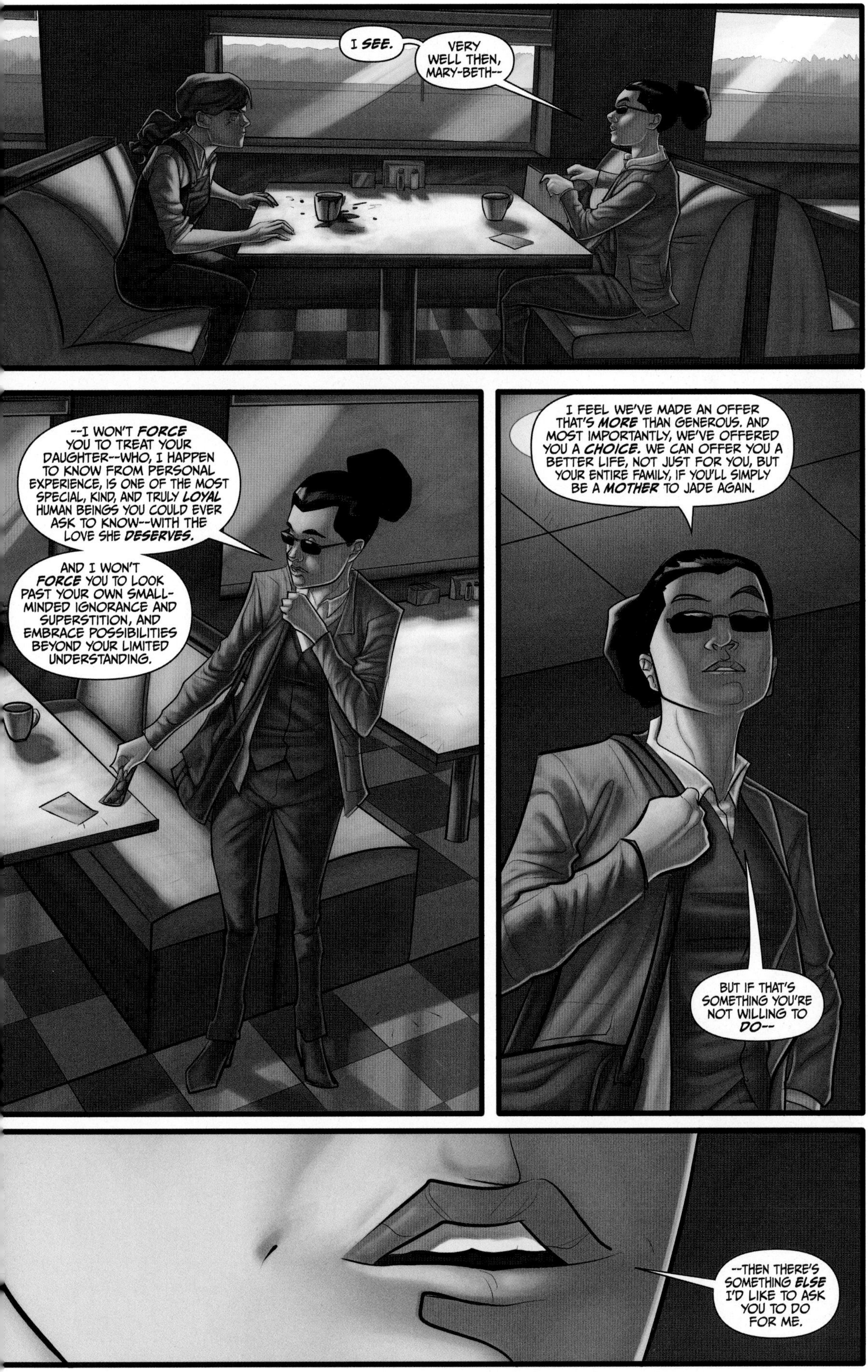
I SEE.
VERY WELL THEN, MARY-BETH--
--I WON'T FORCE YOU TO TREAT YOUR DAUGHTER--WHO, I HAPPEN TO KNOW FROM PERSONAL EXPERIENCE, IS ONE OF THE MOST SPECIAL, KIND, AND TRULY LOYAL HUMAN BEINGS YOU COULD EVER ASK TO KNOW--WITH THE LOVE SHE DESERVES.
AND I WON'T FORCE YOU TO LOOK PAST YOUR OWN SMALL-MINDED IGNORANCE AND SUPERSTITION, AND EMBRACE POSSIBILITIES BEYOND YOUR LIMITED UNDERSTANDING.
I FEEL WE'VE MADE AN OFFER THAT'S MORE THAN GENEROUS. AND MOST IMPORTANTLY, WE'VE OFFERED YOU A CHOICE. WE CAN OFFER YOU A BETTER LIFE, NOT JUST FOR YOU, BUT YOUR ENTIRE FAMILY, IF YOU'LL SIMPLY BE A MOTHER TO JADE AGAIN.
BUT IF THAT'S SOMETHING YOU'RE NOT WILLING TO DO--
--THEN THERE'S SOMETHING ELSE I'D LIKE TO ASK YOU TO DO FOR ME.

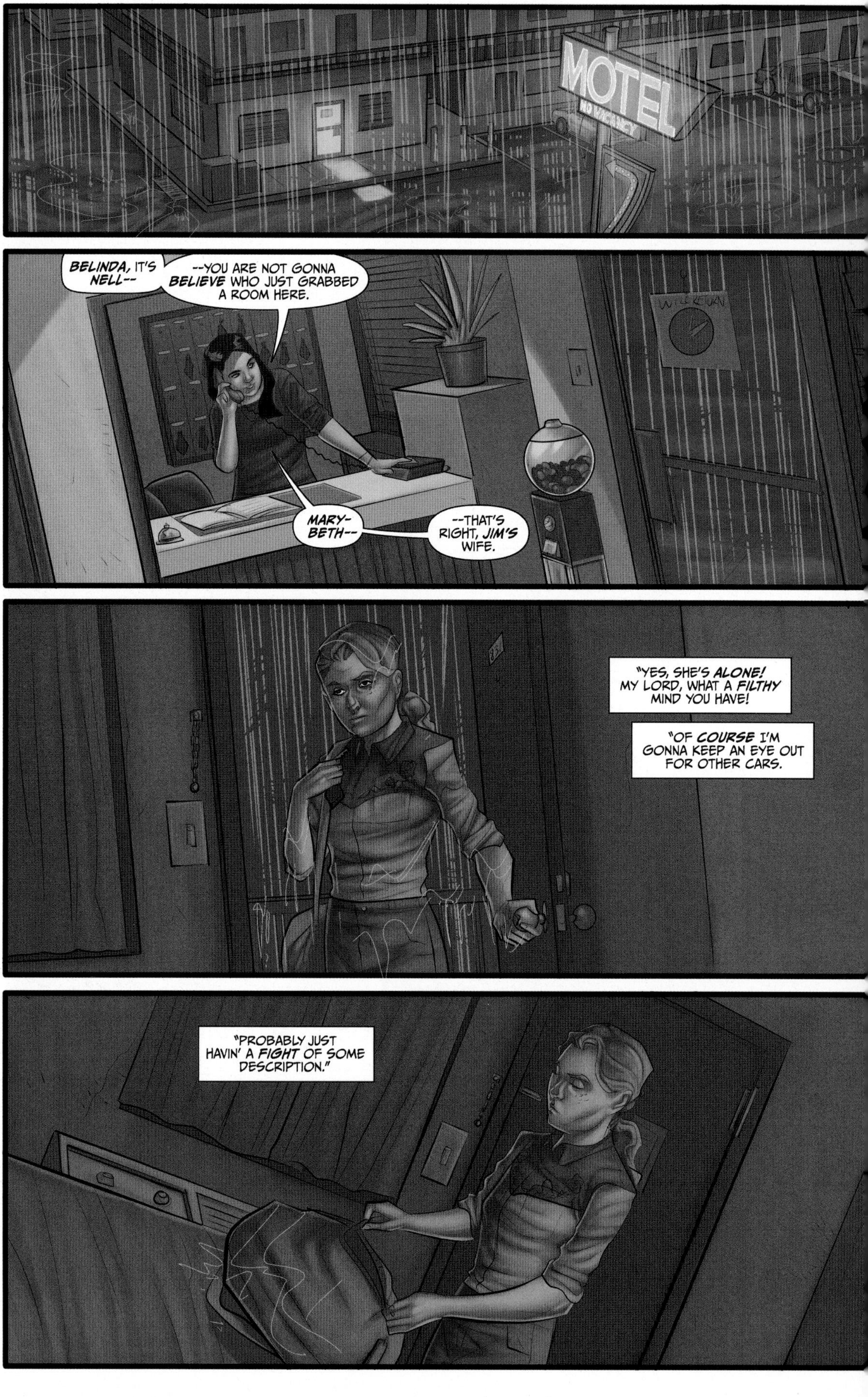
MOTEL
NO VACANCY
BELINDA, IT'S NELL--
--YOU ARE NOT GONNA BELIEVE WHO JUST GRABBED A ROOM HERE.
MARY-BETH--
--THAT'S RIGHT, JIM'S WIFE.
"YES, SHE'S ALONE! MY LORD, WHAT A FILTHY MIND YOU HAVE!
"OF COURSE I'M GONNA KEEP AN EYE OUT FOR OTHER CARS.
"PROBABLY JUST HAVIN' A FIGHT OF SOME DESCRIPTION."

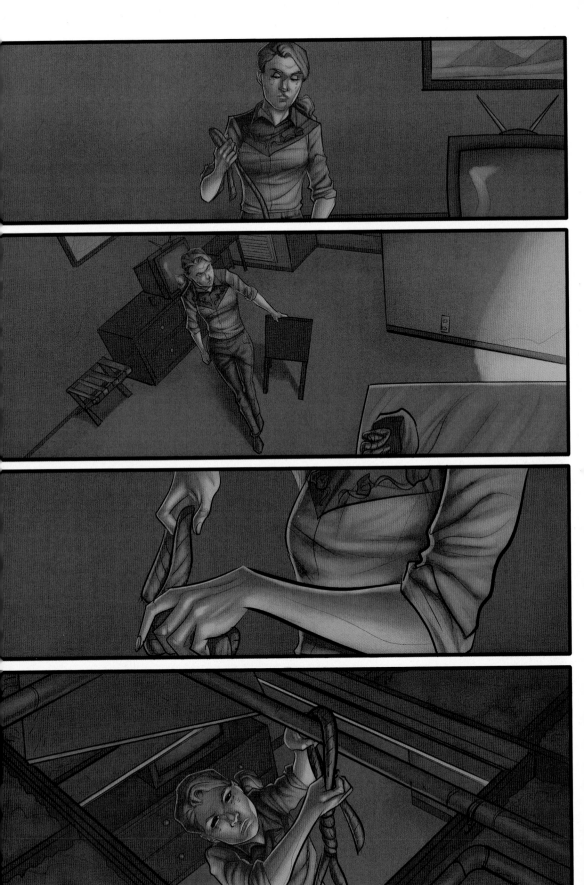

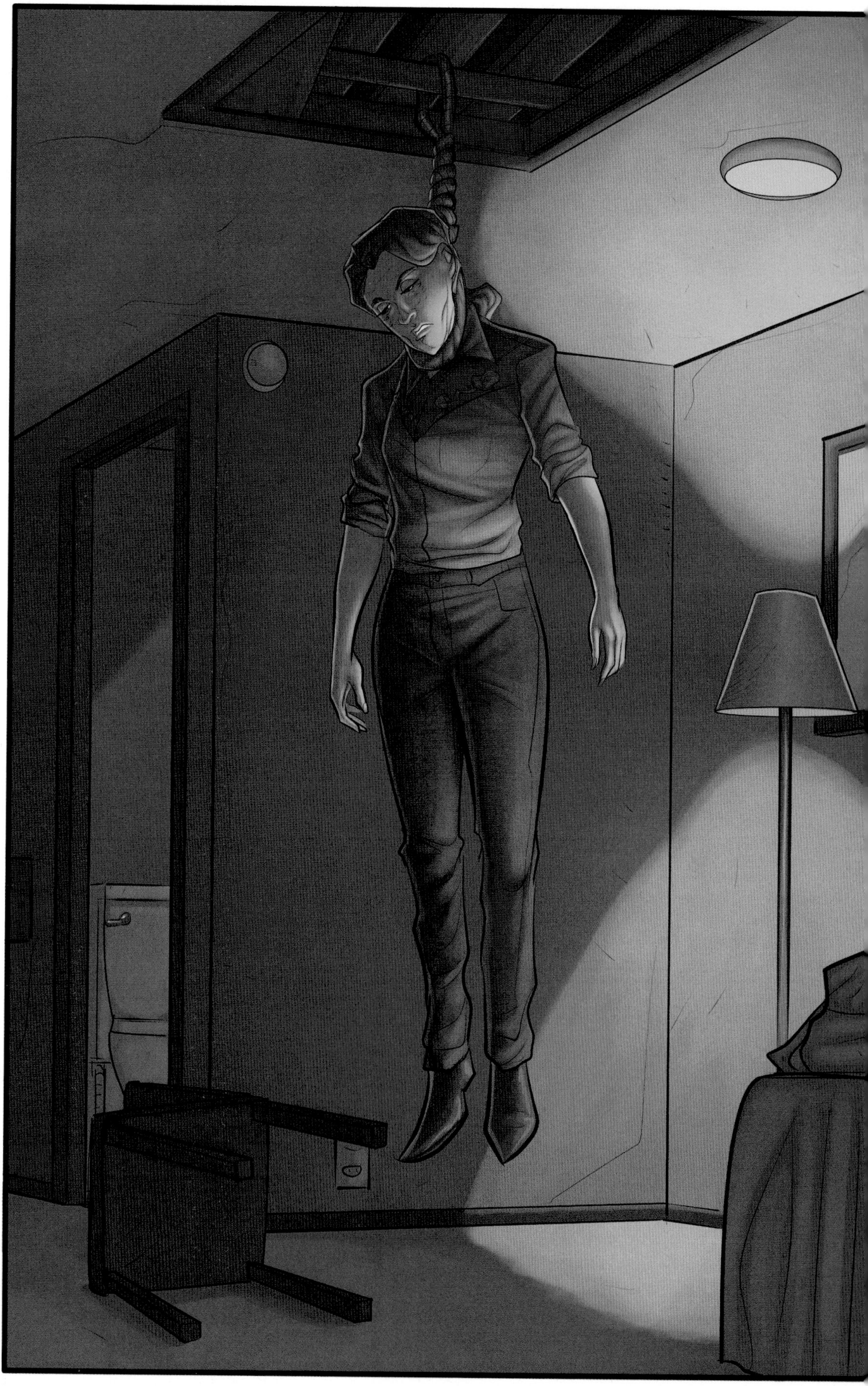

fortysix

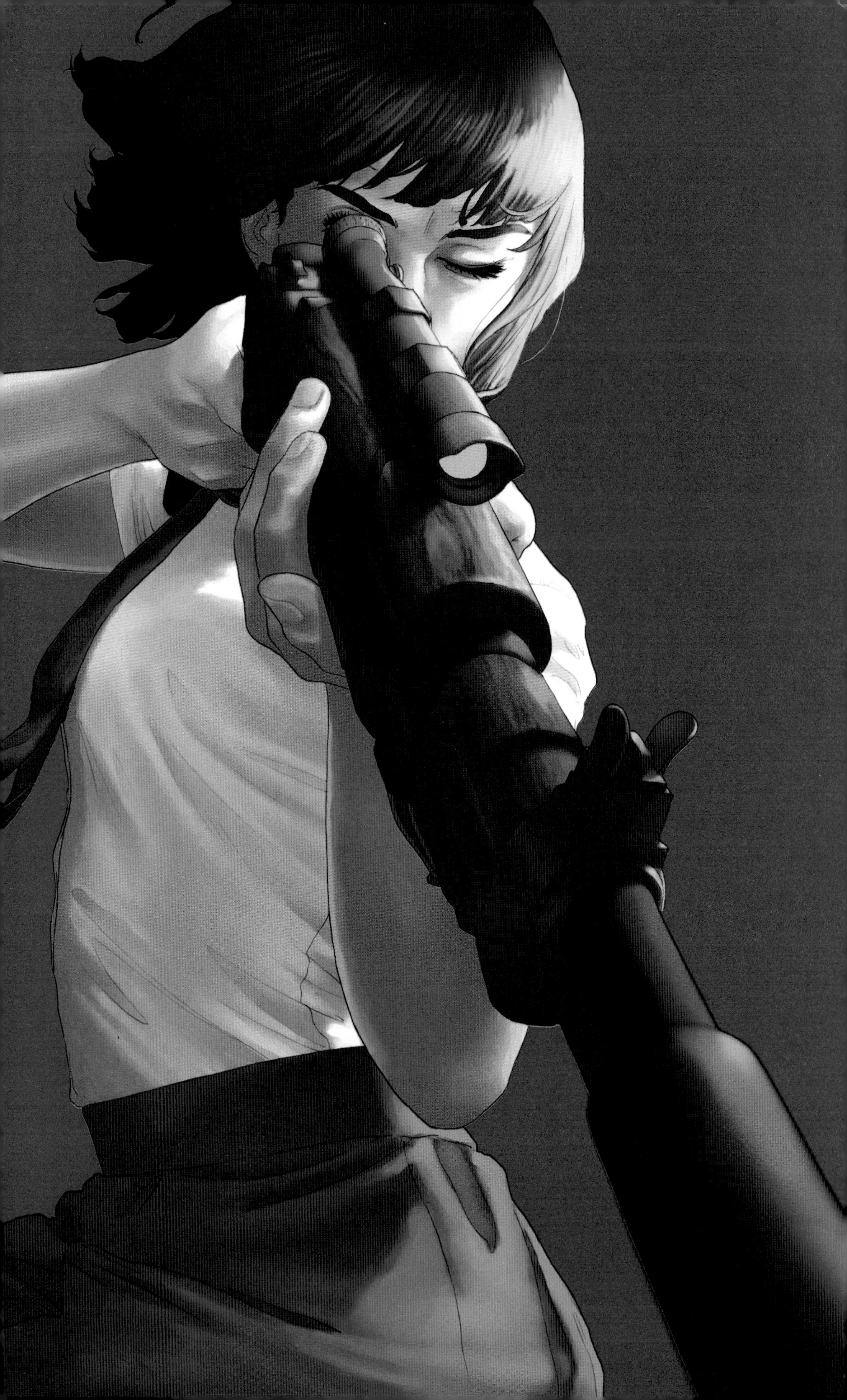

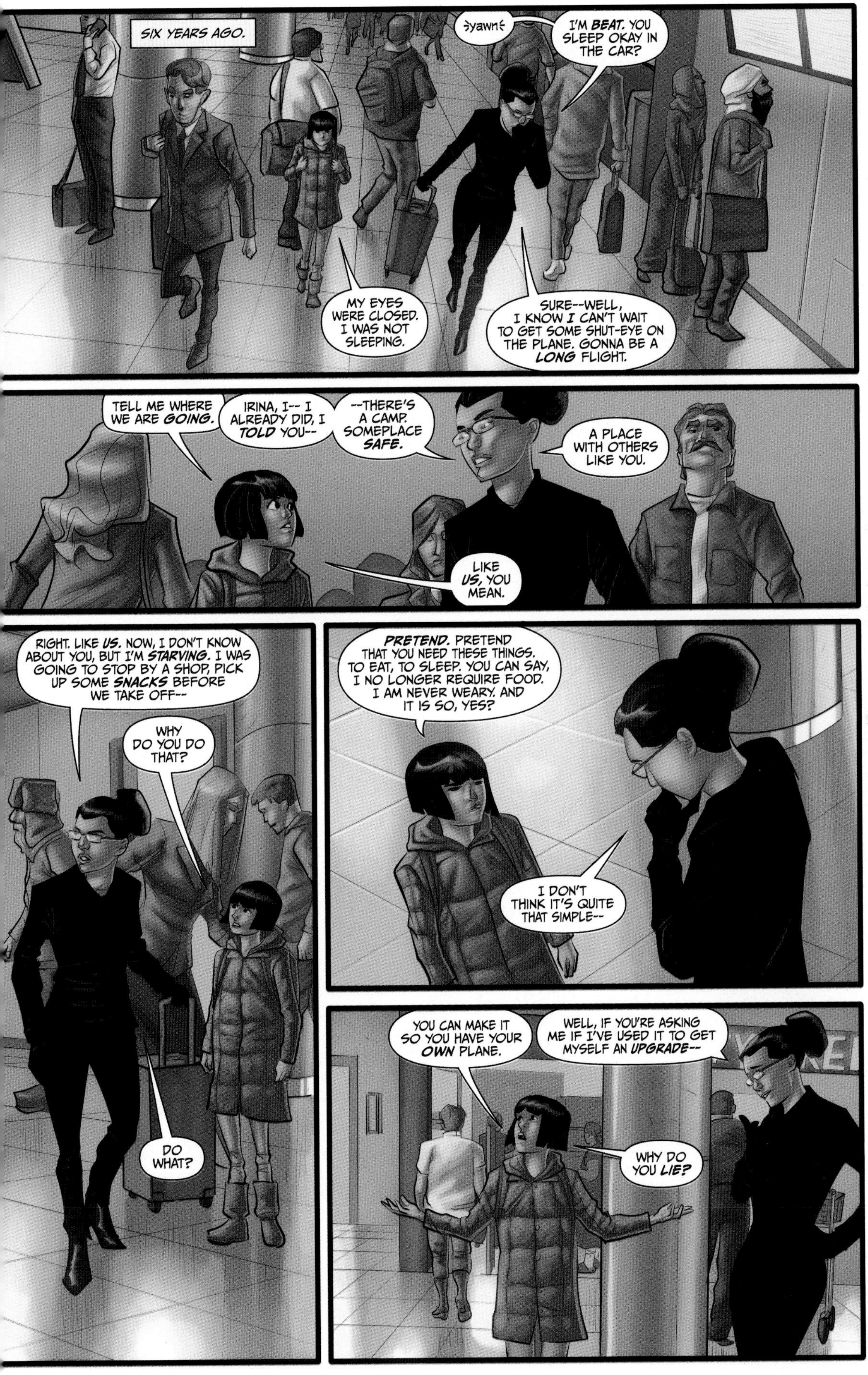

SIX YEARS AGO.
>yawn<
I'M BEAT. YOU SLEEP OKAY IN THE CAR?
MY EYES WERE CLOSED. I WAS NOT SLEEPING.
SURE--WELL, I KNOW I CAN'T WAIT TO GET SOME SHUT-EYE ON THE PLANE. GONNA BE A LONG FLIGHT.
TELL ME WHERE WE ARE GOING.
IRINA, I-- I ALREADY DID, I TOLD YOU--
--THERE'S A CAMP. SOMEPLACE SAFE.
A PLACE WITH OTHERS LIKE YOU.
LIKE US, YOU MEAN.
RIGHT. LIKE US. NOW, I DON'T KNOW ABOUT YOU, BUT I'M STARVING. I WAS GOING TO STOP BY A SHOP, PICK UP SOME SNACKS BEFORE WE TAKE OFF--
WHY DO YOU DO THAT?
DO WHAT?
PRETEND. PRETEND THAT YOU NEED THESE THINGS. TO EAT, TO SLEEP. YOU CAN SAY, I NO LONGER REQUIRE FOOD. I AM NEVER WEARY. AND IT IS SO, YES?
I DON'T THINK IT'S QUITE THAT SIMPLE--
YOU CAN MAKE IT SO YOU HAVE YOUR OWN PLANE.
WELL, IF YOU'RE ASKING ME IF I'VE USED IT TO GET MYSELF AN UPGRADE--
WHY DO YOU LIE?

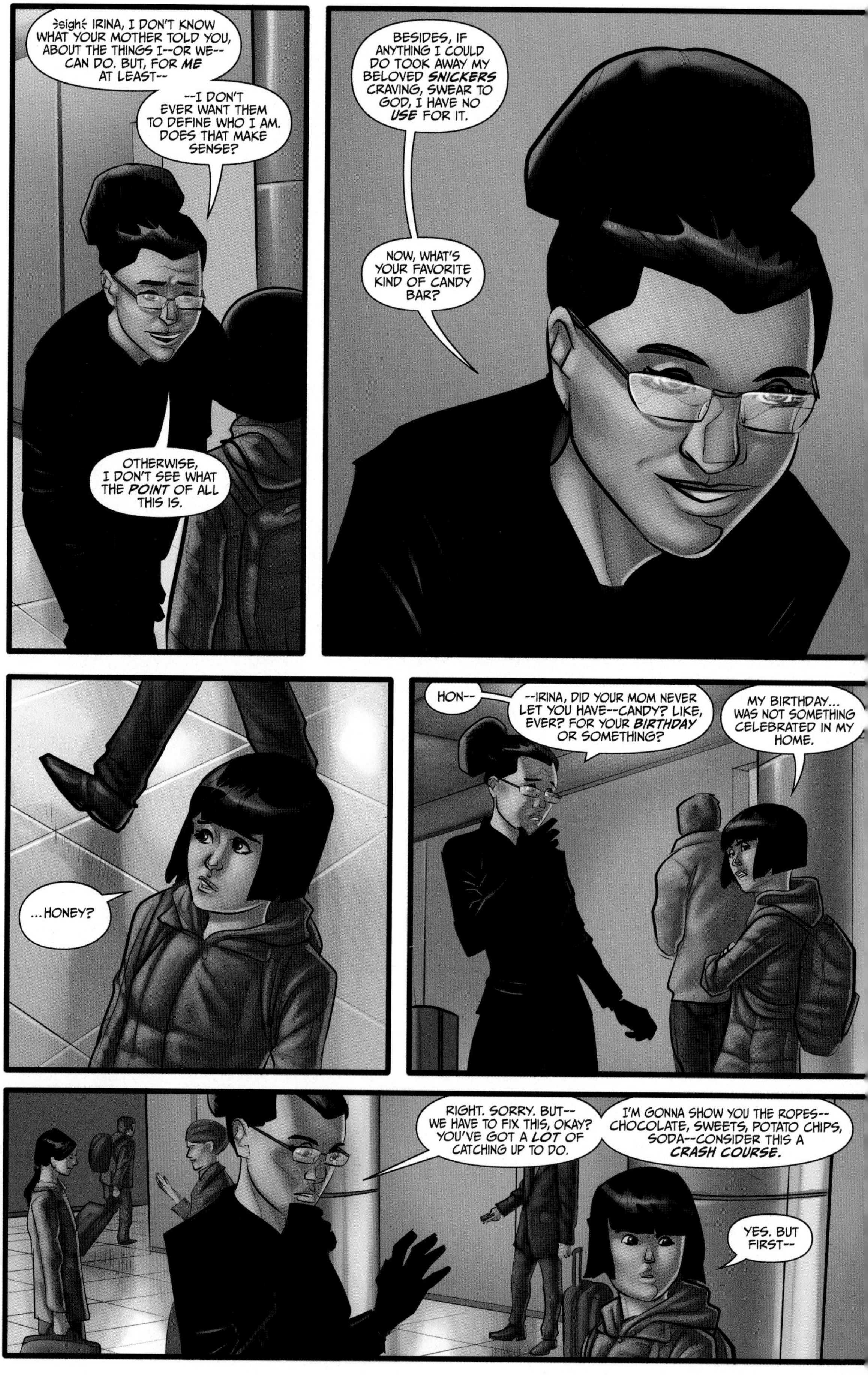

>sigh< IRINA, I DON'T KNOW WHAT YOUR MOTHER TOLD YOU, ABOUT THE THINGS I--OR WE--CAN DO. BUT, FOR ME AT LEAST--
--I DON'T EVER WANT THEM TO DEFINE WHO I AM. DOES THAT MAKE SENSE?
OTHERWISE, I DON'T SEE WHAT THE POINT OF ALL THIS IS.
BESIDES, IF ANYTHING I COULD DO TOOK AWAY MY BELOVED SNICKERS CRAVING, SWEAR TO GOD, I HAVE NO USE FOR IT.
NOW, WHAT'S YOUR FAVORITE KIND OF CANDY BAR?
...HONEY?
HON--
--IRINA, DID YOUR MOM NEVER LET YOU HAVE--CANDY? LIKE, EVER? FOR YOUR BIRTHDAY OR SOMETHING?
MY BIRTHDAY... WAS NOT SOMETHING CELEBRATED IN MY HOME.
RIGHT. SORRY. BUT--WE HAVE TO FIX THIS, OKAY? YOU'VE GOT A LOT OF CATCHING UP TO DO.
I'M GONNA SHOW YOU THE ROPES--CHOCOLATE, SWEETS, POTATO CHIPS, SODA--CONSIDER THIS A CRASH COURSE.
YES. BUT FIRST--

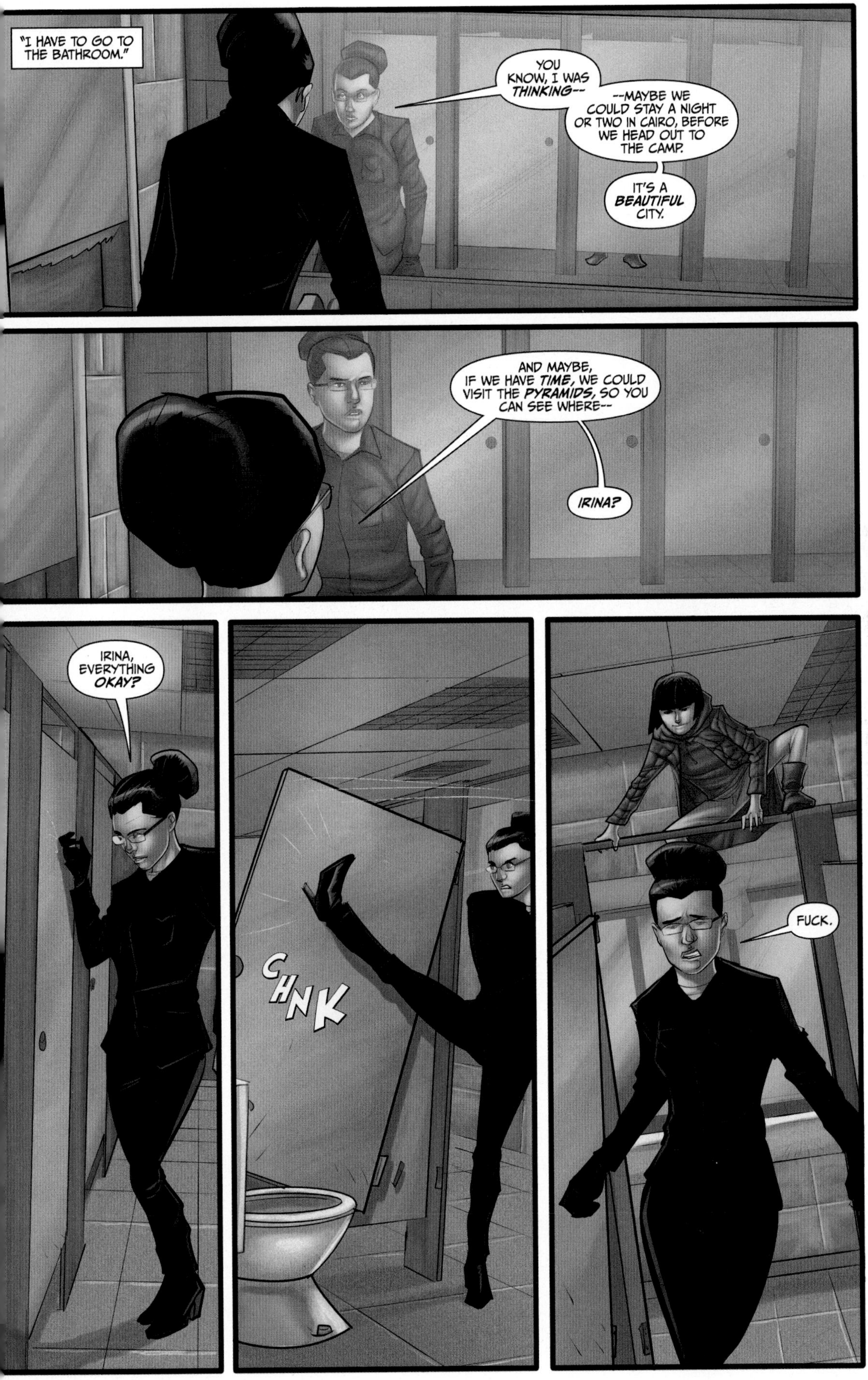
"I HAVE TO GO TO THE BATHROOM."
YOU KNOW, I WAS THINKING--
--MAYBE WE COULD STAY A NIGHT OR TWO IN CAIRO, BEFORE WE HEAD OUT TO THE CAMP.
IT'S A BEAUTIFUL CITY.
AND MAYBE, IF WE HAVE TIME, WE COULD VISIT THE PYRAMIDS, SO YOU CAN SEE WHERE--
IRINA?
IRINA, EVERYTHING OKAY?
CHNK
FUCK.

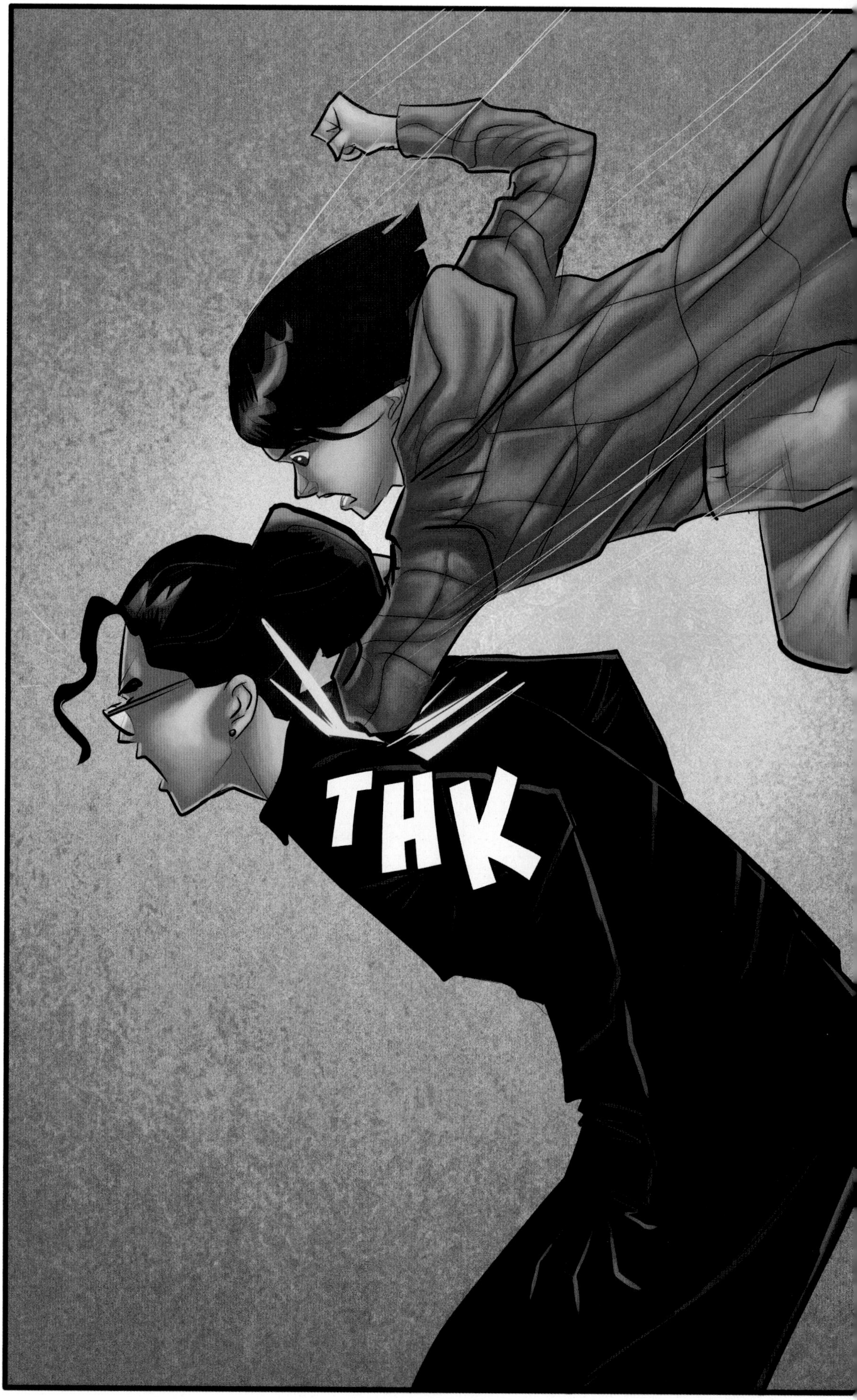
THK

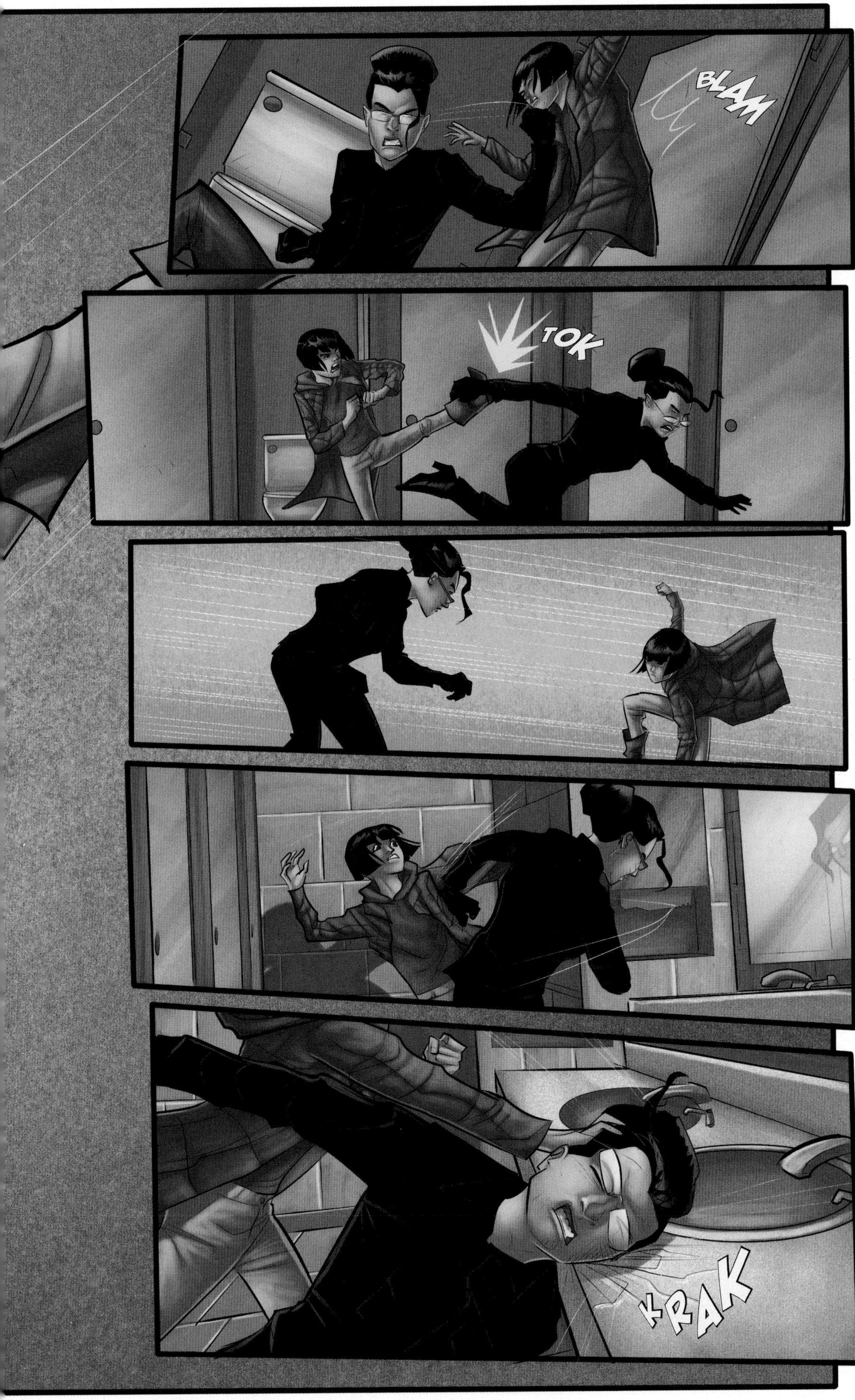
BLAM
TOK
KRAK

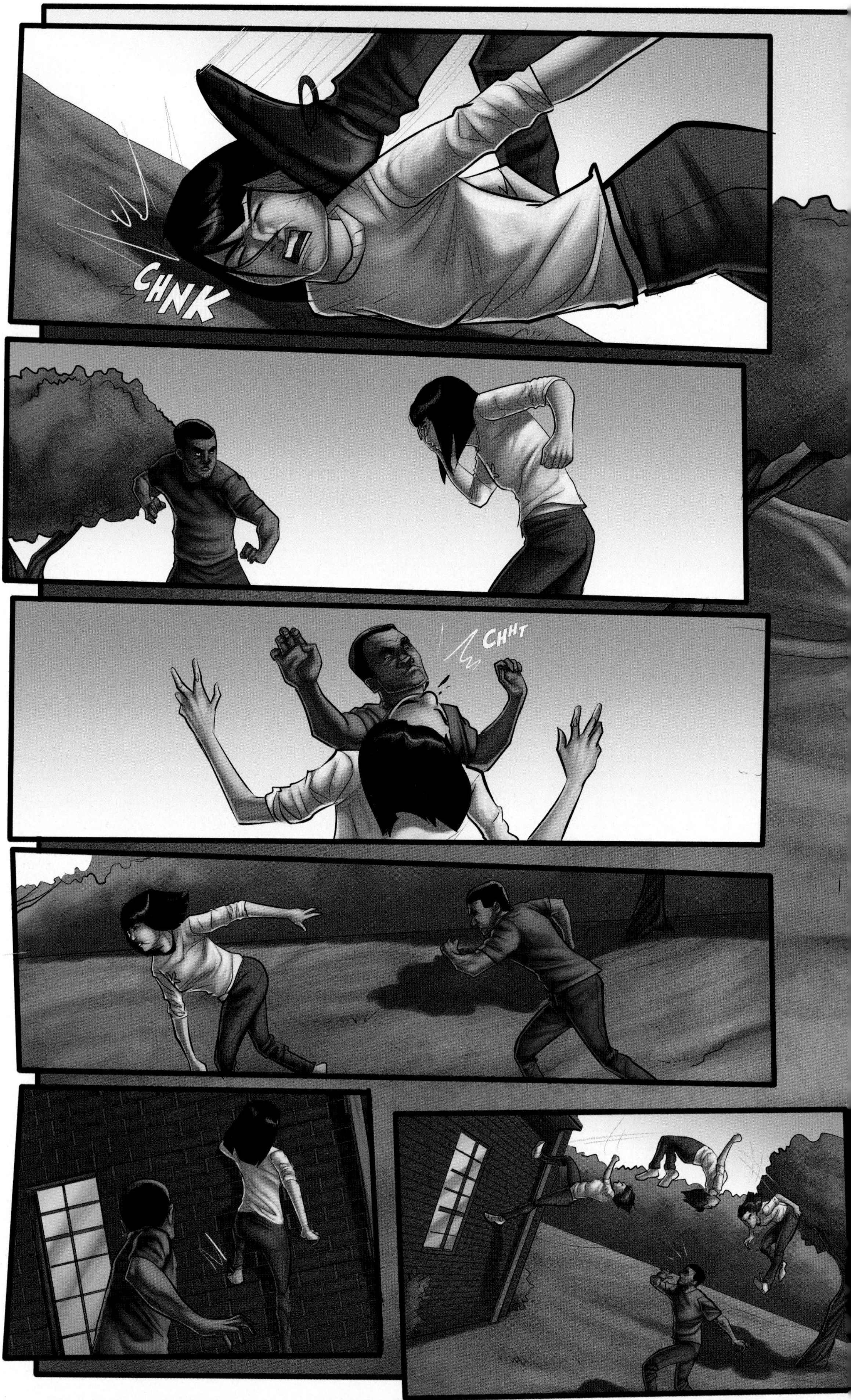
CHNK
CHHT

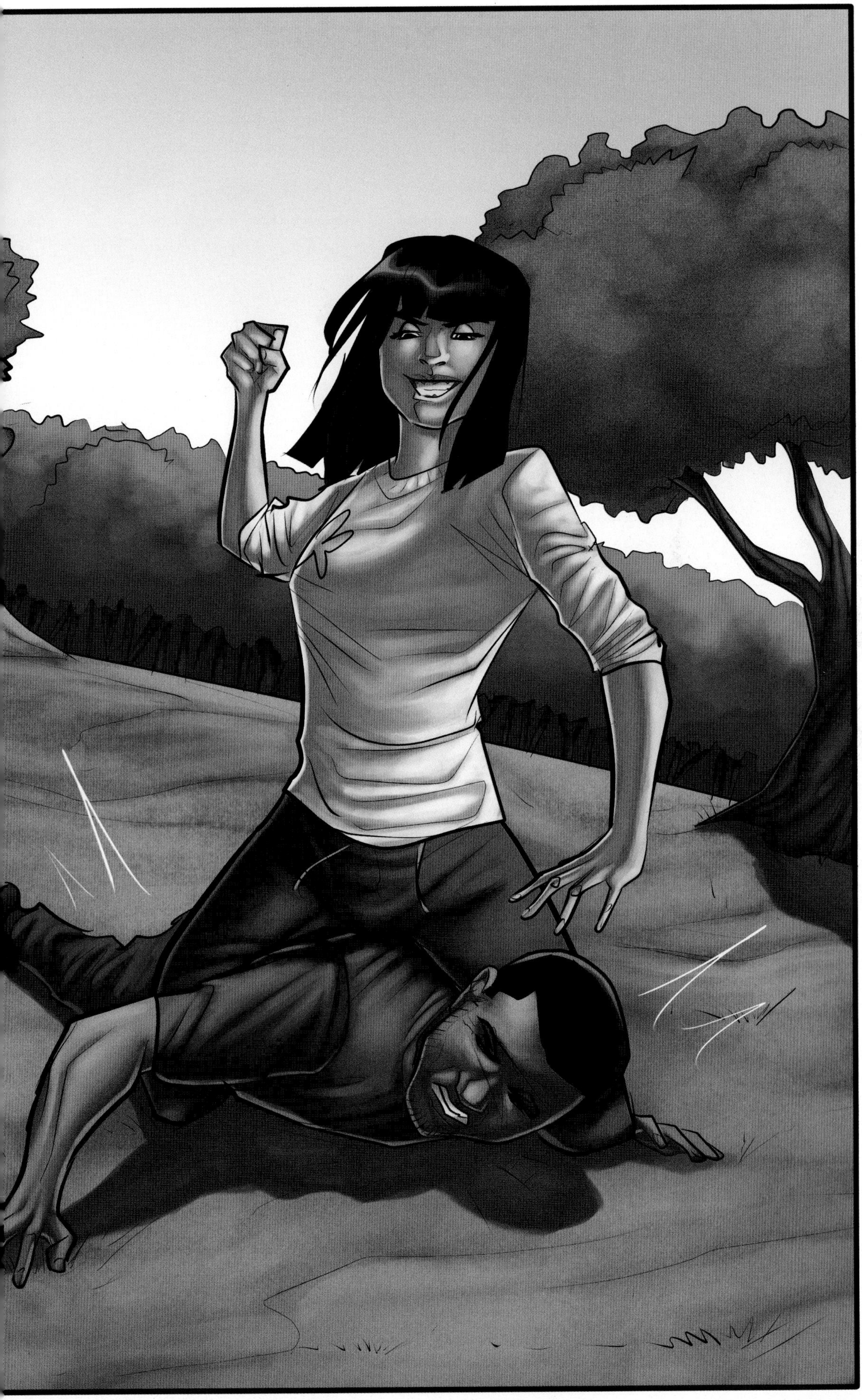

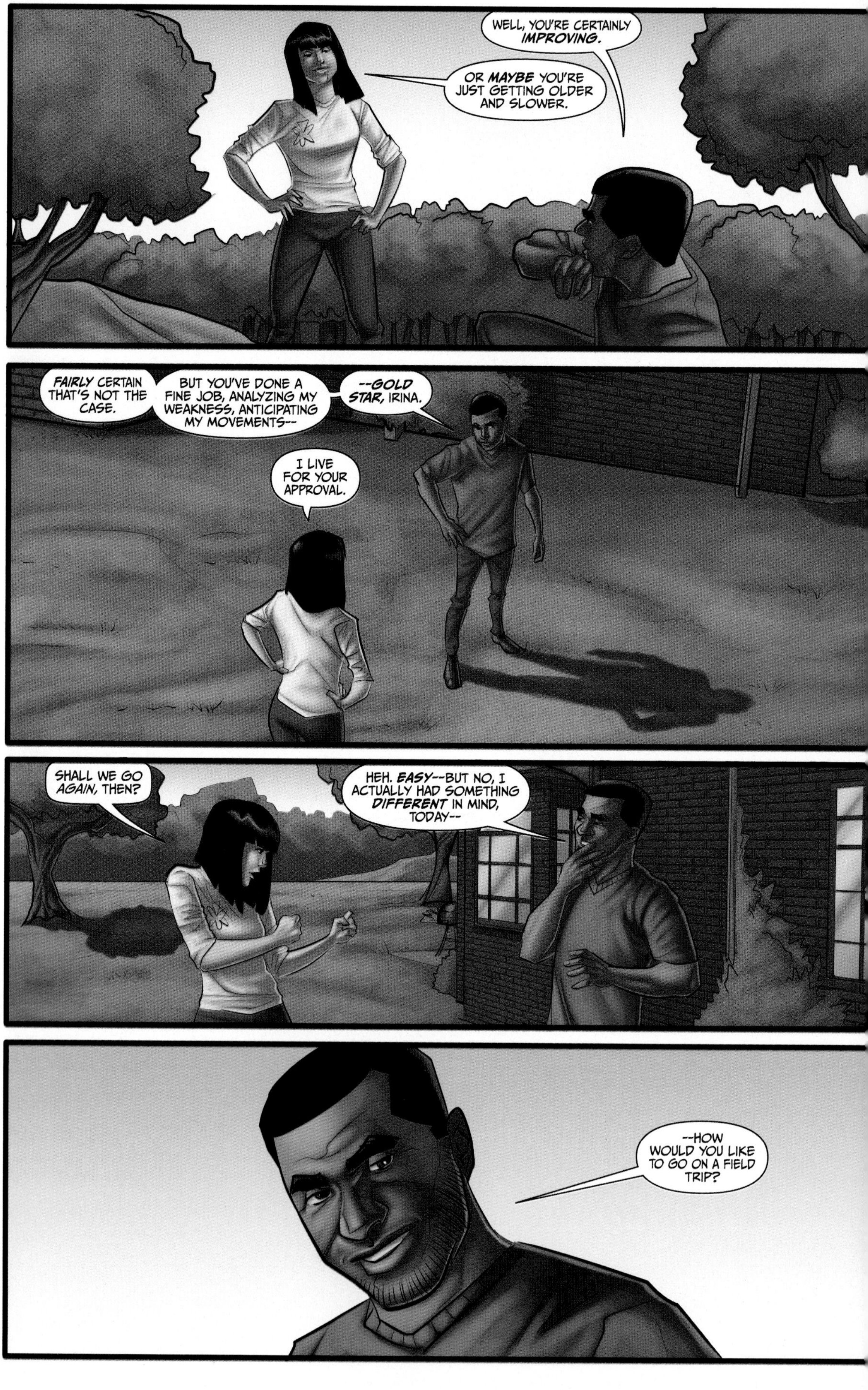
WELL, YOU'RE CERTAINLY IMPROVING.
OR MAYBE YOU'RE JUST GETTING OLDER AND SLOWER.
FAIRLY CERTAIN THAT'S NOT THE CASE.
BUT YOU'VE DONE A FINE JOB, ANALYZING MY WEAKNESS, ANTICIPATING MY MOVEMENTS--
--GOLD STAR, IRINA.
I LIVE FOR YOUR APPROVAL.
SHALL WE GO AGAIN, THEN?
HEH. EASY--BUT NO, I ACTUALLY HAD SOMETHING DIFFERENT IN MIND, TODAY--
--HOW WOULD YOU LIKE TO GO ON A FIELD TRIP?

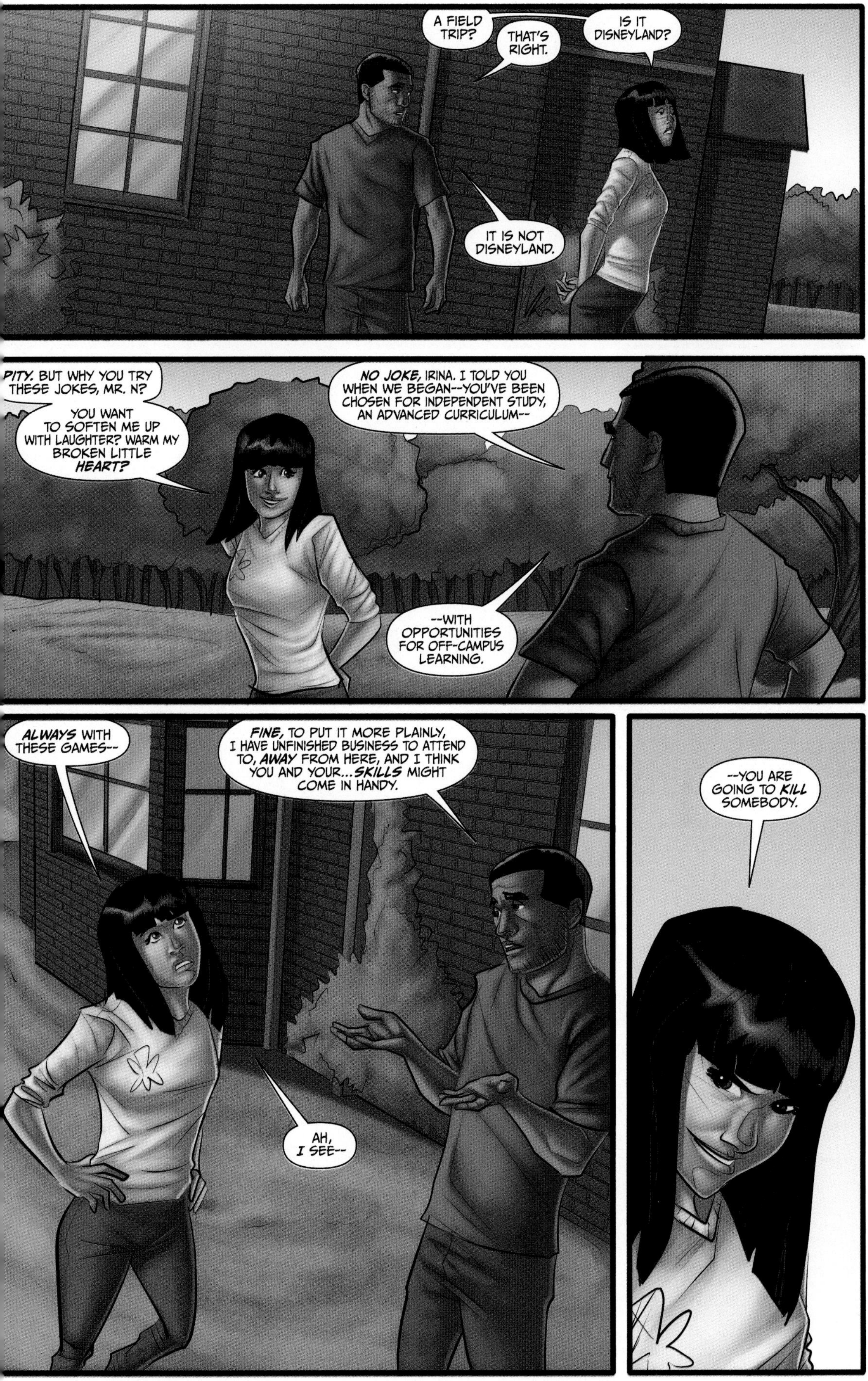
A FIELD TRIP?
THAT'S RIGHT.
IS IT DISNEYLAND?
IT IS NOT DISNEYLAND.
PITY. BUT WHY YOU TRY THESE JOKES, MR. N?
YOU WANT TO SOFTEN ME UP WITH LAUGHTER? WARM MY BROKEN LITTLE HEART?
NO JOKE, IRINA. I TOLD YOU WHEN WE BEGAN--YOU'VE BEEN CHOSEN FOR INDEPENDENT STUDY, AN ADVANCED CURRICULUM--
--WITH OPPORTUNITIES FOR OFF-CAMPUS LEARNING.
ALWAYS WITH THESE GAMES--
FINE, TO PUT IT MORE PLAINLY, I HAVE UNFINISHED BUSINESS TO ATTEND TO, AWAY FROM HERE, AND I THINK YOU AND YOUR...SKILLS MIGHT COME IN HANDY.
AH, I SEE--
--YOU ARE GOING TO KILL SOMEBODY.

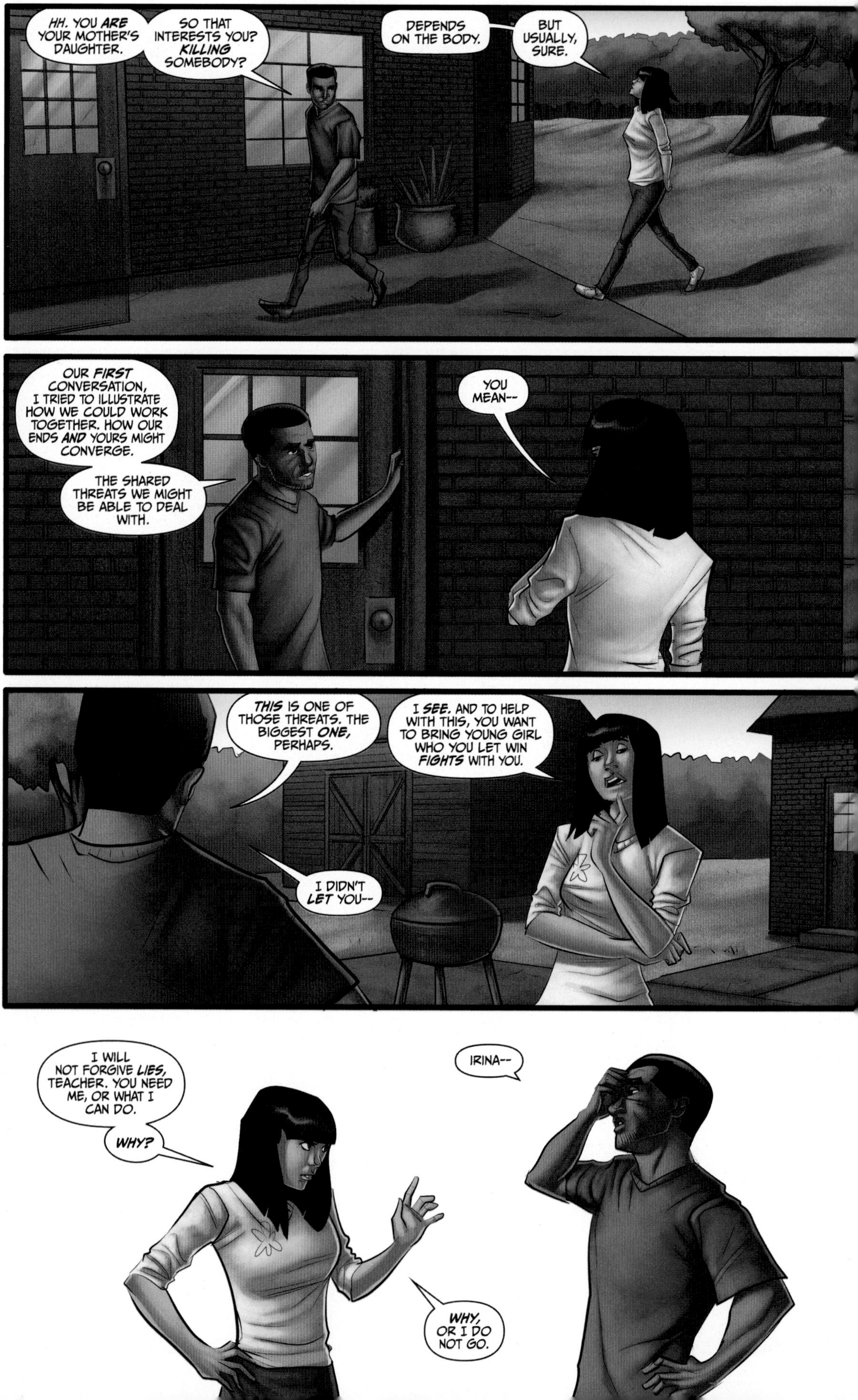
HH. YOU ARE YOUR MOTHER'S DAUGHTER.
SO THAT INTERESTS YOU? KILLING SOMEBODY?
DEPENDS ON THE BODY.
BUT USUALLY, SURE.
OUR FIRST CONVERSATION, I TRIED TO ILLUSTRATE HOW WE COULD WORK TOGETHER. HOW OUR ENDS AND YOURS MIGHT CONVERGE.
THE SHARED THREATS WE MIGHT BE ABLE TO DEAL WITH.
YOU MEAN--
THIS IS ONE OF THOSE THREATS. THE BIGGEST ONE, PERHAPS.
I SEE. AND TO HELP WITH THIS, YOU WANT TO BRING YOUNG GIRL WHO YOU LET WIN FIGHTS WITH YOU.
I DIDN'T LET YOU--
I WILL NOT FORGIVE LIES, TEACHER. YOU NEED ME, OR WHAT I CAN DO.
WHY?
IRINA--
WHY, OR I DO NOT GO.

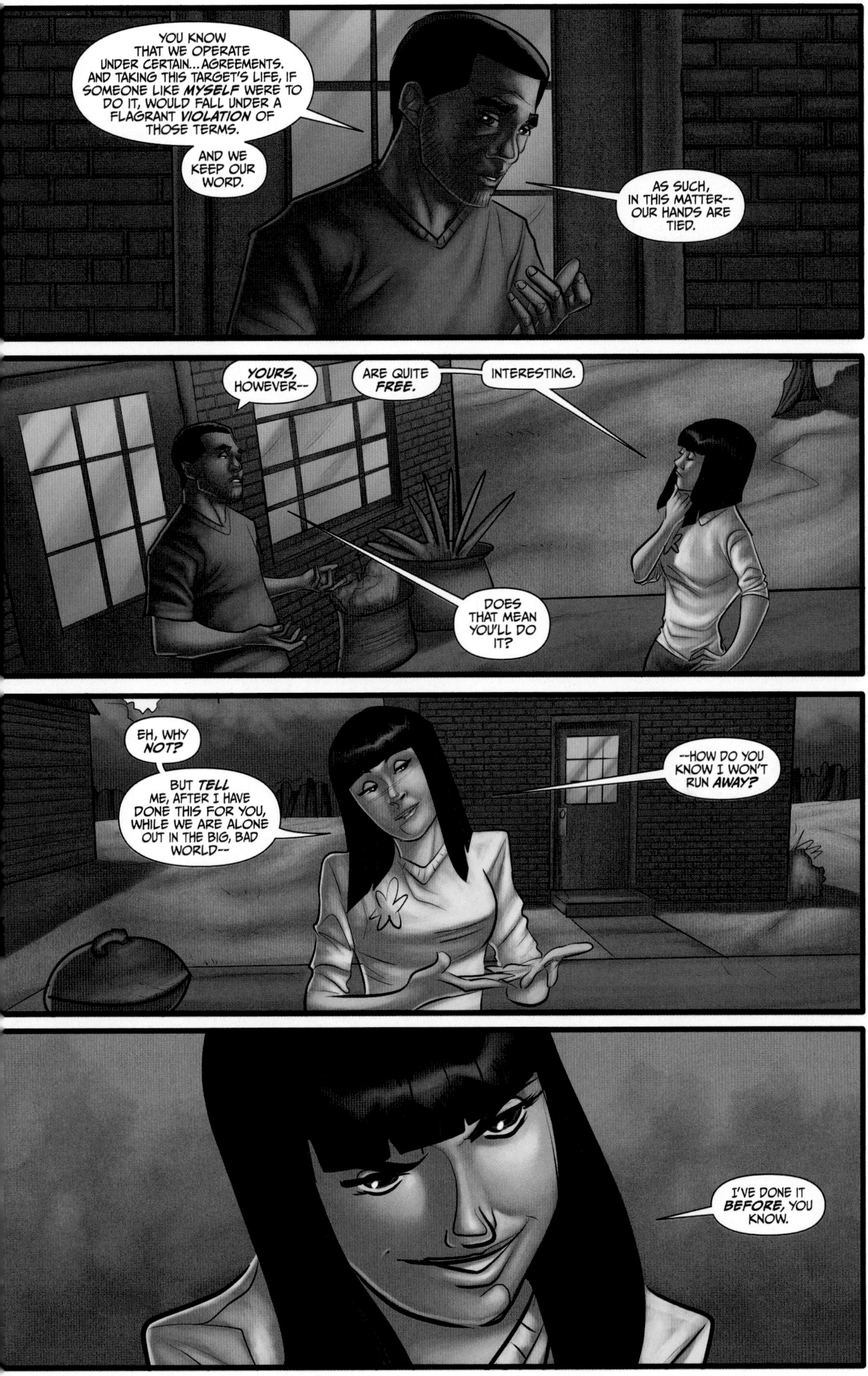
YOU KNOW THAT WE OPERATE UNDER CERTAIN...AGREEMENTS. AND TAKING THIS TARGET'S LIFE, IF SOMEONE LIKE MYSELF WERE TO DO IT, WOULD FALL UNDER A FLAGRANT VIOLATION OF THOSE TERMS.
AND WE KEEP OUR WORD.
AS SUCH, IN THIS MATTER--OUR HANDS ARE TIED.
YOURS, HOWEVER--
ARE QUITE FREE.
INTERESTING.
DOES THAT MEAN YOU'LL DO IT?
EH, WHY NOT?
BUT TELL ME, AFTER I HAVE DONE THIS FOR YOU, WHILE WE ARE ALONE OUT IN THE BIG, BAD WORLD--
--HOW DO YOU KNOW I WON'T RUN AWAY?
I'VE DONE IT BEFORE, YOU KNOW.

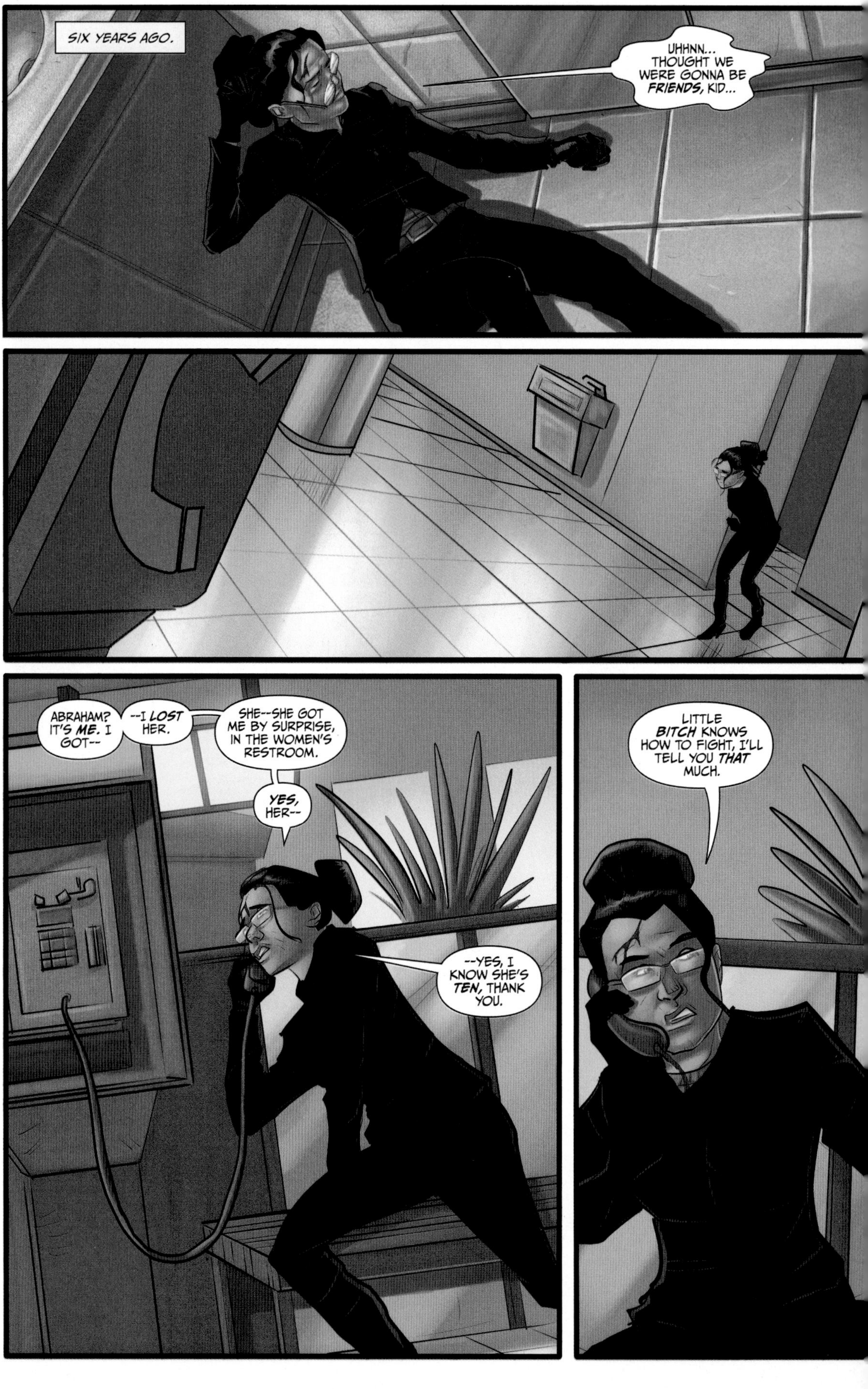
SIX YEARS AGO.
UHHNN... THOUGHT WE WERE GONNA BE FRIENDS, KID...
ABRAHAM? IT'S ME. I GOT--
--I LOST HER.
SHE--SHE GOT ME BY SURPRISE, IN THE WOMEN'S RESTROOM.
YES, HER--
--YES, I KNOW SHE'S TEN, THANK YOU.
LITTLE BITCH KNOWS HOW TO FIGHT, I'LL TELL YOU THAT MUCH.

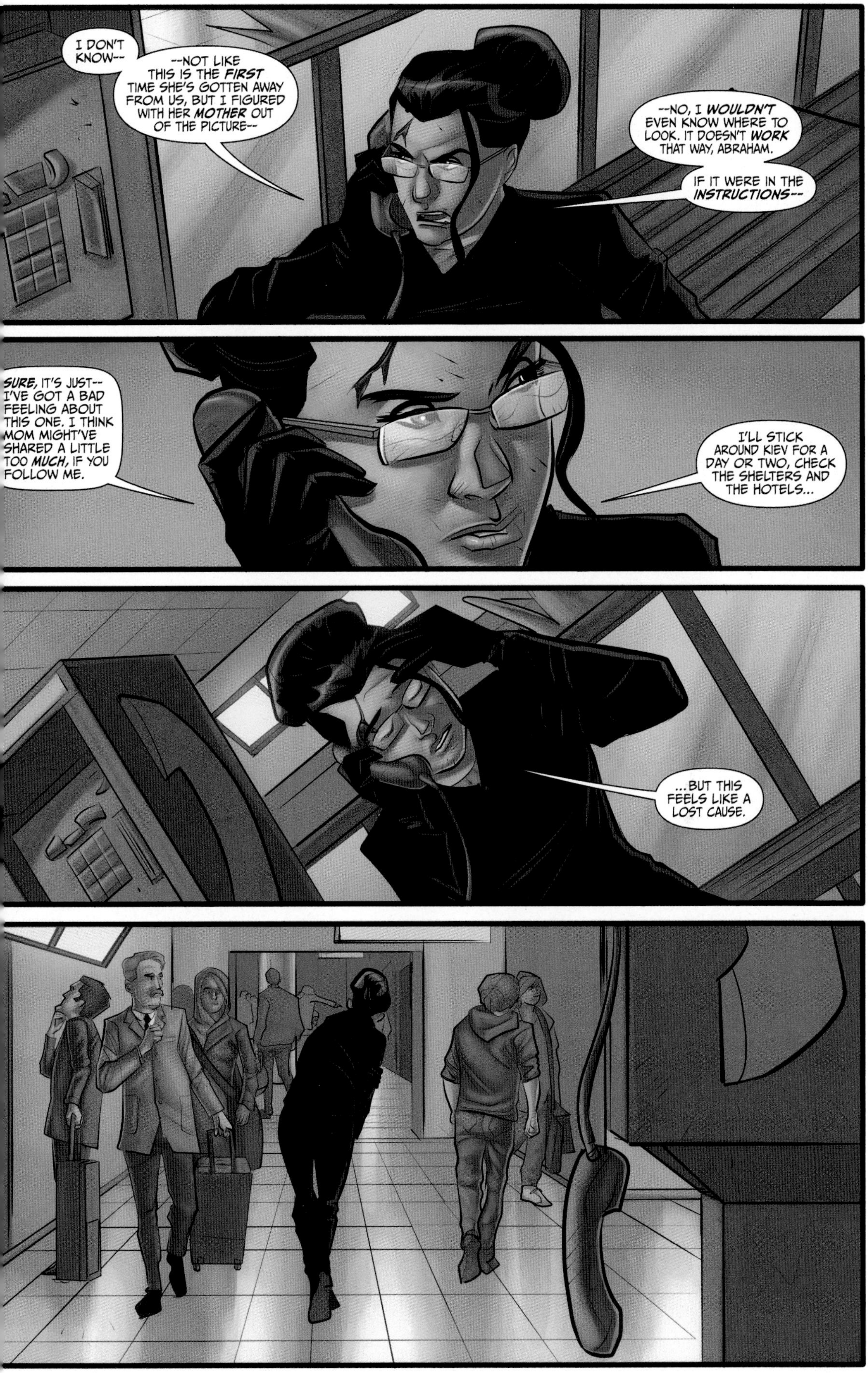
I DON'T KNOW--
--NOT LIKE THIS IS THE *FIRST* TIME SHE'S GOTTEN AWAY FROM US, BUT I FIGURED WITH HER *MOTHER* OUT OF THE PICTURE--
--NO, I *WOULDN'T* EVEN KNOW WHERE TO LOOK. IT DOESN'T *WORK* THAT WAY, ABRAHAM.
IF IT WERE IN THE *INSTRUCTIONS*--
SURE, IT'S JUST-- I'VE GOT A BAD FEELING ABOUT THIS ONE. I THINK MOM MIGHT'VE SHARED A LITTLE TOO *MUCH*, IF YOU FOLLOW ME.
I'LL STICK AROUND KIEV FOR A DAY OR TWO, CHECK THE SHELTERS AND THE HOTELS...
...BUT THIS FEELS LIKE A LOST CAUSE.

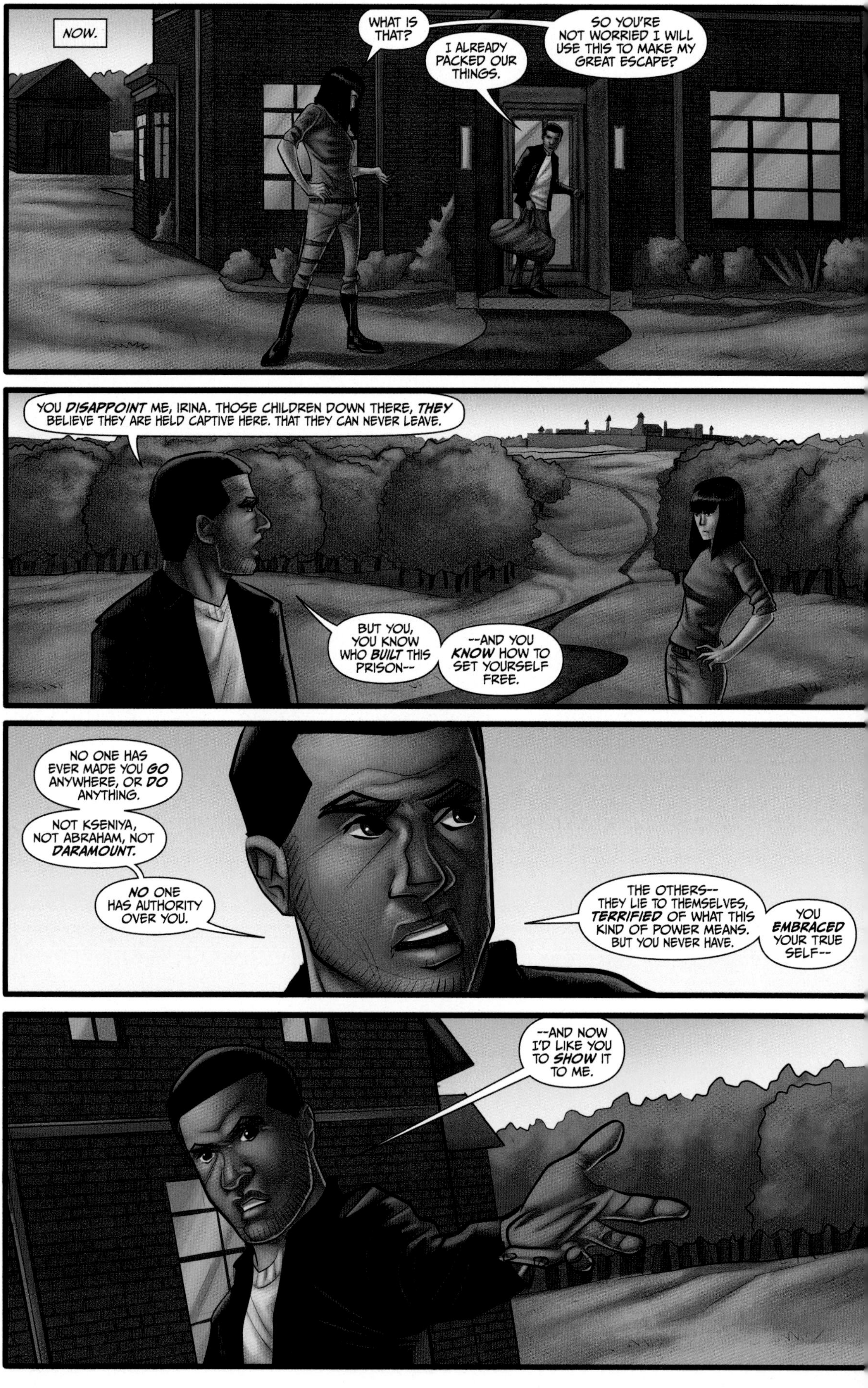
NOW.
WHAT IS THAT?
SO YOU'RE NOT WORRIED I WILL USE THIS TO MAKE MY GREAT ESCAPE?
I ALREADY PACKED OUR THINGS.
YOU DISAPPOINT ME, IRINA. THOSE CHILDREN DOWN THERE, THEY BELIEVE THEY ARE HELD CAPTIVE HERE. THAT THEY CAN NEVER LEAVE.
BUT YOU, YOU KNOW WHO BUILT THIS PRISON--
--AND YOU KNOW HOW TO SET YOURSELF FREE.
NO ONE HAS EVER MADE YOU GO ANYWHERE, OR DO ANYTHING.
NOT KSENIYA, NOT ABRAHAM, NOT DARAMOUNT.
NO ONE HAS AUTHORITY OVER YOU.
THE OTHERS-- THEY LIE TO THEMSELVES, TERRIFIED OF WHAT THIS KIND OF POWER MEANS. BUT YOU NEVER HAVE.
YOU EMBRACED YOUR TRUE SELF--
--AND NOW I'D LIKE YOU TO SHOW IT TO ME.

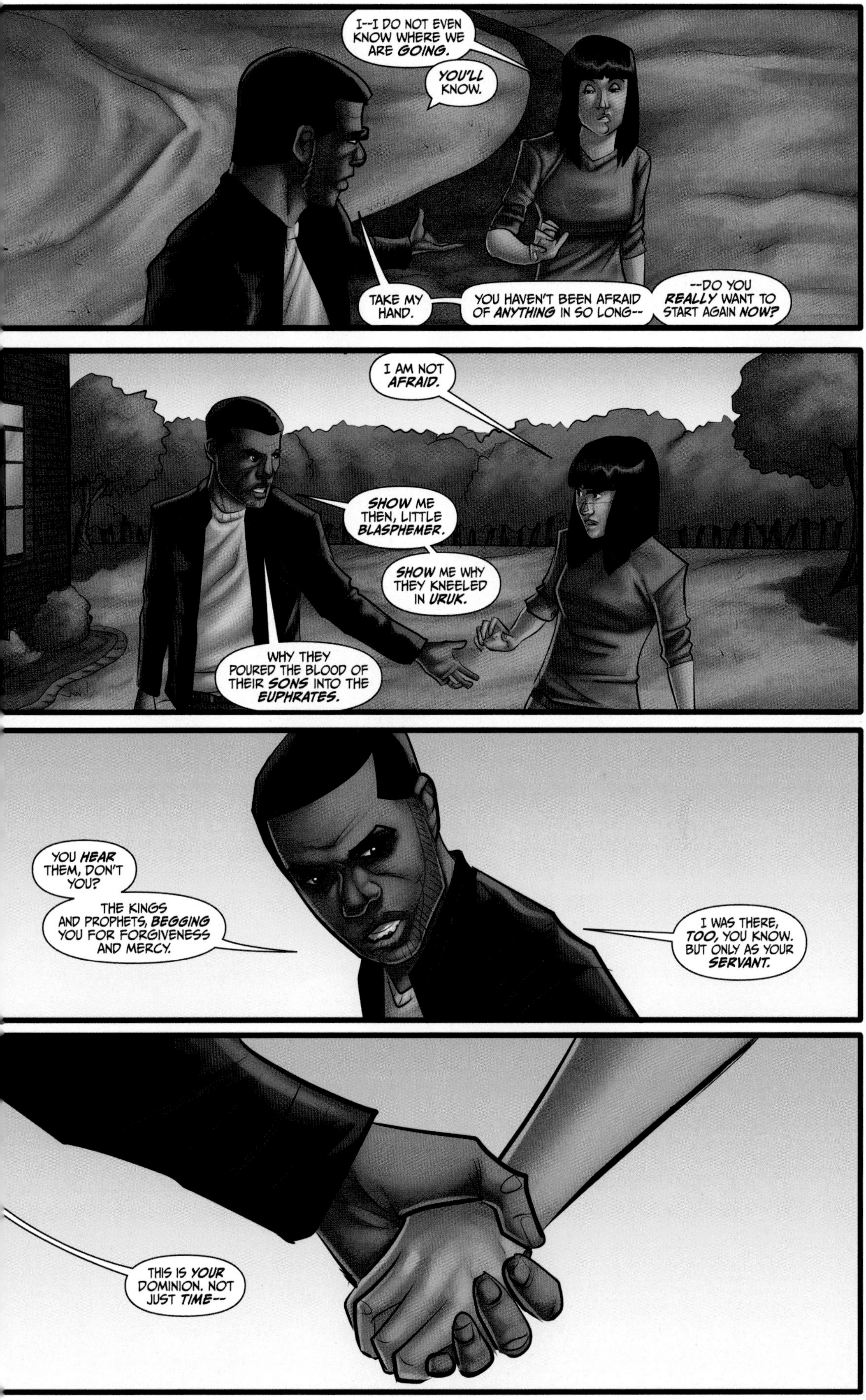
I--I DO NOT EVEN KNOW WHERE WE ARE GOING.
YOU'LL KNOW.
TAKE MY HAND.
YOU HAVEN'T BEEN AFRAID OF ANYTHING IN SO LONG--
--DO YOU REALLY WANT TO START AGAIN NOW?
I AM NOT AFRAID.
SHOW ME THEN, LITTLE BLASPHEMER.
SHOW ME WHY THEY KNEELED IN URUK.
WHY THEY POURED THE BLOOD OF THEIR SONS INTO THE EUPHRATES.
YOU HEAR THEM, DON'T YOU?
THE KINGS AND PROPHETS, BEGGING YOU FOR FORGIVENESS AND MERCY.
I WAS THERE, TOO, YOU KNOW. BUT ONLY AS YOUR SERVANT.
THIS IS YOUR DOMINION. NOT JUST TIME--

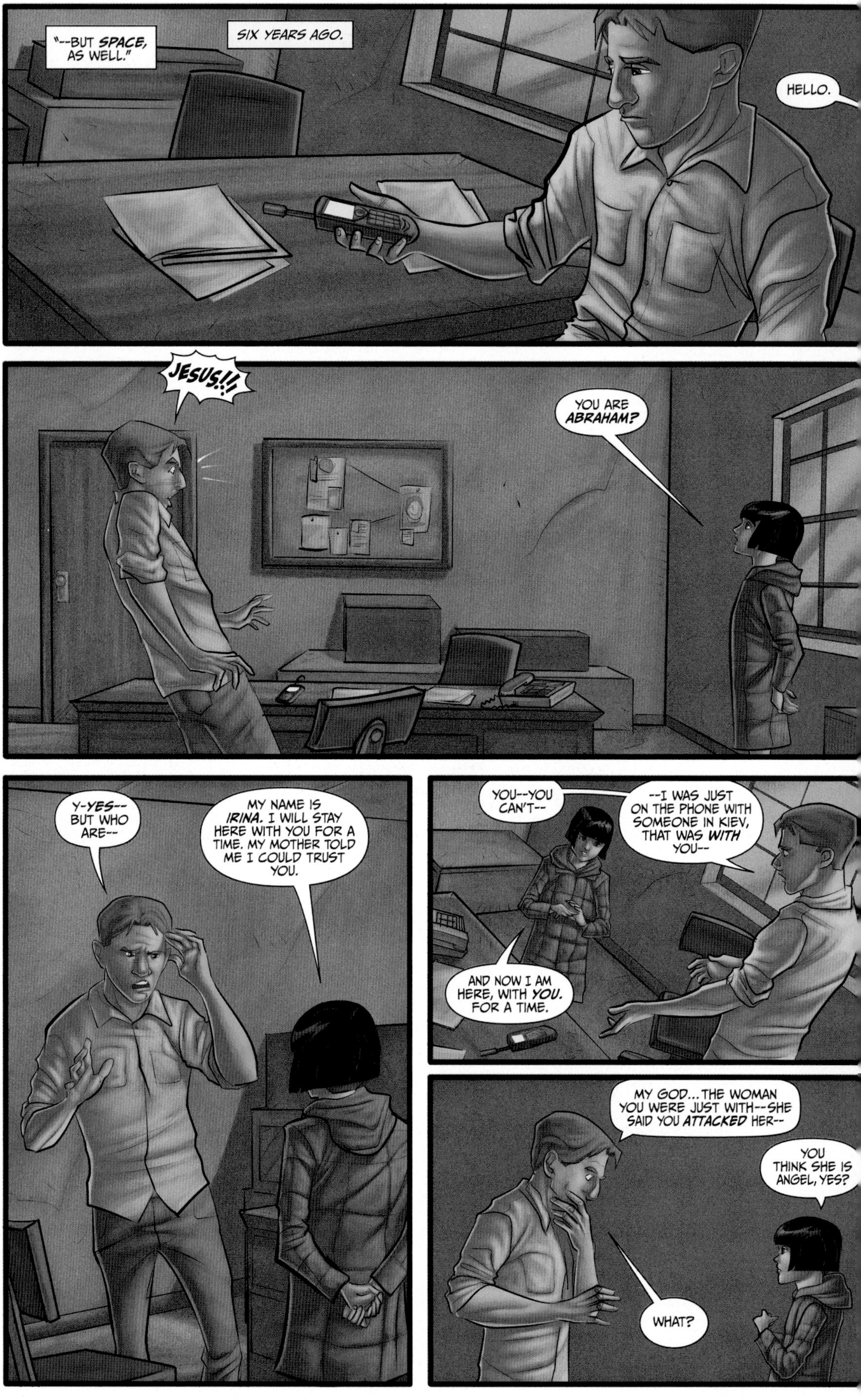
"--BUT SPACE, AS WELL."
SIX YEARS AGO.
HELLO.
JESUS!!!
YOU ARE ABRAHAM?
Y-YES-- BUT WHO ARE--
MY NAME IS IRINA. I WILL STAY HERE WITH YOU FOR A TIME. MY MOTHER TOLD ME I COULD TRUST YOU.
YOU--YOU CAN'T--
--I WAS JUST ON THE PHONE WITH SOMEONE IN KIEV, THAT WAS WITH YOU--
AND NOW I AM HERE, WITH YOU. FOR A TIME.
MY GOD... THE WOMAN YOU WERE JUST WITH--SHE SAID YOU ATTACKED HER--
YOU THINK SHE IS ANGEL, YES?
WHAT?

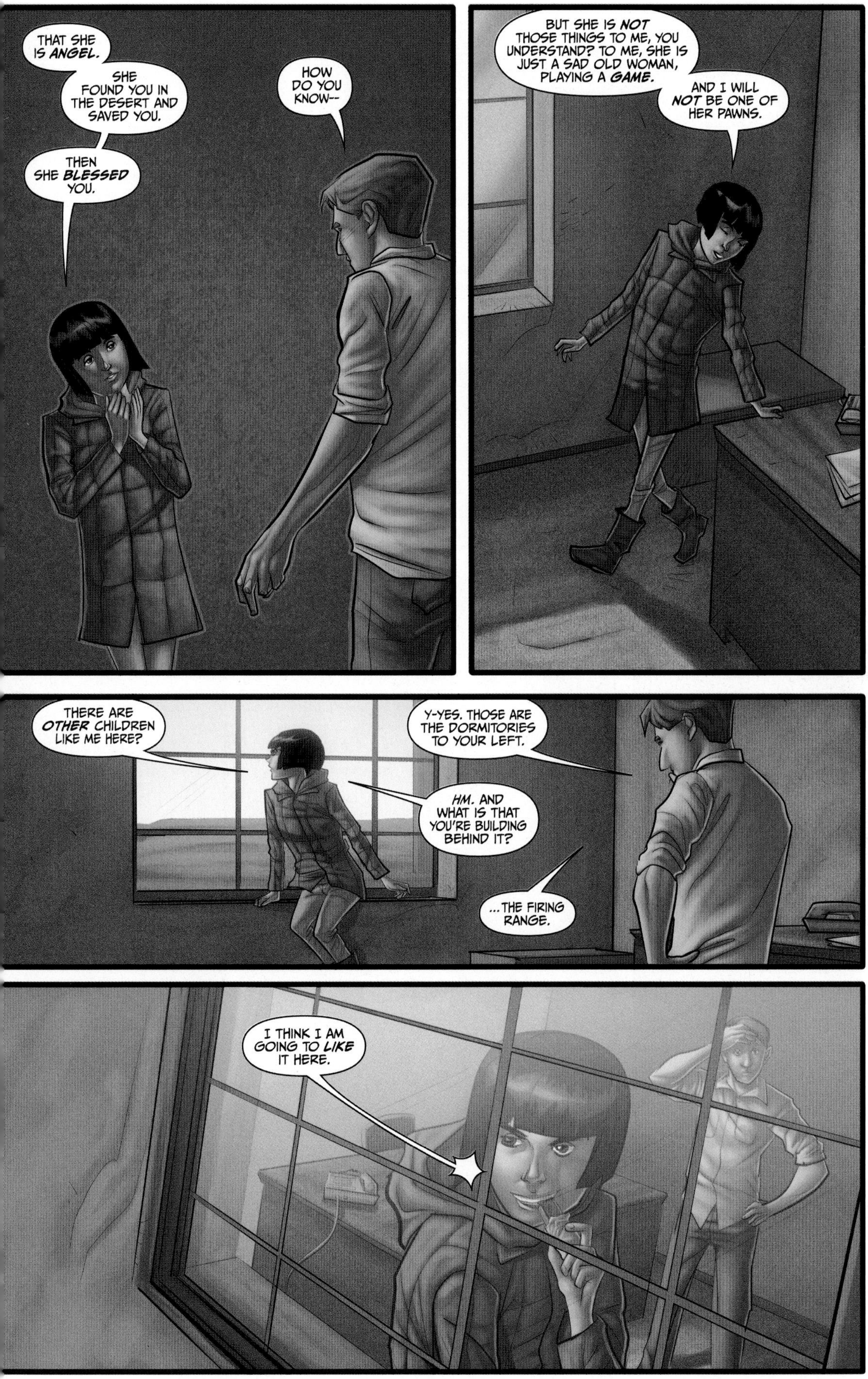
THAT SHE IS ANGEL.
SHE FOUND YOU IN THE DESERT AND SAVED YOU.
THEN SHE BLESSED YOU.
HOW DO YOU KNOW--
BUT SHE IS NOT THOSE THINGS TO ME, YOU UNDERSTAND? TO ME, SHE IS JUST A SAD OLD WOMAN, PLAYING A GAME.
AND I WILL NOT BE ONE OF HER PAWNS.
THERE ARE OTHER CHILDREN LIKE ME HERE?
Y-YES. THOSE ARE THE DORMITORIES TO YOUR LEFT.
HM. AND WHAT IS THAT YOU'RE BUILDING BEHIND IT?
...THE FIRING RANGE.
I THINK I AM GOING TO LIKE IT HERE.

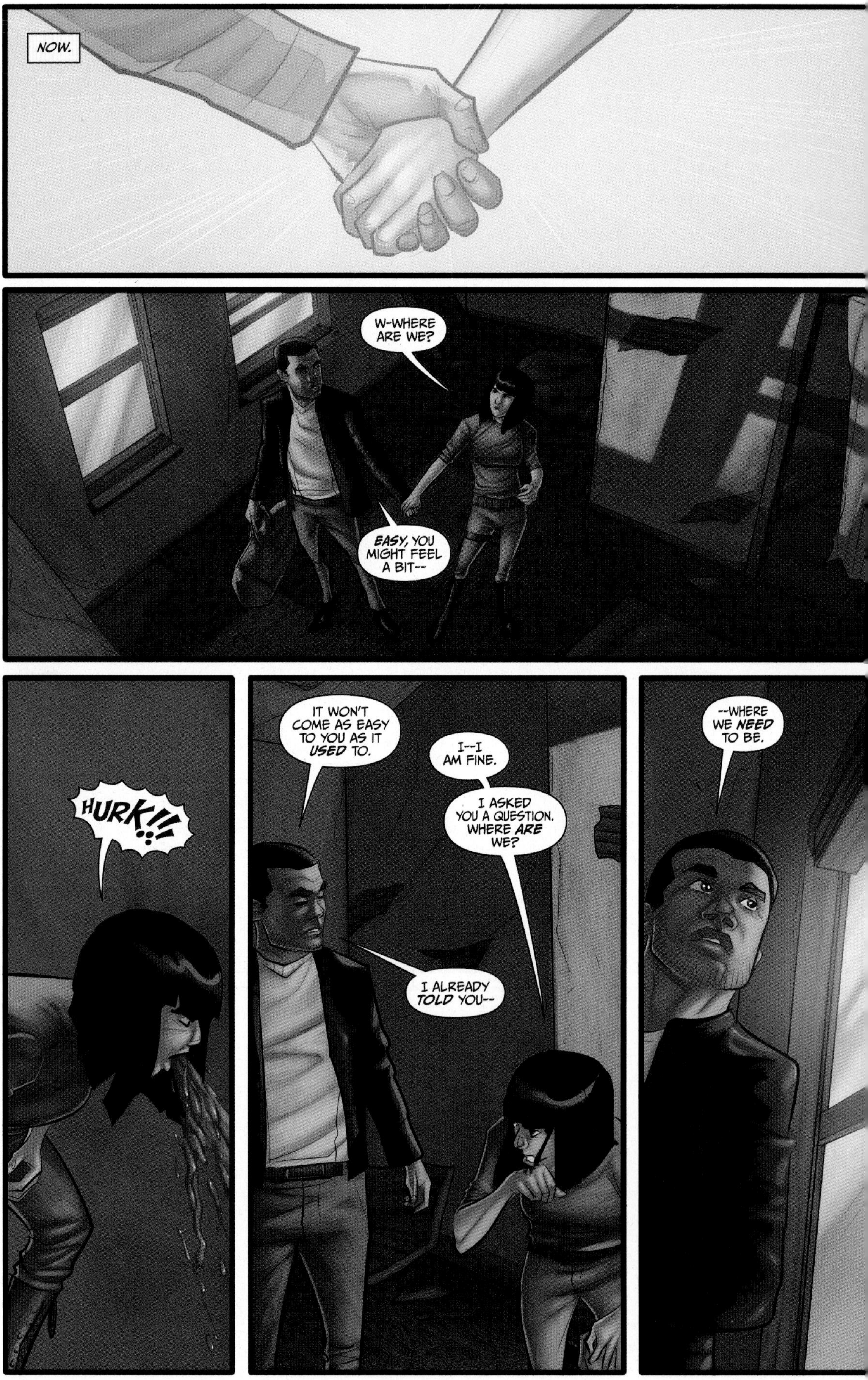
NOW.
W-WHERE ARE WE?
EASY, YOU MIGHT FEEL A BIT--
HURK!!!
IT WON'T COME AS EASY TO YOU AS IT USED TO.
I--I AM FINE.
I ASKED YOU A QUESTION. WHERE ARE WE?
I ALREADY TOLD YOU--
--WHERE WE NEED TO BE.

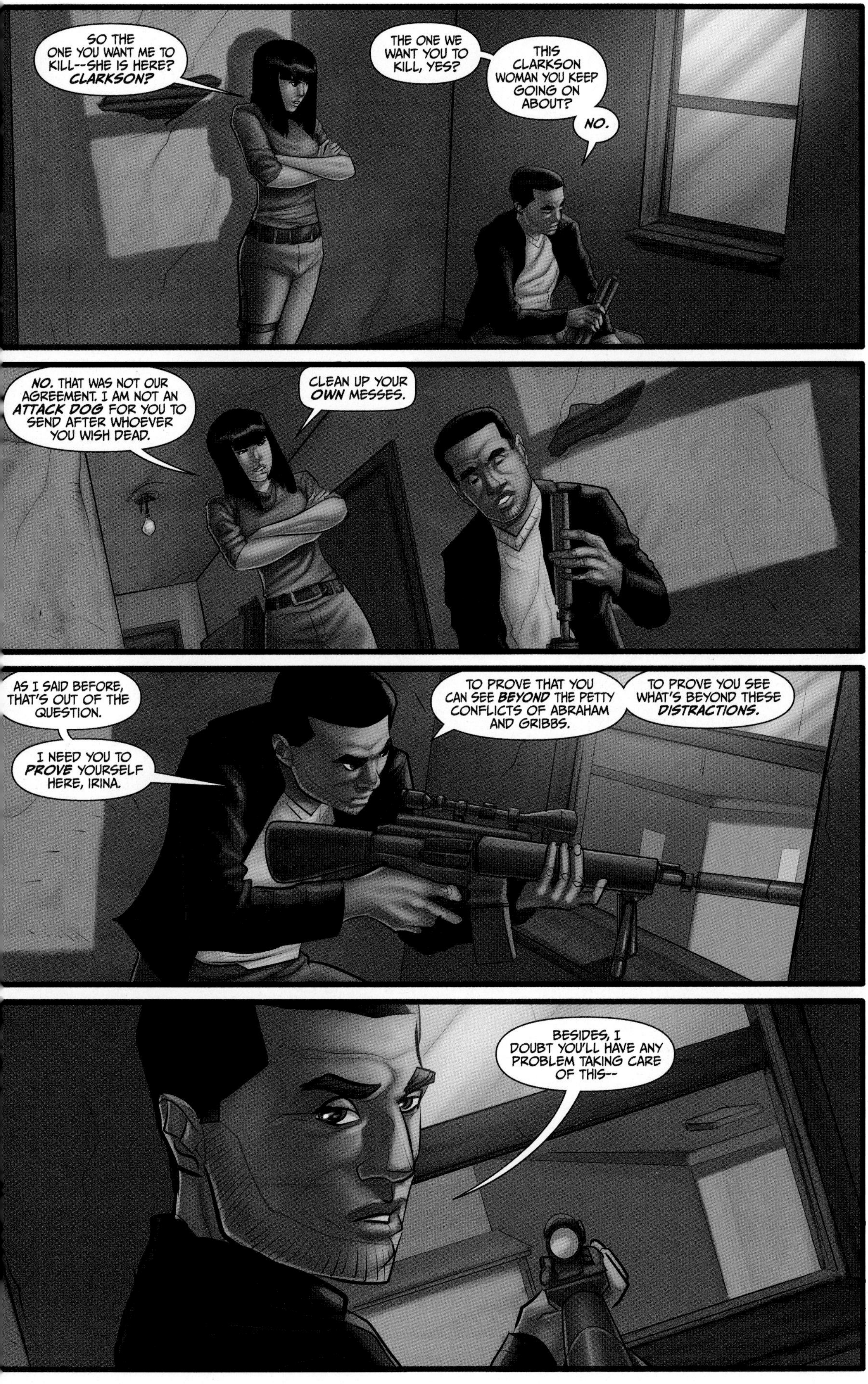
SO THE ONE YOU WANT ME TO KILL--SHE IS HERE? CLARKSON?
THE ONE WE WANT YOU TO KILL, YES?
THIS CLARKSON WOMAN YOU KEEP GOING ON ABOUT?
NO.
NO. THAT WAS NOT OUR AGREEMENT. I AM NOT AN ATTACK DOG FOR YOU TO SEND AFTER WHOEVER YOU WISH DEAD.
CLEAN UP YOUR OWN MESSES.
AS I SAID BEFORE, THAT'S OUT OF THE QUESTION.
I NEED YOU TO PROVE YOURSELF HERE, IRINA.
TO PROVE THAT YOU CAN SEE BEYOND THE PETTY CONFLICTS OF ABRAHAM AND GRIBBS.
TO PROVE YOU SEE WHAT'S BEYOND THESE DISTRACTIONS.
BESIDES, I DOUBT YOU'LL HAVE ANY PROBLEM TAKING CARE OF THIS--

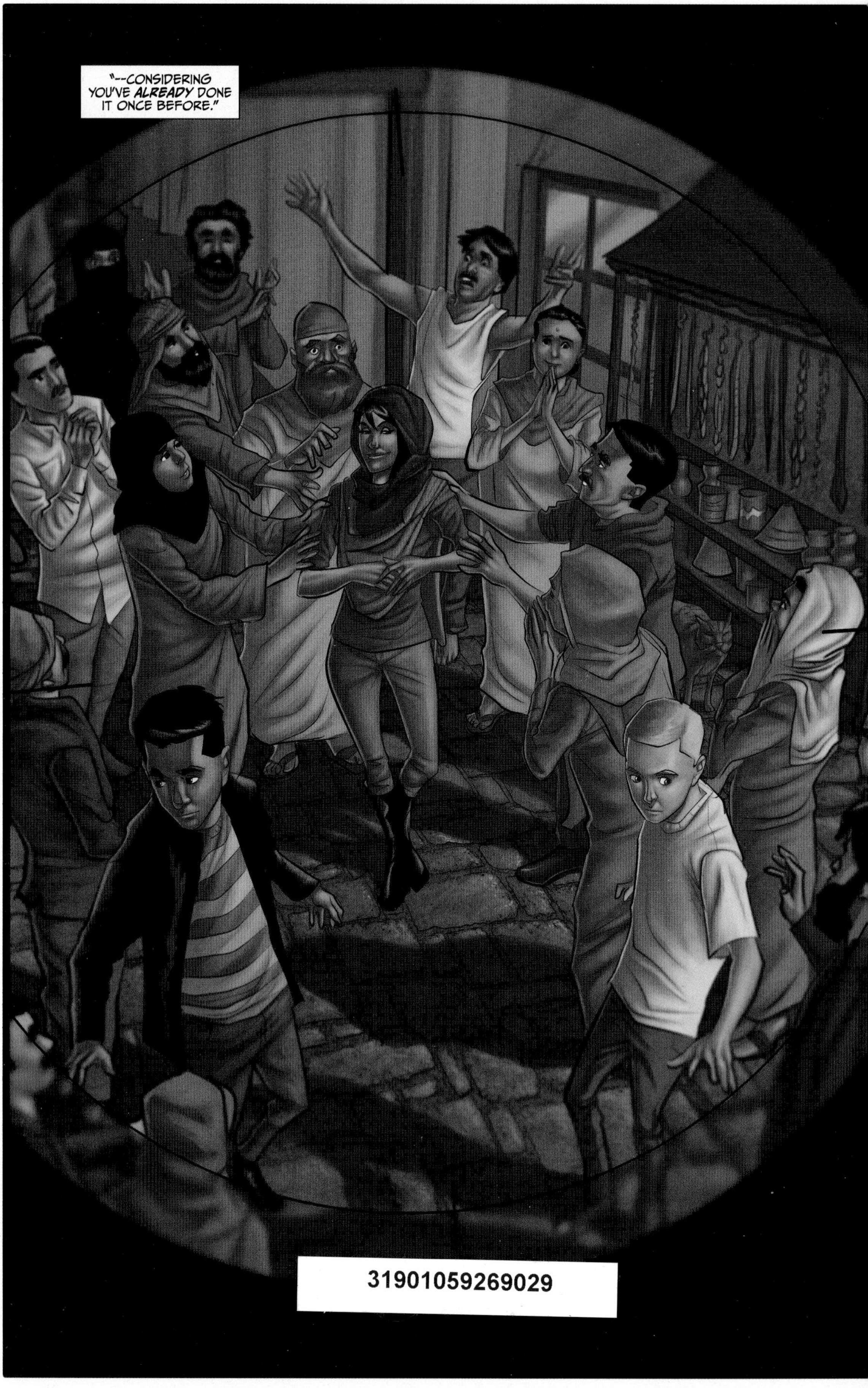
"--CONSIDERING YOU'VE *ALREADY* DONE IT ONCE BEFORE."